D0217093

THE PAPON AFFAIR

THE

PAPON

AFFAIR

MEMORY AND JUSTICE ON TRIAL

Edited by

Richard J. Golsan

Translations by
Lucy B. Golsan and Richard J. Golsan

Routledge

New York   London

Published in 2000 by

Routledge
29 West 35th Street
New York, NY 10001

Published in Great Britain by

Routledge
11 New Fetter Lane
London EC4P 4EE

Copyright © 2000 by Routledge
Routledge is an imprint of the Taylor & Francis Group.

Permissions acknowledgments are printed on pages 271 and 272 of
this volume. The acknowledgments pages shall be considered an ex-
tension of this copyright page. Routledge, Inc. respects international
copyright laws. Any omissions or oversights in the acknowledgments
section of this volume are purely unintentional.

Printed in the United States of America on acid-free paper.

All rights reserved. No part of this book may be reprinted or reproduced
or utilized in any form or by any electronic, mechanical, or other means,
now known or hereafter invented, including photocopying and recording,
or in any information storage or retrieval system, without permission in
writing from the publisher.

Library of Congress Cataloging-in-Publication Data

The Papon affair : memory and justice on trial / edited by Richard J.
Golsan.
    p.   cm.
    Includes bibliographical references and index.
    ISBN 0-415-92364-6 — ISBN 0-415-92365-4 (pbk.)
    1. Papon, Maurice, 1910–   —Trials, litigation, etc.
    2. Trials (Crimes against humanity)—France—Bordeaux.
    3. Jews—Persecution—France.
    4. Holocaust, Jewish (1939–1945)—France—Bordeaux.
    I. Golsan, Richard Joseph, 1952–

KJV135.P37 P37   2000
345.44'0235—dc21   99-088535

KJV
135
.P37
P37
2000

12607851

TO NANCY

UWEC McIntyre Library

DISCARDED

APR 3 2001

Eau Claire, WI

REGROUNDED

CONTENTS

PREFACE

For six months during the fall, winter, and spring of 1997–98, the trial of Maurice Papon in Bordeaux on charges of crimes against humanity dominated the French media as well as the public imagination. The trial had been in the making for nearly twenty years. The accused was a man who had achieved remarkable success as a high-ranking French official, serving various governments for a half a century. For many, the trial was not simply that of a single individual but the symbolic trial of an entire regime, the collaborationist Vichy government, which ruled much of France during the German occupation between 1940 and 1944. No wonder, then, that France's leading historians, legal experts, philosophers, and public figures expressed their views on the trial before it began, during the proceedings, and following the verdict in Bordeaux. They discussed the historical, moral, and legal issues at stake, the nation's difficulty in dealing with a troubled moment in its past, the pedagogical value of the trial, and finally, the controversial role of memory in French public life. As if the issues raised by the history and memory of what the French call *les années noires*—the "Dark Years" of the Occupation—were not enough, early in the trial Papon's role as a Fourth Republican and Gaullist official sparked intense debate, especially his role as prefect of Paris police on the night of 17 October 1961. On that night, Algerian demonstrators protesting a curfew imposed on them by Papon were brutally attacked at several central locations throughout the city. The number of demonstrators killed and wounded is still the subject of controversy, and sentiment is still strong in some quarters that the French government does not want the full truth surrounding the tragedy known. Moreover, when in 1998 the historian Jean-Luc Einaudi called the event "a massacre" and blamed it on the police acting on orders from Papon, he was sued for defamation by Papon and taken to trial in February 1999. This "other Papon trial," as one magazine referred to it, confirmed the extent to which the Papon affair was not just about the Vichy past, but about *another* past with which the French are equally uncomfortable, *la guerre sans nom*, or the Algerian war.

The articles, essays, and interviews included in this volume are intended to familiarize both generalists and specialists with the wide range of issues raised by the Papon affair. They focus for the most part, of course, on Papon's trial on charges of crimes against humanity for his role in the deportations of Jews from the Bordeaux region during the German occupation of France during World War II. But because the trial also brought to light the troubling record of Papon's postwar career, his tenure as prefect of Paris police, and the terrible night of 17 October 1961, these issues are addressed as well.

The introduction focuses broadly on the history of crimes against humanity in France and the legal and historical issues at stake in Bordeaux, and examines some of the important moments of the Papon trial. Part I consists of original essays by five specialists on modern French history, law, and culture. Vann Kelly's essay deals with Papon's postwar career as a colonial administrator, primarily during the Fourth Republic. Christopher Flood discusses the extreme right's — and specifically the National Front's — reaction to the trial. In their essays, Nancy Wood and Nathan Bracher deal with specific aspects of the trial itself. Wood deals with the respective roles of victims and historians as witnesses during the trial, and Nathan Bracher examines the legacy of Gaullism as a source of controversy and dissent before the court. Finally Leila Sadat examines the background of the trial from the perspective of a legal expert and addresses the legacy of crimes against humanity in France in shaping international law.

Part II consists of articles, op-ed pieces, letters, and interviews published primarily in the French press. These texts appeared before, during, and after the Bordeaux trial and verdict, and they are generally organized chronologically. They include a 1995 interview with Papon published in *Libération*, as well as interviews with leading historians of the history and memory of Vichy: Robert Paxton, Henry Rousso, Pierre Nora, Eberhard Jackel, and Philippe Burrin. These interviews originally appeared in *Le Monde* and *Libération*. Also included in this section is a letter from Henry Rousso to Jean-Louis Castagnède, the president of the Assizes Court in Bordeaux, giving his reasons for not wishing to appear as a witness. Finally, assessments of the trial and its implications by philosophers Alain Finkielkraut and Tzvetan Todorov as well as lawyers for the civil litigants (Michel Zaoui) and defense (Jean-Marc Varaut) close out part II. These articles originally appeared in *Le Monde*, and in the case of Todorov's essay, *Salmagundi*.

Part III contains interviews, articles, and essays from *Le Monde* dealing with the controversy surrounding Papon's role in the repression of Algerian demonstrators in Paris on the night of 17 October 1961. In an interview published in February 1999, Benjamin Stora, France's leading expert on the memory of the Algerian war, contextualizes the event in relation to broader issues concerning both the Algerian conflict in 1961 and negotiations that would eventually result in Algerian independence. Essays by the historian Jean-Luc Einaudi then discuss the memory of 17 October and the inadequacies of the Mandelkern report, ordered by Minister of the Interior Jean-Pierre Chevènement in October 1997, and whose findings were made public seven months later. Einaudi also addresses French governmental reticence in allowing researchers access to the archives dealing with the event. The Einaudi essays are followed by journalistic accounts of the "other Papon trial"—Papon's suit against Einaudi for defamation of a public functionary. Finally, a chronology dealing with Vichy, the Final Solution, and the history of crimes against humanity in France has been included at the conclusion of this volume as a reference tool.

A volume of this sort requires the generosity and support of a number of people, in this instance in the United States, France, and England. In the United States, I would like to thank Nathan Bracher, Vann Kelly, and Leila Sadat for agreeing to contribute essays to the book, and for sharing with me their expertise on the career and trial of Maurice Papon. My mother, Lucy B. Golsan, did her usual excellent and expeditious job of translating French texts into English. My colleague Howard Marchitello and my wife Nancy offered much helpful advice to improve the text of the introduction. Teresa Ethridge, a student at Texas A&M University, was most helpful with many aspects of the preparation of the final manuscript. Brendan O'Malley at Routledge has been most supportive of this project from start to finish. And my sons, Jody and James, have put up with me, as usual.

In France, Henry Rousso graciously made available to me his letter to President of the Court Jean-Louis Castagnède included in this volume and opened the archives of the Institut d'histoire du temps présent to me. I have enjoyed many conversations about the Papon trial, the memory of Vichy, and crimes against humanity in France with Rousso, Annette Lévy-Willard, and Tzvetan Todorov, and I wish to thank them here. In England Chris Flood and Nancy Wood generously agreed to write essays for this volume. I have learned much from both of them.

Richard J. Golsan
College Station, Texas
3 November 1999

INTRODUCTION:

MAURICE PAPON AND CRIMES

AGAINST HUMANITY IN FRANCE

Richard J. Golson

On 2 April 1998, Maurice Papon, former mayor of the town of Saint-Amand Montrond, deputy of the Cher department, prefect of Paris police under Charles de Gaulle, budget minister under Valéry Giscard d'Estaing—and Vichy civil servant during the German occupation of France between 1940 and 1944—was convicted of crimes against humanity at the Assizes Court in Bordeaux. The trial of Papon had lasted six months, thus becoming the longest trial in France in this century. The ninety-five days of courtroom testimony from witnesses and speeches by numerous lawyers[1] and officers of the court had exhausted nearly everyone. According to Éric Conan, who covered the trial for the magazine *L'Express*, the jurists, especially, looked "undone" as they entered the courtroom to deliver their verdict after nearly twenty hours of deliberations. When the president of the court, Jean-Louis Castagnède, read the verdict, his voice was "hardly recognizable."[2]

Rather than bring a sense of finality and closure to the proceedings, the verdict seemed instead to capture the ambivalence and uncertainty that had hovered over the trial from the outset. For those who had been legally pursuing Papon for nearly two decades for crimes he had committed as a Vichy civil servant during the Occupation, the verdict marked a victory and brought a sense of relief. But for many others, Papon's conviction, as well as the sentence handed down by the court, were not so satisfying. Papon was found guilty of complicity in the "illegal arrest" of thirty-seven persons and the "arbitrary detainment" of fifty-three others in the context of the roundup and deportations of Jews by train from Bordeaux on four separate occasions dating from July 1942 to January 1944. The deported Jews were sent first to the Drancy internment and transit camp on the outskirts of Paris and then expedited to the death camps to the east.

Papon was found not guilty, however, of "complicity in the murder" of the deportees; that is, he was considered by the jury to be ignorant of the ultimate destination and fate of the deportees in the context of the Final Solution. The *Acte d'accusation*, or charges brought against Papon and read at the outset of the trial, did in fact accuse him of knowingly having sent the Jews to their deaths.[3] To the degree that Papon was found innocent of this charge, the verdict was a victory for the defense, and especially for Jean-Marc Varaut, Papon's chief counsel.

Like the verdict, the sentence also reflected the less-than-decisive outcome of six months of court proceedings. Papon was given ten years in prison. While some of the lawyers for the civil litigants, and especially Arno Klarsfeld, whose background and role in the Papon trial will be discussed in greater detail, were quite satisfied with this "graduated" penalty (Klarsfeld had in fact argued for it in his final plea before the court),[4] others found it simply ludicrous. How could one be found guilty of complicity in crimes against humanity, by definition the most heinous of crimes, and receive a sentence lighter than many of those meted out for far lesser crimes? To which Klarsfeld in essence responded, how could one give the same sentence handed down in the case of Klaus Barbie, the "Butcher of Lyon," to Maurice Papon, a man who had no motives for committing crimes other than his ambition to climb the career ladder in extraordinary times, times when committing "the irreparable" could simply be part of one's job?[5] For his part, Jean-Marc Varaut dismissed the verdict as well as the sentence as "a bastard decision."[6] His sentiments were shared by many, and certainly by some of those who believed in Papon's guilt on all counts and the necessity of giving him the maximum sentence, life imprisonment.

In order to understand the extraordinary length of the trial of Maurice Papon, the many controversies it produced, and the disappointment and frustration it engendered, one must take into account not only the nature and length of the accused's service to four French political regimes—the Third Republic, Pétain's French State, as well as the Fourth and Fifth Republics—but the massive import of the trial in historical, legal, and even moral terms. The trial in Bordeaux was not simply that of a Vichy bureaucrat docilely following orders from a collaborationist regime bent on pleasing the German occupant.

As innumerable newspaper headlines and radio and television reports in France and around the world announced, Papon's trial was, at least in the public's view, the symbolic trial of the Vichy past itself. That past, as historian Henry Rousso and others have argued, has never been successfully integrated into the continuum of French history. The symbolic weight and historical magnitude of the trial was, moreover, not lost on those responsible for preparing for the event at Bordeaux's Palais de Justice. The courtroom itself was fitted out with a tight security system. Video cameras were installed on all four walls to record each moment of the trial for posterity. A second room in the Palais de Justice was equipped with a large video screen so that the overflow crowd of spectators could also witness the proceedings, although not in person.

Rousso observes that outside the courtroom (and viewing room) a second, "virtual trial" took place as well.[7] As the various lawyers and magistrates exited the courtroom during recesses, in the main hall of the Palais de Justice reporters, photographers, and television cameramen awaited them. Powerful television lights were then switched on, and the lawyers not only described the events occurring within but also put their particular spin on them. One of the lawyers present described the atmosphere as a cross between a medieval den of thieves and a parliamentary watering hole.[8] The stars of the show were unquestionably Jean-Marc Varaut, and Arno Klarsfeld, the handsome, longhaired son of famed Nazi hunters and "memory militants" Serge and Beate Klarsfeld. Known for his flamboyance and provocative behavior, Arno Klarsfeld represented the Association of Sons and Daughters of Deported Jews, as he had at the earlier trial for crimes against humanity of Paul Touvier. Despite the seriousness of Papon's trial, Klarsfeld occasionally arrived at the Bordeaux Palais de Justice on roller blades.

Outside the courthouse, protests, vigils, and readings of the names of French Holocaust victims occurred throughout the trial. The organizers of these protests, often the senior Klarsfelds, were frequently interviewed on French television for the evening reports. As news of the day's events, debates, and controversies made their way from Bordeaux to Paris, national political leaders often waded into the fray. In late November 1997, Prime Minister Lionel Jospin stated his opinion that the Papon trial was necessary in order to bring to light the crimes of the Vichy regime—a statement to which Jean-Marc Varaut took strong exception in court. A month earlier, at the moment when Papon's postwar career as a Gaullist was under fire, Philippe Séguin, the leader of the Gaullist RPR Party, bluntly expressed his belief that the Papon trial should not become—if it was not already—the trial of "Gaullism and of France."

Séguin's concern was legitimate to the degree that, from the very outset of the trial in October 1997, the issues raised in court quickly overflowed the historical and legal parameters of the case against Papon. Rather than deal exclusively with the role of the accused in the deportations of Jews from Bordeaux between 1942 and 1944, the trial expanded its focus to include not only Papon's actions on behalf of the Resistance and Gaullism's willingness to embrace former collaborators like Papon at the Liberation, but the excesses of Gaullism itself in the postwar years. The most striking example of the latter occurred during the discussion of the accused's curriculum vitae at the outset of the trial. In the postwar years Papon successfully transformed himself from Vichy functionary and part-time *résistant* into postwar servant of the Fourth Republic, especially in France's colonial possessions. During the Fifth Republic, he became a loyal follower of de Gaulle.[9] It was in this last capacity that Maurice Papon, serving as prefect of Paris police, oversaw the brutal suppression by French police of Algerian protesters on the night of 17 October 1961. That night, Algerian immigrants, objecting to the harsh curfew imposed on them by Prefect Papon, marched on the city of Paris, arriving from the suburban workers' quarters and ghettos where they lived. At a number of locations, including the Neuilly Bridge leading into the heart of Paris, the area around the intersection of rue Saint-Germain-des-Près and boulevard Saint-Michel in the Latin Quarter, and the streets near the Bonne-Nouvelle metro stop not far from the Place de la République, the protesters encountered policemen armed with extralong nightsticks called *bidules* as well as firearms. According to most accounts, the Algerians were brutally attacked by police. In some instances, especially at the Neuilly Bridge, they were fired upon. Hundreds were injured, and thousands were rounded up and taken to internment camps around the city, where they were held, often in terrible conditions, for several days.[10]

Many protesters were killed as well, although the exact figure remains a subject of intense debate. The official government tally made public on the day after the confrontation was three dead and some sixty wounded, but no government investigative report ever followed up on the events or verified the figures just cited. During his trial Papon asserted that some fifteen to twenty protesters had been killed, but not by the police. Rather, he argued that they were the victims of internecine struggles between rival Algerian factions, the well-known FLN (Front de libération nationale) and the more obscure MNA (Mouvement national républicain). Few if any took this claim seriously. Historians who researched the events, read eyewitness accounts, and studied the available archives came up with much larger and more disturbing figures. Jean-Luc Einaudi, who testified at Papon's trial and whose own legal confrontation with the former prefect of Paris police would continue long after the verdict in Bordeaux, stated that between two and three hundred had been killed. As a result of the controversy and media attention generated by the debate over 17 October 1961 during Papon's trial, Minister of the Interior Jean-Pierre Chevènement ordered a new investigation of the archives. The resulting "Mandelkern report," named after its principal author, State Councilor Dieudonné Mandelkern, was released in May 1998. It concluded that between thirty and forty protesters had been killed. Many have expressed strong reservations concerning these figures, criticizing both the thoroughness of the archival research undertaken and the impartiality of the authors' conclusions.[11]

The debate over the actual number of protesters killed is ultimately not as important, however, as is the nature of the events themselves and the responsibility of the prefect of police. By all accounts the events were terrible in their brutality. Bodies of protesters were thrown in the Seine, only to be found washed up downstream several days later. In the courtyard of the prefecture itself, policemen beat protesters mercilessly. There are reports that some of the protesters were strangled with brake cables. Some argue that Papon, who was at the prefecture that night, witnessed the violence and did nothing to stop it. Whatever the case may be, the police attacks on protesters, which Einaudi calls a "massacre," were certainly directed at anyone who *looked* Algerian. Indeed, a dark-complected young American visiting Paris at the time was beaten by police. So for many, speaking out both at the time and more than thirty years later during the trial of Papon in Bordeaux, the Paris police assault on Algerian protesters was a racist crime. The distinguished historian Pierre Vidal-Naquet even went so far as to argue in October 1997 in the *Nouvel Observateur* that Papon should *also* be tried for these crimes as constituting crimes against humanity while standing trial in Bordeaux.[12]

The terrible events of 17 October 1961 and Papon's role both in bringing them about and later in covering them up were, of course, secondary in historical terms and ultimately inconsequential in legal terms in Bordeaux. The historical period that mattered, and the one during which Papon committed the crimes for which he stood trial in 1997–98, was the German occupation of France during World War II, not *la guerre sans nom*—"the war without a name," or the Algerian war. Moreover, a trial for crimes against humanity dealing with Papon's role on 17 October 1961 in Paris would have been legally impossible because by definition crimes against humanity according to French law can, in effect, *only have been committed during World War II and only under the aegis of a government practicing a "politics of ideological hegemony"—for all intents and purposes, Nazi Germany.*[13]

I will return shortly to the historical circumstances, legal precedents, and court decisions that dictated that the law assume this form. (The legal issues will also be dealt with in detail in Leila Sadat's essay in this volume.) But even before consideration of these historical circumstances and legal issues, it is not difficult to see why the airing of Maurice Papon's role in the events of 17 October 1961 during his trial for crimes against humanity created such a stir. In general terms, the Algerian war in contemporary France is very much the subject of continuing controversy, as is the Vichy past. For those who prefer to use psychoanalytical metaphors in analyzing the past, the "war without a name" is one that has been at least as "repressed" as the "Dark Years" of the Occupation, certainly over the last twenty years. So the debate over one of the most troubling and obscure moments of France's struggle with the issue of Algerian independence, especially in the highly charged atmosphere of the Bordeaux Assizes Court, was bound to make waves.

But at least as troubling was the "blurring of boundaries" in legal and historical terms that the debate produced. Ever since the Nuremberg Tribunal, crimes against humanity have *generally* been defined and broadly understood as consisting of the "murder, extermination, enslavement, deportation, and other inhumane acts, committed against any civilian population . . . or persecution on political, racial, or religious grounds."[14] For Pierre Vidal-Naquet, what French police did to Algerian protesters on the night of 17 October 1961 met these basic criteria—although Vidal-Naquet was also certainly aware that these actions did not qualify as crimes against humanity under *French* law. Moreover, as opposed to Papon's situation in Bordeaux—a subprefect taking orders from his French superiors as well as the Nazis—in Paris some fifteen to twenty years later he was acting largely on his own initiative and he was much more in command of the situation. And, as prefect of police, Papon *had* to have been better informed of the fate of the Algerians than he claimed he was of the Jews deported from Bordeaux during the Occupation. In essence, Papon's role in Paris was direct and personal. In Bordeaux during the Occupation, by contrast, Papon's crime was, as many of the lawyers for the civil litigants at his trial agreed, an "office" or "desk" crime—*un crime de bureau*. Papon was a cog in the machine removed from the action. It was in fact because Papon's crimes between 1942 and 1944 were "desk" crimes that Arno Klarsfeld argued in favor of a lighter or "graduated" sentence. Would he have pleaded for a similar sentence had Papon been on trial for crimes committed on 17 October 1961—or perhaps a more severe one?

The blurring of the legal boundaries between Papon's crimes committed during the Occupation and his actions as prefect of Paris police in 1961 stimulated a good deal of discomfort and even more controversy. But it was the tacit comparison between the two governments ultimately responsible for the events in question that prompted the most fireworks, including Séguin's denunciation of the trial as fast becoming the trial of Gaullism and indeed of France itself. The deportation of the Jews from 1942 to 1944 had occurred under a collaborationist, authoritarian regime bent on pleasing the German occupant at all costs—and one whose hegemony Charles de Gaulle had fought against and whose legitimacy he had denied. On the other hand, the suppression of Algerian protesters in 1961 was the action—certainly excessive—of a duly elected government led by the hero of precisely the struggle *against* Vichy and Nazi Germany. For the Gaullists especially, nothing could be more offensive and ludicrous than *any* suggestion of similarities existing between the actions of Pétain's French State and those of de Gaulle's Fifth Republic. And if some of the aging Gaullists who testified at Papon's trial were given to courtroom outbursts against the entire proceedings, it was at least in part because they believed that Gaullism and the Resistance were being tarnished. To the extent, finally, that they defended the accused, it was because of the latter's Gaullist and Resistance credentials, and certainly not because he had served Vichy.

I have emphasized the events of 17 October 1961 and Papon's role as prefect of Paris police at the beginning of this introduction first because these issues stirred tremendous controversy and debate at the outset of the Bordeaux trial for crimes against humanity. But these issues also serve to underscore the difficulties involved in locating and isolating the exact historical context and legal implications of events that occurred more than a half century earlier. And it is precisely these difficulties that have inevitably arisen when individuals have been tried on charges of crimes against humanity under French law. Since Maurice Papon was not the first person accused of or indicted on these charges in France, it is helpful to consider the cases of those individuals who preceded him. Not only did the cases of these men affect the evolution and application of crimes against humanity laws in France, but without the precedents they established—and the public pressures they created—Papon might never have been tried.

Before the former subprefect of the Gironde department stood trial in Bordeaux in the late nineties, two other men were tried on similar charges, and two others narrowly avoided standing trial by dying shortly before their moment had arrived. Of the two men tried, the first was of course the Bolivian citizen "Klaus Altman," better known as SS captain Klaus Barbie, the "Butcher of Lyon." In 1983 Barbie had been brought back to France from South America, where he had been hiding and working as a businessman, an adviser to dictators, and, occasionally, a specialist in training right-wing paramilitary forces. During the Occupation, Barbie had been the scourge of the Lyon Resistance. Among many other crimes, he was responsible both for the torture and death of the great Resistance martyr Jean Moulin as well as the arrest and deportation to their deaths of over forty Jewish children hidden in the village of Izieu. Barbie was convicted of crimes against humanity and sentenced to life in prison on 4 July 1987. He died in jail in 1991.

The second person to be tried for crimes against humanity in France was the Frenchman Paul Touvier. One of eleven children of a profoundly reactionary Catholic family, Touvier was for all intents and purposes a ne'er-do-well before World War II who, during the Occupation, joined Pétain's Légion des combattants and later became an intelligence officer with Vichy's paramilitary police, the Milice, or "Militia," whose purpose it was to fight the Resistance as well as the menace of "Judeo-Bolshevism."[15]

Unlike Papon and other Frenchmen charged with crimes against humanity whom I shall discuss shortly, Touvier was not a bureaucrat, nor was he directly linked to the implementation of the Final Solution in France. Rather, as an officer in the Milice, Touvier used his power and authority to rob, intimidate, and brutalize his victims. In short, during the Occupation (and afterward) he was simply a thug who drove stolen cars, dressed in expensive clothes, and lived in apartments belonging to others. He was also, apparently, a pimp.

When the Lyon region where he operated was liberated, Touvier went into hiding with the help of a Catholic chaplain working with the Milice. There followed many years on the lam, including stints during which Touvier earned his living primarily as a petty thief and confidence man recounting his tale of woe. Among those who took pity on Touvier and helped him out financially were the singer Jacques Brel and the movie star Pierre Fresnay—who had also had a dubious past during the Occupation. But Touvier's most helpful and devoted supporters were members of the Catholic clergy as well as officials of the church hierarchy, who provided Touvier with funds, lodging in monasteries, and, most spectacularly, a presidential pardon from Georges Pompidou in November 1971. Pompidou granted the pardon quietly, against the recommendations of many of his advisers, and only for ancillary penalties stemming from earlier convictions in absentia for crimes committed during the Occupation. (The statute of limitations on the crimes themselves had expired.) The story might have ended there, had not an astute journalist named Jacques Dérogy published news of Pompidou's pardon and details of Touvier's criminal activities in L'Express in June 1972. A veritable storm of controversy followed the publication of Dérogy's article, and in an unsuccessful effort to quell the storm,

Pompidou held a press conference in September of the same year to explain his action and express the view that "it was time to draw a veil over the past," that past being the Dark Years of the Occupation.

Precisely the opposite has of course occurred, as the memory and history of the Vichy years have been anything but forgotten. And where Touvier was concerned, public outcry over his pardon continued, leading in November 1973 to the first accusations of crimes against humanity being brought against him in Lyon. Following a series of protracted judicial maneuvers (discussed in Sadat's essay in this volume), Touvier was finally indicted for crimes against humanity by the examining magistrate Martine Anzani in June 1981. When Touvier failed to appear for his hearing, Anzani issued an international warrant for his arrest. On the lam once again, Touvier continued to benefit from his association with Catholic clerics, frequently taking refuge in monasteries in southern France. Hiding under the name of "Paul Lacroix," Touvier was finally arrested in the priory of Saint-François in Nice, a priory with links to the extreme right-wing *intégriste* movement.[16] After another long series of judicial decisions whose importance will merit further discussion shortly, Touvier stood trial at the Yvelines court in Versailles on charges of crimes against humanity in the spring of 1994. On 20 April, after a trial lasting six weeks, Touvier was convicted of crimes against humanity for ordering the arrest and murder of seven Jewish hostages on the morning of 29 June 1944. He was sentenced to life in prison, where he died in the summer of 1996.

Of the two men charged with crimes against humanity for their actions during the Occupation who did not stand trial, the first charged with and indicted for crimes against humanity was Jean Leguay, the representative in the Occupied Zone of René Bousquet, secretary-general of Vichy police from April 1942 to December 1943. In his role as Bousquet's representative in the Occupied Zone, Leguay oversaw the deportations of Jews to the east from locations including Bordeaux. Indicted in 1979, Leguay was finally on the verge of standing trial when he died in 1989. In an unprecedented move, the official statement announcing the termination of the case against Leguay in July 1989 also confirmed his guilt on charges of crimes against humanity.

Later that year Serge Klarsfeld, acting as the representative of the Association of Sons and Daughters of Deported Jews, brought charges of crimes against humanity against René Bousquet himself. In so doing, Klarsfeld launched the most spectacular and visible of all cases involving charges of crimes against humanity against a Frenchman. This was so not only because of the rank Bousquet held under Vichy and the role he played in implementing the Final Solution in France, but because of the distinction of his prewar and postwar careers. Certainly his prewar and Vichy careers resembled Papon's, only on a grander scale. Essentially for this reason, Papon implied in his 1995 interview with Annette Lévy-Willard (included in this volume) that he was being tried in the place of bigger fish that got away, namely, René Bousquet.

Even more so than Papon, Bousquet enjoyed a distinguished prewar career. In 1930, at the age of twenty-one, he achieved national recognition for saving several people from floodwaters in the south of France. For his efforts, Bousquet was awarded the Médaille de Belles Actions by the president of the Republic, Gaston Doumergue. His heroism, moreover, attracted the attention of other powerful politicians, thus launching Bousquet's career. In short order he was serving as an assistant to various government officials of the center-left Radical-Socialist Party during the early thirties. At the end of the decade he became a subprefect of Vitry-le-François, and later secretary-general of the Marne department. In September 1940, after the French defeat, he was named prefect of the Marne, and in August 1941 prefect of Champagne. From there, Bousquet moved to Vichy and Paris and assumed his role as secretary-general of the police in the Ministry of the Interior.

The scandal over Bousquet's Vichy past broke in October 1978, when *L'Express* published an interview with Louis Darquier de Pellepoix, the former commissioner-general of Jewish Affairs under Vichy, then living in exile in Spain. Among other things, Darquier claimed that "at Auschwitz they only gassed fleas," thus placing himself firmly in the camp of France's "negationists," or Holocaust deniers. But Darquier's biggest "revelation" during the interview, and one that would have very real consequences for the next fifteen years, was the fact that it had been René Bousquet who, as secretary-general of police, had been responsible for the Vélodrome d'hiver roundup of Jews in Paris in July 1942.

In their classic study *Vichy France and the Jews*,[17] Michael Marrus and Robert O. Paxton offer a brief and harrowing summary of events that took place on 16 and 17 July 1942. For many of the French, these are two of the darkest days in the nation's history. Early on the morning of the sixteenth, more than 9,000 French policemen fanned out across Paris with orders to arrest 28,000 stateless and foreign Jews, who were to be interned and then deported. More than 900 arrest teams, usually consisting of three or four men each, were given clear instructions and precise lists of those to be arrested. No one on the list was to be spared. The sick were to be taken along with the healthy, and there were no exceptions for children. Those arrested were instructed to bring clothing and food for two days, and the arresting officers were to turn off gas and electricity in their abandoned lodgings.

The destination of the majority of the Jews rounded up was the Vélodrome d'hiver, a bicycle-racing stadium in the fifteenth arrondissement used for political rallies. (Ironically, it would later serve in 1961 as an internment center for Algerians arrested on the night of 17 October.) According to Marrus and Paxton, the conditions at the Vel d'hiv in July 1942 were atrocious. No provisions for food or water or for maintaining sanitary conditions had been made. Seven thousand internees, including four thousand children, were packed into a space where there was hardly room to lie down. The heat was terrible during the day, followed by cold at night. At first, those interned suffered from hunger and thirst, then diarrhea and dysentery. The situation lasted for five days, before those inside the Vel d'hiv were moved and eventually deported to the death camps.

The Vel d'hiv roundups of 16–17 July 1942 were carried out as a direct result of meetings between René Bousquet and German authorities in Paris earlier that month. During a meeting on 2 July, Bousquet had agreed to use French police to round up some 10,000 foreign Jews in the Unoccupied Zone. He had, however, initially resisted the Nazis' desire to use French police to round up Jews in Paris, the capital being under German occupation. Faced with German pressure, Bousquet caved in. The Vel d'hiv roundups, carried out with virtually no German participation, were the result. From the German perspective, to use their own forces for the implementation of the Final Solution in France was not only a manpower drain, it was "bad publicity" and would lead to greater French resistance.

The fact that the Germans pressured Bousquet to use French police in the Paris roundups did not mean, however, that Vichy's secretary-general of police got nothing in return, or, at least, thought he did. As a result of accords between Bousquet and Karl Oberg, head of the SS in France, that were concluded later that month and renewed the following spring, the French police were given a "free hand" in areas that "did not affect German interests." Moreover, the Germans agreed to give orders to French police only through proper channels—something they had not previously done—and allowed them to establish reserve units of Mobile Guards. Finally, the Germans relieved French police of the onerous task of designating hostages among the French population. The Germans usually executed these hostages in reprisal for acts committed against them by the Resistance.

But any "independence" on the part of the French police that these accords appeared to guarantee was for all intents and purposes illusory. Not only were the French police obliged in return to help carry out the struggle against "the enemies of the Reich," but the concessions they secured from the Germans were soon thereafter ignored. In effect, the only real accomplishment of the Bousquet-

Oberg accords, according to Philippe Burrin, was a higher degree of ideological complicity.[18]

The Vel d'hiv roundups of July 1942 were not the only roundups of foreign *and* French Jews under Bousquet's tenure. Of course some of the convoys sent from Bordeaux were at issue in the Papon trial, but not those that occurred after 1943, because Bousquet had resigned under pressure on 31 December of that year. Just the same, to get a sense of the damage done under Bousquet's tenure, it is enough to note that already by 31 December 1942, almost 42,000 Jews had been deported from France to Auschwitz.

As opposed to Maurice Papon, Bousquet did not make a seamless career transition into the postwar world. After returning from a brief exile in Germany at the end of the war, Bousquet was imprisoned for three years. In June 1949 he stood trial before the High Court of Justice, whose function it was to pass judgment on the most important Vichy officials who had collaborated with the Nazis. However, for reasons that will be explained shortly, Bousquet stood trial not for crimes against humanity, but rather for treason. The trial lasted three days and was dominated by the accused. Very little attention was paid to the deported Jews; the transcript of the trial reveals that the subject of the Vel d'hiv roundups was, incredibly, completely glossed over. At the end of the trial, Bousquet was sentenced to five years of dégradation nationale ("national degradation"), which includes the loss of civil rights. The sentence was immediately commuted for Bousquet's reported "acts of resistance." Bousquet was a free man.

For roughly the next twenty years, Bousquet enjoyed a remarkable career in the private sector. He sat on the boards of numerous banks and corporations and was the associate director-general of the Bank of Indochina by 1960. He counted among his friends the rich and powerful, including François Mitterrand, for whose 1965 presidential campaign he secured funds from the influential Toulousian newspaper the *Dépêche du Midi*. Without the Darquier interview in *L'-Express*, Bousquet might well have lived out his life in comfortable and wealthy obscurity. As it was, his last years were spent trying to avoid a trial on charges of crimes against humanity for his role in the deportation of the Jews during the Occupation. Shortly before he was finally due to stand trial, Bousquet was gunned down in his apartment building by a crazed publicity seeker on the morning of 8 June 1993. Bousquet's assassin, one Christian Didier, would later tell the press that, in shooting Bousquet, he felt he was "killing a serpent."[19]

This introduction has sketched out the careers and crimes of Barbie, Leguay, and especially Touvier and Bousquet primarily in order to fill in part of the historico-legal background to the trial of Maurice Papon. But these brief descriptions also point to a number of considerations that help to explain why cases involving crimes against humanity in France have proven so vexed and controversial over the last two decades. First, in all cases the accused was tried or would have been tried at least forty years after the crimes themselves were committed. This fact alone raises a number of historical, legal, and moral concerns and dilemmas, which for some are enough to undermine the validity of these trials from the outset.[20] From an historical perspective it is exceedingly difficult to ascertain the exact political and social circumstances that are necessary to contextualize properly the crimes being judged. In the case of Papon, the conflation of events during Vichy with those of 17 October 1961 presented such difficulties. In the Touvier and especially the Papon trials, historians were called as "expert" witnesses in circumstances that some scholars, and especially Henry Rousso, found unacceptable. In his discussion of the Papon trial in *La Hantise du passé*, Rousso notes first of all that the historians were asked to testify about events in which the accused was involved—*and about which the historians themselves had no firsthand knowledge.*[21] Moreover, unlike the lawyers in Bordeaux, they did not have access to all the documents specifically concerning Papon, nor, ironically, had they been consulted for their archival expertise when the case was being prepared. The solicitation of their opinions therefore presumed a certain level of ignorance that made some of them ill at ease. Finally, the fact that they testified just like any other witnesses and subjected their knowledge to the mediation of lawyers and the media made it possible for the latter to manipulate, "instrumentalize" (to use Rousso's expression), or even dismiss the expert views they expressed. An excellent example of this occurred during the Touvier trial. Touvier's lawyer, Jacques Trémolet de Villers, dismissed the testimony of the dean of Vichy historians, Robert Paxton, as just "one version" of the past, neither more nor less reliable than any other. In subjecting historical expertise and exactitude to the rhetorical manipulation of the lawyers (and others) in this fashion, History itself, with a capital "H," was, in effect, put on trial as well.

Trémolet's efforts to distort and dismiss Paxton's observations concerning Vichy point to one very real danger that emerges when the often contradictory exigencies of history and the law are forced to confront each other in proceedings such as these. (Whatever one might think of Trémolet's attack on Paxton's expertise, it was, after all, simply part of his defense of his client.) But there are other, more serious dangers from the standpoint of history that emerged in the events leading up to the Touvier trial. In April 1992 the Paris Court of Appeals shocked the nation by dropping all charges against Touvier. The court argued that because Touvier was acting as an agent of Vichy, and since Vichy did not practice a politics of "ideological hegemony"—a qualification that, according to French law, was essential if crimes against humanity were to be committed in the name of the regime in question—Touvier was not guilty of crimes against humanity. And since the statute of limitations had run out on war crimes with which Touvier could legitimately be accused, the former Milice member had to be freed.

I will return shortly to the legal precedents and context of the April 1992 Court of Appeals decision, but it is important to stress here the damage done to historical truth both prior to and during the 1994 trial of Touvier. First, in whitewashing Vichy, the court took real liberties with the historical realities of the Pétain regime. According to the court, Vichy consisted of "a constellation of 'good intentions' and political animosities." The court also claimed that although a "certain ideology" consisting of a nostalgia for tradition and the rural past and a celebration of an archaic Christianity did reign at Vichy, diversity was also tolerated, and therefore no specific, monolithic ideology held sway. Moreover, the court also insisted that there was a huge difference between the ideology of some of Vichy's institutions, including especially the Milice, to which Touvier belonged, and the ideology of Nazi Germany. Finally, as regards the question of an official state anti-Semitism, the court acknowledged that the policies of Vichy were not "devoid of anti-Semitism," but denied that there was ever an "official proclamation of anti-Semitism." To prove this last point, the court noted that none of Pétain's speeches made anti-Semitic pronouncements.

As historians have argued subsequently, on each of these counts the court was completely misguided.[22] Vichy was an authoritarian, hegemonic regime with a coercive ideology that did, however, evolve somewhat over time. But this did not mean that it tolerated ideologies other than its own—quite the reverse. Moreover, institutions like the Milice certainly *were* close to the Nazis, both ideologically as well as in practical terms. One only has to consider their charter and study their close links with the Nazis in policing the French, rounding up Jews, and carrying out collaborative military actions. As for the issue of anti-Semitism, both Vichy's anti-Jewish statutes, instituted *independently of the Nazis* and promulgated in 1940 and 1941, and, later, Vichy's willing participation in the deportation of Jews from France, flatly contradicted the court's claims.

In November 1992 a higher court partially overturned the April Court of Appeals verdict. The Criminal Chamber of the High Court of Appeals ruled, in effect, that Touvier could indeed stand trial for crimes against humanity for the murder of the seven Jews at Rillieux-la-Pape. But it refused to challenge the lower court's reading of the Vichy regime, which meant in effect that crimes against humanity could not be committed in Vichy's name. Perhaps the court felt that one more judicial intervention in rewriting the Vichy past would only make matters worse. But whatever its intention, the net effect was to put history and justice irretrievably at odds when Touvier actually stood trial in 1994. In order to convict the ex-Milice member of crimes against humanity, it had to be proven that the murders were undertaken at the behest of the Nazis, who *did* practice a politics of "ideological hegemony." The problem was that, as the trial revealed, no German orders or initiatives of any kind led Touvier to act. The murder, as Touvier's own slip of the tongue on the stand seemed to confirm, was a gesture of reprisal for the Resistance's murder the day before of Philippe Henriot, Vichy's minister of propaganda and a favorite of the Milice. The crime was, as Arno Klarsfeld's published plea asserted, *un crime français*[23]— a French crime.

Ironically, it was Klarsfeld himself who argued successfully for a strong enough linkage between the Milice and the Gestapo to make Touvier's crime at Rillieux fall under the category of an action undertaken on behalf of a regime practicing a policy of ideological hegemony. This paved the way for Touvier's conviction. But any satisfaction that could be derived from the verdict had to be tempered by the knowledge that it had had to be secured by taking very serious liberties with the historical record. Some of the expert witnesses even changed their tune during the trial, arguing that the murders at Rillieux had been undertaken at the behest of the Germans, even though they knew full well that this was not the case. Some had in fact earlier testified that it was indeed a French crime.

The April 1992 Court of Appeals decision and its impact on the Touvier trial certainly provide the most dramatic examples of legal decisions relating to crimes against humanity having an adverse effect on the proper understanding and representation of historical truth. But these are not the only instances where this has occurred. As historians have noted, the considerable and perhaps excessive interest in Vichy anti-Semitism—especially Vichy's role in aiding and abetting the Final Solution—which has been encouraged to a very significant degree by the cases involving crimes against humanity, has tended to distort the *overall* understanding of the regime, its policies and practices. At the same time, it has occasionally tended to blacken through guilt by association the reputation on this score of *all* of the French who lived through the Occupation. As books like Susan Zuccotti's *The Holocaust, the French, and the Jews* confirm, however, there were many instances where the French attempted, often successfully, to save the Jews despite the will of Vichy and the Germans. The well known example of dozens of Jews saved by the villagers of le Chambon-sur-Lignon, recounted movingly in the film *Weapons of the Spirit*, comes to mind.

If cases involving crime against humanity in France have tended to do a disservice to historical understanding and, in the case of the Papon trial, even to mark a "regression" in historical knowledge (see the interview with Henry Rousso in *Le Monde* included in this volume), legal efforts to cope with the individuals and crimes in question have also put serious strains on the consistency and coherence of French law. Since the trial of Klaus Barbie, in fact, French courts have repeatedly modified the law to the point where the French legal expert Christian Guéry wondered in 1994—*before* the Papon trial further muddied the waters—if crimes against humanity even *existed* in any coherent shape or form in French law.[24] Other legal experts working outside France have expressed this view as well.[25]

In order to make sense of Guéry's claim, it is necessary to review briefly the strange legal history of crimes against humanity in France. One must emphasize first of all that despite French participation at Nuremberg, crimes against humanity were not incorporated in French law until 1964. On 26 December of that year, crimes against humanity as defined by the London accords of August 1945 were declared imprescriptible—that is, not subject to a statute of limitations—under French law. The target the legislators had in mind were Nazis like Klaus Barbie, who had eluded prosecution, and *not* Frenchmen.

It is important to stress that the actual text of the London accords was not included in the legislation, nor was any jurisdiction established for trying cases involving crimes against humanity. As Henry Rousso and Éric Conan assert in *Vichy: An Ever-Present Past*, these omissions would give rise over time to a number of problems. First, given that no definition of the crimes in question was provided in the legislation, how were these statutes to be incorporated in domestic law? Second, what court could try these cases, given that the Nuremberg Tribunal no longer existed?[26]

But the larger moral, ethical as well as legal concern raised by the 1964 law was the declaration that crimes against humanity were imprescriptible. Imprescriptibility was not included in the definition of crimes against humanity provided in the London accords, in large part because, as Rousso and Conan explain, Anglo-American law does not recognize a statute of limitations in criminal cases. But its inclusion in French law meant that crimes against humanity statutes could, and would, be applied retroactively and indefinitely. For many, including even those who wished to see the likes of Bousquet, Touvier, and Papon prosecuted, the retroactivity of the law was a source of very real discomfort, since it ran counter to the spirit of French, and, in most instances, international law as well.[27]

All of these issues manifested themselves in one form or another in the cases of those accused of crimes against humanity in France. Defense counsels from Barbie's lawyer, Jacques Vergès, to Touvier's lawyer, Jacques Trémolet de Villers, to Jean-Marc Varaut decried the injustice of applying laws retroactively. Vergès gleefully asserted that the last time this occurred in France was under Vichy, when the infamous *Sections spéciales* were created to deliver summary executions against "terrorists." As for jurisdictional questions, these were particularly pronounced in the Touvier and Bousquet cases. Throughout the 1970s a number of courts declared themselves incompetent to try Touvier on charges of crimes against humanity, only to have these decisions overturned by higher courts. At one point, the Ministry of Foreign Affairs was consulted, since the issue at stake was the incorporation of an international statute into French domestic law.

Jurisdictional issues also played an important role in the case against Bousquet, but here things were complicated by the fact that Bousquet had already stood trial in 1949 before the High Court of Justice. As should now be clear, the reason that Bousquet was not tried in 1949 for crimes against humanity was that the statutes governing such crimes were not incorporated into French law until 1964. However, this distinction did not prevent Bousquet's allies, including François Mitterrand, from muddying the historical and legal waters by arguing on several occasions during the early 1990s that Bousquet had already stood trial for *all* of his crimes during the Occupation. And for those unaware of or inattentive to the important, indeed crucial, legal distinctions between the crimes for which Bousquet was tried in 1949 and those of which he was accused by Serge Klarsfeld in 1989, the effort to bring Bousquet to trial in the 1990s looked like a clear case of double jeopardy.

Moreover, as a consequence of Bousquet's having been tried before the High Court of Justice in 1949, the jurisdictional issue took a particularly controversial turn in 1990. In October, the prosecutor-general Pierre Truche, who had earlier prosecuted the state's case against Klaus Barbie, asked the Criminal Division of the Paris Court of Appeals which had been assigned the Bousquet case to declare itself incompetent to handle it. To great public consternation, Truche argued that Bousquet's case should be handled by the High Court that had originally tried him in 1949. The difficulty was that the High Court had been dissolved for years, many of its members were long since dead, and any effort to reconstitute it would take years, if it could be reconstituted at all. By that time Bousquet would in all likelihood be dead of old age himself.

For all but the most naive, Truche's gambit was clearly a delaying tactic, one whose inspiration, as it turned out, came indirectly from the president of the republic. Later, in November, the Paris Court of Appeals refused to declare itself incompetent, but not before government officials lamely attempted to explain Truche's ploy on the grounds that it was undertaken in the interest of "civil peace."

If jurisdictional issues played a crucial role in the entire Bousquet affair and the early stages of the Touvier affair, the definition of crimes against humanity, not clearly spelled out in the text of the 1964 law, came to the fore as preparations were being made to try Klaus Barbie in the mid-1980s. In essence, the definition of crimes against humanity in the London accords made things fairly straightforward for trying Barbie on charges of crimes against humanity for his participation in the Final Solution and specifically the arrest and deportation of the children of Izieu. The problem was that, for many of the French, and especially former Resistance members, Barbie was first and foremost the SS officer who imprisoned, tortured, and killed many of their former colleagues, and especially Jean Moulin. In order to address the concerns of this latter constituency, in 1985 the Court of Criminal Appeals amended the definition of crimes against humanity in French law to include "inhumane acts and persecutions which, for the sake of a State practicing a policy of ideological hegemony, were committed systematically *not only against individuals because they belonged to a racial or religious group, but also against adversaries of this policy, whatever may be the form of their opposition* [my emphasis]."[28] Now Barbie (and potentially others) could be tried for their crimes against the Resistance as well as for their crimes against the Jews, all within the framework of crimes against humanity. Within the context of the trial of Barbie, this may have been helpful and even necessary, but it is not difficult to see how the definition of crimes against humanity itself was being modified to suit the purposes of the moment. A dangerous precedent was being set.

As it turned out, the 1985 Court of Criminal Appeals amendment of the definition of crimes against humanity also contained a "time bomb" of sorts, which, as we have seen, "exploded" in April 1992 in the context of the Touvier case. The Court of Criminal Appeals introduced the phrase "a regime practicing a policy of ideological hegemony,"[29] the interpretation of which led the Paris Court of Appeals to whitewash Vichy and drop charges against Touvier in April 1992. Moreover, as also noted, it hamstrung Touvier's trial so that the conviction of the accused could only be accomplished at the expense of historical truth.

If the cases of Barbie, Touvier, and Bousquet underscore the contortions and questionable adjustments the French legal system was obliged to make in order to try, or, in Bousquet's case, make possible the trial of the accused, the Papon case would have its own pretrial twists and turns. Some of the difficulties involved in the earlier cases could, however, be ignored. First, in comparison with the Barbie case, there was no question of actions against the Resistance. In fact, as previously noted, Papon stressed his assistance to and participation in the Resistance as part of his defense. Second, there was no question of a "French crime" as in the case of Touvier because, even though Papon was a Vichy civil servant, the deportation of Jews was clearly part of the *German* plan to exterminate them in the context of the Final Solution. Finally, unlike Bousquet, Papon had not been tried during the postwar period for any of his actions during the Occupation, so there was no jurisdictional question of the sort Pierre Truche raised in 1990.

However, there were other very serious legal difficulties where Papon was concerned that had not come up in the cases involving the other men. First, some doubted that Papon would even be brought to trial in a conservative city like Bordeaux, one that had earned the reputation of being the "capital of collaboration" during the war. But a larger issue concerned the incrimination of Papon in light of the November 1992 decision in the Touvier case. In effect, this decision required that in order to be convicted of crimes against humanity, one had to be the direct and willing accomplice of the Nazis. It was difficult enough to convict Touvier on these grounds, but in the case of Papon, as Éric Conan asserts, "[n]othing in the comportment of this member of the hierarchy of state permitted one to establish direct and willing complicity with the Nazis."[30] So in 1995, the advocate-general charged with writing the indictment following the conclusion of the investigation of the case against Papon decided that a dismissal of charges was in order. When the decision was referred to the Chancellery, however, Jacques Toubon, the minister of justice under the Gaullist president Jacques Chirac, concluded that nothing would prove more scandalous under the circumstances than the dismissal of charges against a former Gaullist minister. Toubon therefore told the prosecutor in Bordeaux to arrange things so that the case would be sent before the Assizes Court.

In a complicated series of maneuvers over the next few years, the various individuals and branches of the court charged with handling the Papon case succeeded each other in accomplishing the painful legal and verbal acrobatics necessary to bring Papon to trial. In December 1995 the prosecutor concluded that Papon "had associated himself, in a complex process of participation, with the anti-Jewish operations decided on by the German authorities, one of whose aims of which the accused was not ignorant was the deportation [of Jews to Germany]." But the prosecutor also acknowledged that the accused "was ignorant of the Final Solution." In order to establish Papon's willing complicity with the Germans, the prosecutor was obliged to fall back on the weak argument that merely accepting the job of secretary-general of the Gironde prefecture "was an implicit sign [on the part of the accused] of favoring the projects of the occupant."

For its part, the Criminal Division of the Court of Appeals came to a different conclusion. Even before Papon accepted his assignment in Bordeaux in 1942, the Criminal Division concluded that he had a "clear, reasoned, and detailed understanding" of the Nazis' intentions to "take the lives of these persons." This conclusion was, of course, highly speculative and indeed quite dubious, and when Papon's lawyer Jean-Marc Varaut challenged it before the Court of Appeals, the Court of Appeals did not hesitate to modify the law again. In its 23 January 1997 decision, the court concluded that it was no longer necessary for the accomplice of crimes against humanity to "adhere to the politics of ideological hegemony of the principal authors of the crime." It was this decision, obviously, that made the April 1998 conviction of Papon possible.

Cases involving crimes against humanity in France have often pitted History (with a capital "H") against the law and even against the interests of justice itself, and, moreover, have forced the law into a series of damaging contortions and contradictions. Unfortunately, these are not the only dilemmas these trials have raised. Those who have opposed the trials on principle have articulated other concerns of a moral and ethical nature, some of which have been dispensed with during the trials themselves, and some not. In the former category, the objection has been raised that it is unjust to try an individual for crimes committed forty to fifty years earlier, especially because, given the time elapsed, the accused may have changed completely. But as the trials of Barbie, Papon, and especially Touvier revealed, this concern proved to be illusory. None of the accused showed any sign of repentance or change in outlook. During his trial Papon brazenly asserted that if he had it to do all over again, he would do the same thing.[31] As for Touvier, among the items found in his possession at the time of his arrest was a notebook dating from the 1980s, which he had filled with the same anti-Semitic invective that had characterized his attitudes during the war. By all accounts he seemed to be, as much of his rambling testimony revealed, a man "frozen in time."

Shortly before the Papon trial got under way in Bordeaux, the distinguished editorialist Paul Thibaud published an essay in the political and cultural review Le Débat in which he raised another concern having to do with the anachronistic nature of the trial and the imprescriptibility of the crimes in question.[32] In effect, Thibaud argued that a trial like Papon's ultimately gave a greater sense of false satisfaction to members of subsequent generations than it did real satisfaction to Papon's actual victims. This was so because it allowed the former to indulge in a facile morality in judging a past in which they themselves had not been actors, in which they had no real vested interest, and in which they themselves could not be compromised. In the uncertain times of the present, after the collapse of ideological metanarratives like communism, which had made sense of history for so long and for so many, the trial at least provided a moral anchor to grasp, even though the morality it afforded had been purchased much too cheaply. Regardless of the cogency of Thibaud's argument, it does not seem to have made the jurors' job in Bordeaux any easier.

Given these numerous shortcomings and indeed dangers, what possible benefits could counterbalance them in order to make these trials serve a valuable historical, social, or political function? The most frequent response to this question was that they fulfill a so-called duty to memory by belatedly bringing the criminals in question to justice and rescuing the majority of their victims from the terrible anonymity of the Holocaust and the gas chambers. In the Papon trial, the desire to preserve the memory of the victims was evident not only in the reading of their names at vigils outside the courthouse, but in efforts to project photos in the courtroom itself of those deported from Bordeaux who had died in Auschwitz. In at least one such attempt, the interests of memory and the law were clearly at odds.

On 16 December 1997 Arno Klarsfeld requested that a photograph of the mother of a witness, Georges Gheldman, be projected in the courtroom. When President Castagnède refused, Klarsfeld, caught up in the emotion of the moment, insulted Castagnède, arguing that for the president of the court as well as for the accused, there were "interesting Jews" and others who weren't. (Klarsfeld was referring to Papon's practice during the Occupation of saving some Jews and not others on the basis that those who were spared were more "interesting" for various political reasons.) As if comparing the president to the accused were not enough, Klarsfeld went a step further, arguing that Castagnède would not be in the exalted position of presiding over a trial of this magnitude if it weren't for the efforts of the association Klarsfeld represented to bring Papon to justice. The affront to the president was severe enough to get Klarsfeld thrown out of court, even according to other lawyers for the civil litigants.[33] Indeed, this might well have happened had Klarsfeld not apologized in court the next day.

From the standpoint of the law, it was the president's decision as to whether or not to show the photograph, and he would certainly have been within his rights to demand sanctions against Klarsfeld for his courtroom behavior. But from Klarsfeld's perspective, the president's action was an inexcusable affront to the memory of Gheldman's mother and an attempt on the part of the court to leave the victims of the deportations in the "hell of anonymity" in which the Nazis, with Vichy's assistance, had sought to consign them.[34] And although Klarsfeld's behavior was certainly outrageous, it was in keeping with his motivation for participating in the trial in the first place. As he stated on numerous occasions, he was there primarily to rescue the memory of the victims, and in difficult moments during the proceedings, he notes in his memoir of the trial, it was the thought of each of the victims he represented that kept him going.

Of course few would question the validity and necessity of commemorating the victims of the Holocaust, especially since denial of the Holocaust rears its head periodically in French public life, most recently in the spring of 1996 with the Father Pierre–Roger Garaudy scandal.[35] But the question remains as to whether a court of law is the appropriate arena in which to fulfill the "duty to memory," as the controversy over the Gheldman photograph suggests. In Bordeaux there were certainly those who felt that the activism of the "memory militants" ultimately ran counter to the interests of justice in bringing undue pressure on the court in the latter's efforts to observe the letter of the law. Conversely, for the memory militants, pressure of this sort was necessary not only to save the victims from anonymity, but to ensure that the court's interpretation of the law did not incline unfairly in the direction of the accused, who was after all a powerful politician involved in public service for a half a century. This last concern, in fact, also sparked an earlier confrontation between Klarsfeld and Castagnède, this one having to do with Castagnède's decision to release Papon from custody, primarily on grounds of the poor health of the accused. In announcing his decision, however, Castagnède did not restrict his justifications solely to the issue of Papon's health:

> Given that freedom is the rule and detention the exception . . . Given the extreme old age of the accused and the serious downturn in his health . . . Given that there is no evidence to support the hypothesis that the accused might flee . . . Given that a perturbation of public order is not of a sufficient nature to support provisional detention, the court orders that the accused be released.[36]

In his assessment of the president's decision to release Papon, Éric Conan argues that there was absolutely "nothing exceptional" about it in legal terms. The decision was taken, moreover, by "one of the best presidents of the Assizes Courts of the southwest," a judge known for being "rigorous and attentive to the rights of the defense." And as final proof of the validity and consistency of Castagnède's decision, Conan notes that it was in keeping with the earlier decision of the prosecutor to leave Papon at large during the long years that the case against him moved slowly through the legal system. [37]

When Castagnède announced his decision, Arno Klarsfeld got to his feet, expressed his view that what the president had done was an insult to the victims of the deportations, and concluded that the trial itself "had lost its purpose." He then stormed out of the courtroom. In his memoirs Klarsfeld explains his extreme hostility to Castagnède's clemency toward Papon by contrasting it to the fact that questions of age and health did not deter or defer the deportations of Jews from Bordeaux. Klarsfeld also expresses his belief that Castagnède caved in to pressure not to imprison a man of the accused's social stature.[38]

In these comments, Klarsfeld evokes the two primary motivations of the memory militants: respect for the memory of the victims and a necessary vigilance to ensure that the court did not incline in favor of the accused. In the same discussion, however, Klarsfeld also calls attention to a *legal* consequence of Castagnède's decision that, for many, ultimately compromised the validity of the decision from the standpoint of justice itself. Once Papon was released from custody in this fashion, French law stipulates that *even if convicted, he could not be imprisoned until his appeal was exhausted.* This explains why Papon was still at large and able to pursue a normal, unfettered existence for more than a year after his conviction. And to add insult to injury, at the time of Castagnède's decision, in the days following his release Papon made a point of visibly and ostentatiously dining in the four-star restaurants sprinkled through the Bordeaux region. He then arrived in court by limousine, unaccompanied by the guards who had been present by law before Castagnède's decision. As Nicolas Weill would later remark bitterly, once Papon was released, his appearance in court was more like that of a luminary attending a colloquium devoted to him rather than a criminal against humanity on trial for his actions.[39]

While one might well find sympathy with Klarsfeld's criticism of Castagnède's decision to release Papon, it is harder to accept the imperatives of the "duty to memory" as Klarsfeld interpreted them in his final confrontation with Castagnède. In his memoir Klarsfeld reports that in late January 1998 he received a visit from Micheline Castagnède, the president of the court's cousin. Micheline Castagnède informed Klarsfeld that three of the president's cousins had been deported to Drancy on the convoy of 30 December 1943. Klarsfeld states that he wondered at the time why Castagnède had not revealed the connection and recused himself from presiding over the trial. But what really interested Klarsfeld were the potential consequences and implications of this revelation. Had Jean-Marc Varaut, Papon's lawyer, been aware of this compromising relationship all along and used it to force Castagnède to release Papon at the outset of the trial? Did the same deal guarantee that Papon would attend the trial, since without the presence of the accused the trial would certainly lose much of its cachet? Finally, if Castagnède could be shown to have a familial link to some of the victims of the deportations, could he be pressured into going along with the acquittal of the accused, since any guilty verdict would be tainted by the president's link to the victims?

Rather than confront Castagnède, whom Klarsfeld admits he completely distrusted by this point, or consult the other lawyers for the civil litigants (who were cozy with the president of the court, according to Klarsfeld) or the prosecutor, Klarsfeld opted to release the information directly to the press. He had three objectives in mind. First, he wanted to make sure that if Varaut was not already aware of Castagnède's family connection to the three deportees, he would not use the revelation to the advantage of his client. Second, as Klarsfeld readily admits, in releasing the information he wanted to weaken Castagnède's position in relation to the jurors, especially if the latter assumed the president had deliberately hidden something compromising from them. Since Castagnède was already, in Klarsfeld's opinion, too much under the sway of his first Assessor,[40] Jean-Pierre Esperben, known to hold right-wing sympathies and to be in favor of acquittal, he, Castagnède, might well be inclined to come out for acquittal as well. And, if the jurors had no reason to distrust or lose respect for him, they might also be swayed in the same direction simply by virtue of Castagnède's prestige as president. But all of these considerations were inconsequential if Klarsfeld could achieve his third objective: to force Castagnède to resign.

As one might expect, Klarsfeld's press release created a stir. For his part, Castagnède immediately denied any knowledge of his deported relatives, and Varaut quickly expressed his continued confidence in the president of the court. But the other lawyers for the civil litigants were outraged. Gérard Boulanger, the first lawyer to begin the effort to bring Papon to trial on charges of crimes against humanity many years before, stated that Klarsfeld had taken France back to the darkest days of Vichy. The question, he continued, was not whether or not Castagnède should resign but whether Klarsfeld himself should be thrown out of court. Michel Zaoui called Klarsfeld's action "scandalous, shameful and infantile."[41] Michel Lévy, another civil litigants lawyer, argued that Arno *and* Serge Klarsfeld were trying to sabotage the trial because they were afraid that Papon would be given a life term rather than the shorter sentence they advocated. Éric Conan believed, conversely, that the Klarsfelds were afraid of an acquittal and they would do anything they could to prevent it.[42] Klarsfeld's memoir confirms, obviously, that Conan was closer to the truth.

Whatever Klarsfeld's motivations, the real issue lies elsewhere. Even if Klarsfeld feared an acquittal, and even if this would have been an intolerable insult to the memory of the victims, in essentially blackmailing the president he violated any sense of "fair play" and justice. Furthermore, he attempted to force the court to conform to his wishes by bringing *external* pressures to bear on it. In this instance at least, the duty to memory, as at least one of the most visible memory militants interpreted it, could not be exercised in a court of law without compromising the integrity of the court itself.

Should confrontations such as the one just described lead one to conclude that trials like Papon's, or Touvier's, or Barbie's for that matter, should not be undertaken, at least in the name of a "duty to memory"? This is a difficult question, first, because for many observers who feel that the historical and legal disadvantages of these trials far outweigh any advantages they may have, the *only justification* of these trials is that they serve memory. For others, however, the problem is compounded because the whole notion of a "duty to memory" is a very vexed and indeed counterproductive notion. In France (as in the United States) there are those who question the value of memory for memory's sake, especially where Vichy and the Holocaust are concerned. During the war in the former Yugoslavia in the early 1990s, Alain Finkielkraut argued that the obsession with the "Dark Years" of the Occupation and the effort to right the wrongs committed by Vichy, especially against the Jews, prevented the French from seeing or caring about the fact that the Serbs were at that very moment accomplishing crimes comparable to the worst crimes of the Nazis. The duty to memory, according to Finkielkraut, was just the latest form of navel contemplation.[43] Finkielkraut was referring at the time to the trial of Paul Touvier, but as his editorial on the Papon trial included in this volume confirms, he has not changed his opinion. In the recent *Les Abus de la mémoire* (The Abuses of Memory), Tzvetan Todorov argues that the cult of memory can just as easily result in a sterile wallowing in the role of the victim as it can in creating a positive morality in the present.[44] And as commentators from Henry Rousso and Éric Conan to Charles Maier in the United States have argued, a "surfeit" of memory, as Maier calls it, may not only undermine constructive action in the present but may also compromise a rigorous historical understanding of the past. Finally, as the Papon trial demonstrated in at least one instance, the duty to memory may function only selectively, retrieving some of the victims and consigning others to oblivion. In his journal of the trial, Éric Conan notes that two convoys departing on 2 February and 7 June 1943, and which took 206 individuals to their deaths, were not even examined in the Assizes Court in Bordeaux. The reason, Conan explains, is that Papon was not charged with involvement in these deportations, and no civil parties represented the dead. For the victims of these deportations, the duty to memory failed completely.[45]

So what remains of the Papon trial, what is its legacy, and what has it taught us? In the numerous books, articles, and interviews that have appeared since the verdict in Bordeaux, the reviews, so to speak, are decidedly mixed. Among the more positive is that of Arno Klarsfeld, in part because the jury and the court ended up seeing things his way in handing down the sentence of ten years' imprisonment, and in part, as he explains, because of what would have happened had Papon been acquitted:

> A fracture would have traversed all of French society, the partisans of Vichy would once again have raised their heads, the extreme right would have been reinforced, the image of France would have been tarnished, and finally, what happened yesterday could have occurred again tomorrow with complete impunity.[46]

Unlike Klarsfeld, most commentators on the Papon trial neither were happy with its outcome nor did they offer dire predictions as to what the consequences of an acquittal would have been. Three months after the conclusion of the proceedings in Bordeaux, the lawyer for the civil litigants Michel Zaoui lamented what he described as the "silence" that followed the Assizes Court's conviction of Papon (see Zaoui's commentary in this volume), a silence he attributed in part to the delaying tactics of the defense. Having successfully steered the court's attention away from the crimes with which Papon was charged for the first two months of the trial, the defense had managed to exhaust the interest of the media, which had already moved on to other issues by the time the verdict was in. In an interview published later in the review *Esprit*, Zaoui would change his tune, arguing that if the trial had concluded in December 1997 as planned, the court would have only scratched the surface of the case.

Éric Conan was more specific in his assessment of the trial, focusing his attention primarily on the unsatisfactory nature of the verdict. In the final pages of his book *Le Procès Papon: Un Journal d'audience*, he argues first that the verdict was sadly consistent with the impossible situation in which the jurors found themselves. Since the prosecution failed miserably to make its case against the accused, the jury might well have been inclined to acquit him. But having bought into the so-called symbolism of the trial, they felt they could not acquit Papon without acquitting Vichy in the same gesture. The irony then was that if one *did* accept the notion that the Papon judgment was somehow the symbolic judgment of Vichy, then a verdict that found Papon guilty of complicity in arrests and detentions but *not* complicity in murder actually *reduced* Vichy's culpability, which was in fact much greater at the higher administrative levels.

But perhaps the trial's and verdict's worst failing, in Conan's eyes, was that the court simply did not engage with the real heart of the debate over crimes against humanity. It was Jean-Marc Varaut's position that a crime against humanity necessitated a personal adherence to Nazi objectives. Only then could it measure up to the definition Varaut assigned it in an interview in *Esprit*: "an absolute crime, a metaphysical crime against the human condition." (Because Papon did not qualify in this regard, to try him was in Varaut's view to "banalize" crimes against humanity.) As opposed to Varaut, according to Conan, for Michel Zaoui and Michel Lévy (another lawyer for the civil litigants) crimes against humanity were not to be determined on an act-by-act basis but in the "conscious participation in a process whose criminal intent was evident." As Zaoui explained in the same *Esprit* interview, in directing the Jewish services offices at the Bordeaux prefecture, Papon was already guilty because he was working in an office that was *by definition* criminal.

As it turned out, the conviction of Papon failed to come to terms with *either* of these approaches, thus avoiding the real debate over the nature and definition of crimes against humanity as it applied to the case at hand. So Varaut and Zaoui and Lévy were all losers, according to Conan, but so too were history, memory, and the law. At the end of *Le Procès Papon*, Conan concludes that future historians will look upon the trial as severely as those who advocated trying figures like Papon, Touvier, and Bousquet now look upon the postwar trials of the Purge. Éric Conan's gloomy epitaph of the Papon trial is in many ways all too accurate. But it is perhaps fitting that an event of the magnitude of the trial of Maurice Papon for crimes against humanity should outlive its epitaph both in its capacity to generate *new* controversies and to inspire unusual and provocative interpretations—global in their import—of what was really at stake in Bordeaux.

In February 1999, Maurice Papon, free on appeal form his conviction in Bordeaux, took the historian Jean-Luc Einaudi to court for "defamation of a public official in the person of Maurice Papon, the prefect of Paris police in October 1961." At issue was an editorial published by Einaudi in *Le Monde* in May 1998, which was in effect a thoroughgoing critique of the Mandelkern report discussed earlier. (Einaudi's editorial is included in this volume under the title "For the Truth, at Last.") At the conclusion of the editorial, Einaudi wrote that in Paris on the night of 17 October 1961, there had been a "massacre perpetrated by police forces acting on the orders of Maurice Papon." It was this assertion that led Papon to sue for defamation.

The court deliberated for several days, heard testimony from the accused and his accuser, and concluded that although Einaudi's statement was "on the evidence" defamatory, it was made in the good faith context of a body of serious and well-documented research. In essence, the court found in favor of Einaudi, and concluded moreover that "certain members of the forces of order, relatively numerous, acted with extreme violence" on the night in question. This was the first time that the French justice system had recognized the brutality of Parisian police against Algerian protesters in 1961. Furthermore, the court's acknowledgment of police brutality occurred, as Philippe Bernard remarked, at precisely the moment when Papon was seeking the court's assistance in silencing a man who had long characterized the 1961 events in this fashion. After the trial, Einaudi asserted that justice was at last done to the victims of 1961, and his lawyer pronounced the verdict "a great victory." So if the first trial of Maurice Papon had failed to serve memory and justice, what *L'Express* called the "other Papon trial"—a trial in which Papon was not the accused but the accuser and crimes against humanity and the Holocaust were not at stake—had, at least for some, accomplished that goal.

In moving from Bordeaux under the Occupation to Paris during the Algerian war, from the deportation of Jews to the beatings and murder of Algerians, and from the Nazi Final Solution to the excesses of French democracy in the throes of decolonization, the "two Papon trials" have tended to call forth historical comparisons that are both explosive and ultimately untenable. But the historical strata that the Bordeaux trial unearthed, inadvertently or not, does suggest that in reflecting on the meaning and lessons of the trial, it is legitimate to move beyond the historical context of Bordeaux during the Occupation—and even World War II—and ask why trying Papon fifty years after the event seemed such an urgent necessity. This is precisely the question to which the legal expert Jean de Maillard seeks to respond in an article provocatively entitled "À quoi sert le procès Papon?" (What Purpose Does the Papon Trial Serve?)[47]

For Maillard, the trial was a monumental failure, not only because of the contradictions it reinforced rather than resolved and the historically dubious understanding of the past it fostered, but because it obscured rather than exposed its own motive and raison d'être. To begin with, according to Maillard, in order for the court to arrive at the judgment it rendered, it was necessary to posit that the Holocaust was a whole from which one could not subtract a single piece—Papon—without compromising the significance and coherence of that whole. But, at the same time, the court had to maintain that the Holocaust could include "detachable" actions, detachable in the sense that, like Papon's deportation orders, they were committed completely outside any *intention* to exterminate.

As if this skewed logic were not enough, in historical terms the trial was equally flawed in that, at least at the outset, it promoted an anachronistic and simplistic interpretation of the war. According to this interpretation, on one side were the Jews and their allies, and on the other the Nazis. Moreover, from the beginning of the conflict, *everyone* knew the Nazis intended to exterminate all the Jews. On all accounts, this is of course a preposterous reading of history. Not only was the fate of the Jews generally a secondary consideration for the Allies (it certainly did not figure at all in Soviet motivations), but the Nazi plan to exterminate the Jews was only put into effect piecemeal in 1941 and 1942. And as for the Final Solution, the Nazis made every effort to cover it up. In this they were largely successful, so certainly not everyone knew of the Nazis' murderous intent.

The fulfillment of the "duty to memory" in Bordeaux, according to Maillard, only made matters worse. The commemorations during the trial of the victims of the Final Solution in no way contributed to a better understanding of the historical forces and circumstances that gave rise to nazism, nor, for that matter, did they provide real insights into the nature of the beast itself, so to speak. So any moral satisfaction which might be gained from the commemorations of the victims should be counterbalanced by the fact that failing to explain nazism, they failed to prepare anyone to recognize it should it recur.

But for Maillard the most crucial failure of the Papon trial is that its larger meaning was not understood. In reality the trial was less an exercise whose purpose was to come to terms with the past than the expression of a complete loss of faith in the nation-state as the guarantor of the rights of the individual. The perfect bureaucrat and thus servant of the nation-state, Papon had repeatedly violated the rights of others, not only in the name of Vichy but also in that of the Fourth and Fifth Republics. The taint of nazism, contracted through Vichy, only served as a kind of indelible proof of the absolute evil that the nation-state—in the abstract—had come to embody. The only way for citizens to seek justice against the state and its representatives was through a court of law. So it was now the judge, according to Maillard, who alone could protect the individual and guarantee his or her rights. The judge had become "the phantasmagoric defender of the individual isolated in the political and social desert of the new global reality," a global reality where *any and all* nation-states were criminal by definition.[48] Rather than simply condemning the crimes of Vichy and Nazi Germany ex post facto, the Papon trial marked the first, spectacular staging of an impulse whose ultimate aim was the symbolical and systematic rejection of the nation-state—past, present, and future. In this sense, the trial's real message was nothing less than a call for radical change on a global scale.

One need not agree with the particulars of Maillard's assessment of the implications of the Papon trial to recognize that it offers much food for thought in legal-historical, political, and even philosophical terms. And certainly these and other issues raised by what some call the "trial of the century" will be debated, discussed, and written about for years to come. But in the short run, the legacy of the Bordeaux trial is evident less in far-reaching and abstract debates than in the almost farcical coup de théâtre surrounding the hearing of Papon's appeal. On 21 October 1999, Papon's appeal was scheduled to be heard by the Court of Appeals. According to French law, the night before the appeal is heard, the convicted individual must surrender himself or herself to the authorities and enter prison. In Papon's case, he could either turn himself in to the maison d'arrêt de Gradignon in the Bordeaux region or to the Santé prison in Paris. An effort by Papon's lawyers to exempt him from imprisonment on the grounds of poor health was rejected.

As the date the appeal was to be heard approached, rumors circulated—shortly to be confirmed—that Papon had fled the country, and reports from Swiss police suggested that he was in hiding in their country. On 21 October, with Papon still at large, the Court of Appeals rejected his appeal, which it was obliged to do automatically if the convict failed to turn himself in the day before. Papon's lawyer Jean-Marc Varaut announced that he would appeal to the European Court on the grounds that surrendering the day before the appeal was heard was a violation of Papon's human rights. In fact, the European Court had already criticized French law on this point in earlier cases.

Varaut's appeal did not stop the French court from signing out an international warrant for Papon's arrest, and shortly thereafter Swiss police apprehended Papon in a small hotel in Gstaad where he was staying under the alias "Robert Rochefoucauld." He was returned to France and began serving his prison sentence at Fresnes prison near Paris—the prison where many wartime collaborators had been held at the Liberation before their execution for treason.

If Papon's flight provided enormous grist for the media mill and put to rest any lingering doubts that Papon might be, as he said, a courageous man who "stood by his post" and accepted the consequences of his actions, it also rekindled important debates that had occurred during the trial itself. Most importantly, Jean-Louis Castagnède's decision to free Papon at the outset of the trial on grounds of poor health now looked particularly ill-advised, especially since it came out during Papon's flight to Switzerland that the authorities had not even taken away his passport. Seconding members of President Jacques Chirac's entourage that there was "guilty negligence" in the entire affair, Arno Klarsfeld argued that the Bordeaux prosecutor's office should be sanctioned. (Presumably its negligence created the favorable circumstances that allowed Papon to flee.) He also concluded sadly that the entire affair had made a mockery of French justice, and that when France called for the prosecution of war criminals in

Kosovo and East Timor the response would be derision. France, after all, had "let its own war criminals go."

Klarsfeld's pessimism is certainly legitimate. But it is also important to remember that a man who avoided justice for fifty years and arrogantly denied any wrongdoing is now finally serving his time. For the relatives and descendants of those deported to their deaths from Bordeaux between 1942 and 1944, this, at least, offers some solace.

NOTES

1. In French courts, lawyers representing civil litigants, including aggrieved individuals or organizations, are permitted to attach themselves to the prosecution. During the Papon trial several lawyers, representing primarily the victims of the deportations, their relatives, and their descendants, were present.

2. Éric Conan, *Le Procès Papon: Un Journal d'audience* (Paris: Gallimard, 1998), p. 313.

3. The full text of the *Acte d'accusation* was published by the Communist newspaper *L'Humanité* on 15 October 1997.

4. Klarsfeld's plea was published as *Papon: Un Crime français* (Paris: Ramsay, 1998).

5. Klarsfeld discusses the verdict and many other aspects of the trial in his memoir of it, *La Cour, les nains et le bouffon* (Paris: Robert Laffont, 1998). His reasons for arguing for a reduced sentence are found on pp. 26–28.

6. Jean-Marc Varaut, *Plaidoirie de Jean-Marc Varaut devant la cour d'assizes de la Gironde au procès de Maurice Papon, fonctionnaire sous l'Occupation* (Paris: Plon, 1998), p. 7.

7. See the interview with Rousso published in *Le Monde* following the trial included in this volume.

8. Arno Klarsfeld, *La Cour*, p. 28.

9. For details of Papon's postwar career, especially in the colonies, see Vann Kelly's essay included in this volume.

10. For details of the night of 17 October 1961 in Paris, see my "Memory's *bombes à retardement*: Maurice Papon, Crimes against Humanity, and 17 October 1961." *Journal of European Studies* 28 (1998), pp. 153–72, and especially Jean-Luc Einaudi, *La Bataille de Paris: 17 octobre 1961* (Paris: Seuil, 1991).

11. See Jean-Luc Einaudi's "For the Truth, at Last," included in this volume.

12. Pierre Vidal-Naquet, "Ce qui accable Papon," *Le Nouvel Observateur*, 23–29 October 1997, pp. 56–57.

13. Actually, the countries defined under French law as practicing a politics of ideological hegemony are the Axis powers, and thus Fascist Italy would be included

along with Nazi Germany. But in terms of the cases involving crimes against humanity, only Nazi Germany has been at issue.

14. The definition of crimes against humanity is included in W. Michael Reisman and Chris T. Antoniou, eds., *The Laws of War: A Collection of Primary Documents of International Laws Governing Armed Conflict* (New York: Vintage Books, 1994), p. 319.

15. For a more detailed account of Touvier's life, see the introduction to my *Memory, the Holocaust, and French Justice: The Bousquet and Touvier Affairs* (Hanover, N.H.: University Press of New England, 1996).

16. The *intégriste* movement had been led for years by Monsignor Lefèvre, and was eventually denounced by Rome. By the end of his years on the run, Touvier's church supporters were limited to the far-right fringes of French Catholicism.

17. Michael R. Marrus and Robert O. Paxton, *Vichy France and the Jews* (New York: Schocken Books, 1983), pp. 250–52.

18. Philippe Burrin, *La France à l'heure allemande* (Paris: Seuil, 1995), p. 164.

19. For an account of the murder of Bousquet as well as his 1949 trial, see my "Memory and Justice Abused: The 1949 Trial of René Bousquet," *Studies in Twentieth Century Literature* 23:1 (1999), pp. 93-110.

20. See, for example, Tzvetan Todorov's essay in this volume.

21. Henry Rousso, *La Hantise du passé* (Paris: Textuel, 1998), pp. 101–9.

22. See, in particular, François Bédarida, *Touvier, le dossier de l'accusation* (Paris: Seuil, 1996), pp. 20–43.

23. Arno Klarsfeld, *Touvier, un crime français* (Paris: Fayard, 1994).

24. Christian Guéry, "Une Interrogation après le procès Touvier: Le Crime contre l'humanité existe-t-il?" *Le Genre humain* 28 (1994), pp. 119–38.

25. See Leila Sadat Wexler, "The Interpretation of the Nuremberg Principles by the French Court of Cassation: From Touvier to Barbie and Back Again." *Columbia Journal of Transnational Law* 32:2 (1994), pp. 363–64.

26. Éric Conan and Henry Rousso, *Vichy: An Ever-Present Past.* Trans. Nathan Bracher (Hanover, N.H.: University Press of New England, 1998), p. 88–90.

27. The Nuremberg statutes were, of course, also applied retroactively, which gave rise to a good deal of criticism, especially, as Rousso notes, among the losers.

28. Cited in Conan and Rousso, p. 90.

29. It is important to note that the phrase "practicing a politics of ideological hegemony" was inserted precisely to prevent Barbie's lawyer, Jacques Vergès, from muddying the legal waters by arguing that the French torture of Algerians during the Algerian war could *also* be considered crimes against humanity. Since the Fourth and Fifth Republics, under which these actions took place, were democracies, they could not be described as practicing a politics of ideological hegemony. And no crimes against humanity could therefore be committed in their names.

30. Éric Conan, "La Casse-Tête juridique," *L'Express*, 2–8 October 1997, pp. 54–56. The discussion of the legal negotiations over the Papon case in the nineties is taken from Conan's account in this article.

31. Quoted in Klarsfeld, *La Cour*, p. 68.

32. Paul Thibaud, "Un Temps de mémoire?" *Le Débat* 96 (September–October 1997), pp. 166–83.

33. See Conan, *Le Procès Papon*, p. 96.

34. See Klarsfeld, *La Cour*, p. 131.

35. Father Pierre unfortunately lent his support to a negationist text published by his old friend, Roger Garaudy, a former Communist whose credibility had long since been dismissed in most quarters. For a discussion of the affair, see my introduction to Alain Finkielkraut, *The Future of a Negation: Reflections on the Question of Genocide* (Lincoln: University of Nebraska Press, 1998), pp. xi–xxx.

36. Quoted in Klarsfeld, *La Cour*, p. 65.

37. Conan, *Le Procès Papon*, pp. 17–21.

38. Klarsfeld, *La Cour*, pp. 55–57.

39. Nicolas Weill, "Penser le procès Papon," *Le Débat* 103 (January–February 1999), p. 108.

40. Castagnède was assisted by two Assessors, or associated judges, Esperben and Irène Carbonnier.

41. Klarsfeld, *La Cour*, p. 176.

42. Conan, *Le Procès Papon*, pp. 152–53.

43. See Alain Finkielkraut, *Comment peut-on être Croate?* (Paris: Gallimard, 1992).

44. Tzvetan Todorov, *Les Abus de la mémoire* (Paris: Arléa, 1995).

45. Conan, *Le Procès Papon*, p. 144.

46. Klarsfeld, *La Cour*, p. 253.

47. Jean de Maillard, "À quoi sert le procès Papon?" *Le Débat* 101 (September–October 1998), pp. 32–42.

48. Maillard, p. 40.

Part I

THE PAPON AFFAIR

Historical, Legal, and Psychoanalytic Perspectives

PAPON'S TRANSITION

AFTER WORLD WAR II

A Prefect's Road from Bordeaux, through Algeria, and Beyond, August 1944–October 1961

Vann Kelly

. . . an anonymous person in prefect's clothes.

—*Sartre,* Nausea

. . . weakness is generally what creates crises.

—*Papon,* Les Chevaux du pouvoir

The political scientist Charles-Louis Foulon, an expert on France's return to democracy after the Nazi military occupation, has reconstituted the organizational chart of Gaston Cusin, Gaullist commissioner of the French Republic for Bordeaux and the region of the Gironde during their liberation in August 1944. Immediately underneath Cusin's name, we read:

MAURICE PAPON——PREFECT
CABINET DIRECTOR[1]

This bit of Cusin's flowchart continues to have an impact today on the French politics of memory. Papon, far from being stigmatized in summer and fall 1944 for his previous work as Vichy's subprefect and secretary-general in the Gironde prefecture at Bordeaux, seems to have negotiated an immediate transition, without hiatus, through the liberation of France and the subsequent punishment of civil servants who had collaborated with the German occupiers. He then turned this smooth transition slowly and methodically into a successful, even brilliant postwar prefectorial career that included positions of authority in Corsica, Algeria, Morocco, and Paris.

Papon's career from roughly 1945 until Algerian independence in 1962 is solidly linked to the French crisis of decolonization in North Africa. It can be plausibly argued, moreover, that his service under pressure during the German occupation, combined with his audacious navigation of the dangerous moments of the Liberation and the administrative purge, gave him a reputation for survivorship and toughness that made him one of the Interior Ministry's *hommes à poigne,* or enforcers, capable of mastering difficult situations and hot spots. His assignments as superprefect in Algeria at the height of its war for independence, from 1956 to 1958, and as Paris police prefect in the politically troubled period from 1958 to 1962, are not coincidental. His service under the compromised Vichy regime, from 1940 through early summer 1944, does not seem to have impeded his professional advancement. A series of promotions through challenging, difficult jobs enabled him to reach the apogee of his career in 1978, outside the Interior Ministry's corps of prefects, when he was appointed budget minister under President Valéry Giscard d'Estaing. These revelations came at a crucial moment in the 1981 presidential election that pitted Giscard, the conservative incumbent, against the Socialist challenger and eventual winner, François Mitterrand. To state the obvious, there would have been no revelations about Minister Papon's blemished prefectorial past under Vichy had Cusin in August 1944 not rehabilitated him politically by making him his personal cabinet director. In 1981, however, Papon suddenly began to resemble a bit less the anonymous person in prefect's clothes whose portrait Roquentin, the Sartrean antihero of the novel *Nausea,* fleetingly notices in the Bouville museum. As Papon had come to occupy ever greater positions of power, his actions had begun to occasion greater scrutiny. Prefectorial discretion notwithstanding (and partly, indeed, because of his career success), he was unwittingly creeping toward the moment of truth and remembrance when his fragile world would collapse.

Did Papon change his patterns of behavior after the Liberation in 1944, or do his postwar actions confirm his bleak record as Vichy's secretary-general in the Gironde prefecture? His name appears infrequently in the histories of Algeria, whereas governors-general, ministers, military generals, and colonels figure quite often: Naegelen, Soustelle, Lacoste, Gaillard, Massu, Salan, and Bigeard.[2]

This agrees with what Jeanne Siwek-Pouydesseau, a political scientist who has studied the institutional history and traditions of the French prefect, says about the "very circumspect character of prefectorial style," "the goal being not to embarrass the government of the moment." Papon deviated somewhat from this model, however, in crucial moments as the subprefect of the Gironde from 1942 to 1944, as the superprefect of Algeria from 1956 to 1958, and as the Paris police prefect in 1961, when he overstepped the bounds. These moments best explain his career path, yet they also eventually got him more notoriety than he wanted. Whereas Siwek-Pouydesseau specifies "reserve" as the greatest prefectorial virtue, the resister who recommended Papon to Commissioner of the Republic Cusin in 1944, career bureaucrat Roger-Samuel Bloch, considered Papon a "fonceur," a risk taker who treaded into touchy situations enthusiastically and, we might surmise, with blind spots.[3] Papon's career seems a battle between careerism and a deeper impulsiveness, and this is the dilemma I will explore: professional discretion versus an insensitive sort of audacity that only succeeded in the short term.

Papon's own renditions of his move beyond Vichy are not without irony. One of his first accusers, Michel Slitinsky, has noted the conveniently abridged biographical blurbs that Papon used in 1960 on the inside cover of his essay *L'Ère des responsables* and again in a 1978 interview for the magazine *Jours de France*, "skipping over the Bordeaux years during Nazi occupation."[4] Papon adopts a similar strategy of ellipsis on the back cover of his 1988 memoirs, *Les Chevaux du pouvoir*, where he conveniently skips his wartime prefectorial career and recounts his role only in the Liberation, without a whisper of prior government service from 1940 to 1944 during the collaboration with German occupation forces. Furthermore, he agilely dovetails his service as a secretary-general of the Gironde prefecture (under the oppressive Vichy regime) and his stint as Cusin's cabinet director at the Liberation (after democracy had been restored): "Secretary-general of the Gironde prefecture at the Liberation, Maurice Papon is named prefect by General de Gaulle's government because of his action in the Resistance. . . ."[5] By 1988, however, the blurb was indirectly part of Papon's legal strategy, a public relations version of the curriculum vitae he offered the court first in 1988 and again during his 1997–98 trial for crimes against humanity committed during World War II.[6] The ellipsis in *Les Chevaux du pouvoir* foreshadows his legal defense, namely, that he served as secretary-general of the Gironde prefecture from 1942 to 1944 only so he could shield the regional French resistance from hostile German authorities.

Éric Conan, a French reporter who covered Papon's trial and who later published a diary of his own courtroom impressions, has asked if someone who was just a subprefect in 1944, and not at the time a prefect or a minister, can legitimately be taken as a symbol "for the overall context" of French administrative collaboration during the war. Is he the "standard by which the entire epoch can be measured"? Perhaps he was just the anonymous person in prefect's clothes, a civil servant whose trial in 1997–98 was forced to carry the excessive burden of France's collective memory. Gérard Boulanger, the lawyer who initiated the court case and who remained active throughout the trial, has alleged that "career motivation" best explains Papon's wartime behavior, in contrast to the deep ideological convictions that drove Marshal Pétain and other notorious collaborators, such as Marcel Déat or Robert Brasillach, to cooperate willingly and even enthusiastically with the Nazi occupiers. During Papon's trial, Michel Tubiana, a lawyer for the plaintiffs, alleged in a similar vein that Papon "understands nothing about this trial because he does not understand how one can reproach a civil servant for having done his work," when circumstances instead dictated civil disobedience.[7] Papon's craftily abridged versions of his own biography show that he considered his transition from Vichy to the postwar problematical indeed.

Some discussion of commissioner Cusin's background and of de Gaulle's management of the Liberation will show how a Vichy civil servant like Papon escaped the Purge so readily, when we might have expected a different outcome, one that entailed less forgetfulness.

THE LIBERATION OF BORDEAUX

Cusin began his career in the French customs bureau, and he held important positions in French government ministries from 1936 to 1940. During the German occupation, Vichy demoted him, and he was briefly imprisoned. He escaped and became active in the clandestine CGT (Confédération générale du travail), a left-wing French labor union. He also belonged to the resistance movement Libération-Nord. As the Allied invasions unfolded and during the liberation of France, Cusin served as Gaullist commissioner of the French Republic (commissaire de la République) for Bordeaux and the Gironde region. He served in this capacity from May 1944 until April 1945.[8] He came recommended by Robert Lacoste, a cofounder of Libération-Nord, and later, coincidentally, the resident minister in Algeria during Papon's service as superprefect of Constantine from 1956 to 1958.[9] (Such initially coincidental connections played a determining role in Papon's postwar career, as we shall see.)

Cusin's written deposition, which was read into the record at the 1997–98 Papon trial, is very detailed. Although he was obliged to work undercover during the period that preceded the liberation of Bordeaux, Cusin was able to "follow personally through privileged channels of information the evolution of the relationship the Resistance had with the [Bordeaux] administration." (It should be added, however, that he did not reach Bordeaux until spring 1944.) There was anecdotal evidence that Papon, despite his affiliation with the collaborationist Vichy regime, had aided Allied aviators downed in the region. It was, however, the recommendation of the aforementioned Roger-Samuel Bloch, a Jewish resister who had good contacts with civil servants in Bordeaux, that convinced Cusin to rely on Papon. Bloch, a former French civil servant, worked during the last half of the war for the Marco-Kléber intelligence group, an undercover network of agents busy gathering military intelligence for the Allies. Bloch had made Papon's acquaintance in 1938–39 in government circles but was himself dismissed because of Vichy's anti-Semitic statutes and had migrated to the Unoccupied Zone. Papon did indeed lodge and hide Bloch several times from November 1943 through June 1944, on the recommendation of an intermediary both men knew before the war.[10] Such friendly gestures were common enough for administrators like Papon who wished to turn vest and convert from Pétainism to resistance. Bloch's deposition confirms the ad hoc nature of Cusin's recruitment of Papon, which appears unavoidable under the circumstances. Bloch says that he "considered Maurice Papon reliable at the time," furthermore, "without hesitation, when I came to the Bordeaux region on 6 June 1944, the day of the Allied landing . . . I gave Maurice Papon's name to Gaston Cusin who sought a man of discretion and competence to be his assistant."[11] To test Papon, Cusin asked him to arrange a clandestine meeting in the Bordeaux prefecture itself with "those in charge of the police and gendarmes, so as to maintain order during the upcoming liberation." Papon complied. The meeting took place without a problem on 23 August 1944. Cusin took this as "uncontestable proof of a deliberate commitment" to the Resistance.[12]

Commissioners of the Republic had executive, legislative, and judicial powers. Cusin enjoyed the right to suspend and appoint prefectorial personnel, but his decision to retain Papon in his cabinet reflected the priorities of de Gaulle's political organization, the French Committee for National Liberation (Comité français de libération nationale, or CFLN). The thrust of Cusin's mission, as established in the CFLN's ordinance of 10 January 1944 defining the powers of the commissioners of the Republic, was to consolidate the victory behind the battle lines by restoring public services and "republican legality."[13] Well before the Allied landings, the idea of a thorough purge of Vichy elements was tempered by the realization that too much change in administrative personnel would create havoc. Does Papon represent not just the sins of Vichy France, but also, abetted by Cusin, the infamy of a Gaullist restoration that valued the return to order over the demands of justice?[14] Whatever one's final judgment, the CFLN did face a complex situation and concluded that some Vichy personnel with administrative and technical competence had to remain in place at the Liberation if France was to avoid a Communist-inspired revolution or an Allied military government.[15] This policy echoed de Gaulle's hostility toward a number of resistance movements that had developed in France itself, outside his direct control. Some elements of this internal resistance favored a more thorough renovation from the grass roots upward. Due to the isolation of French regions during the Allied invasions, the Liberation was likely to be (and indeed turned out to be) an uncommon experience of decentralization for the French. The CFLN wished the commissioners to pursue a gradual, methodical return to the centralized organizations that defined French political culture, irrespective of the opprobrium heaped upon the prewar Third Republic by virtually all factions of the Resistance, including the Gaullists.[16] Future French prime minister Michel Debré, then an important cog in the Gaullist internal resistance, personally chose Cusin. Debré describes him as a man of character who knew when to "give priority to the needs of the State."[17] In turn, it was Emile Laffon, Cusin's administrative superior, who made a recommendation to the commissioners that might explain Cusin's decision to retain the services of the Vichy subprefect Papon: "Vichy prefects must be relieved of duty, you will make sure that none remain at their post . . . (for your cabinet). You must have an excellent clerk for composing texts and official proclamations, undoubtedly a jurist, *and certainly a civil servant who has sufficient knowledge of administrative affairs, and whom you ought to choose among the subprefects or members of the prefectoral council of your region*" [emphasis added].[18] Papon, far from risking his career at the Liberation, moved into a position to advise Cusin on the Purge.

Cusin had arrived in Bordeaux in April 1944 and had begun to exercise his functions secretly before D-Day.[19] On 22 August 1944 he suspended all government functionaries from duty, effective as of the liberation of the city, which occurred six days later. On 23 August Cusin appointed Papon prefect and named him cabinet director.[20] This appointment immediately brought protests from resisters in Bordeaux and the region, though the objections, which lasted through early 1945, did not implicate Papon in the deportation of Jews but concerned the general fact that he had served under Vichy.[21] Commissioners during the Liberation often temporarily suspended questionable prefects, but this was far from universal.[22] In this context, it is conceivable that someone like Papon was recuperated for the sake of expediency, given that his role in the Jewish deportations remained hidden at the time. In February 1942, former prefect

Jean Moulin stipulated that a Vichy civil servant be deemed "undesirable" only if, "in public opinion," he had harmed resisters or the nation *and* if he had done one of three things: shown hostility toward Gaullists, demonstrated excessive pro-German sentiments, or exhibited brutality.[23] It should be noted, too, that until 1988, neither was much attention paid to the role that Papon's boss, the regional prefect Sabatier, had played under the Occupation. At the Liberation, Sabatier, like Papon, had a relatively easy conversion and became chief civilian administrative adviser for the French occupation army in Germany.

Foulon has claimed that Cusin agreed to overlook Papon's role in the deportations of Bordeaux Jews because of other contributions to the Resistance, but this interpretation has been strongly contested by Jean Morin, a resister and the director of personnel for de Gaulle's Interior Ministry in 1944 and 1945.[24] It is very unlikely that Cusin had any knowledge of Papon's role in the deportation of Jews. Even in more visible instances of the Bordeaux administration's collaboration with the German policy of deportation, arrests often took place at night. Lesser officials in the administration and police, especially Pierre Garat, Jacques Dubarry, and agents of the regional head of police, René Duchon, arrested the victims and on occasion guarded them on the train trip to Drancy, which was the prison camp near Paris that served as the point of departure for convoys to Auschwitz. Papon's association with the deportations does not seem to have been public knowledge. The populace of Bordeaux tended to blame the police or French agents like Lucien Déhan, who worked for the overtly collaborationist anti-Semitic government bureau the CGQJ (Commissariat général aux questions juives), an organization that was not directly attached to the prefecture.[25] Only an examination of confidential prefectorial documents would have revealed to Cusin the extent of Papon's collaboration in the *rafles,* or roundups, of 1942–44, and these documents lay filed away in the departmental archives until 1981 when the historian Michel Bergès by chance requested and examined an incriminating bundle of dusty papers. In an interview, Bergès says that no search had been requested at the Liberation for documents from the Gironde prefecture's Office of Jewish Questions (Service des questions juives, under Papon's supervision, as distinct from Déhan's rival CGQJ): "Those documents had been deposited in a bundle there, by the archival services, without even having been inventoried."[26] The same sort of forgetfulness affected the availability of police archives for 1942 through 1944, according to Bergès. Jean Morin, privy to the deliberations of the Interior Ministry's internal purge committee at the Liberation, affirms as much: Cusin used Papon "for services rendered during the Resistance and for his administrative competence." As to Papon's role in Jewish deportations, "no one accused Papon at the time."[27]

These elements give a plausible explanation for Cusin's decision to retain Papon, while not excusing Papon's opportunism. Claude Bouchinet-Serreulles, a Gaullist delegate in France and one of the key reorganizers of the Resistance after the death of Jean Moulin, characterizes the difficulties Cusin faced in recruiting qualified personnel to help him govern: "the commissioners of the Republic had at their disposal limited means of investigation. They did not have access to archives and were not in a position to conduct exhaustive inquiries. They had to act quickly and rely on the recommendations that others gave them. In Cusin's place, I would have done the same."[28] Even if Papon's record of resistance had been sterling, which was hardly the case, this would obviously not absolve him of complicity for the crimes against humanity of which he stood accused in 1997. Jumbled circumstances played in Papon's favor in 1944, since Cusin was forced to choose his personnel in the absence of perfect information. Like the typical French prefect, Papon served the powers that were strongest from 1942 through midsummer 1944—Vichy and the SS—while cultivating behind the scenes the most likely magnates of the future (the Resistance in the persons of Bloch, Cusin, and others).[29]

Moments of public visibility and controversy were exceptional, however, for Papon. Indeed, an ability to go more or less unnoticed characterizes prefects in general. Too much public attention can ruin a career, and the prefectorial ideal is one of quiet efficiency. Prefects under the Third Republic had become used to serving rapidly changing regimes, whether it be the archconservative Laval government or the left-wing Popular Front. The instability of the parliamentary system in prewar France had created habits that made the notion of serving the *État français* seem unremarkable to many members of the prefectorial corps. Siwek-Pouydesseau notes that the purge of Vichy prefects was in many cases draconian, but that the treatment of subprefects like Papon was "a little less severe."[30] In point of fact, Papon emerged mostly unscathed by the prefectorial purge. On 6 December 1944, the Interior Ministry's national purge commission cleared Papon and confirmed his promotion.[31] As a good prefectorial careerist should, he had passed without undue scandal from government positions under the Third Republic, to Pétain's *État français*, to the Gaullist provisional government, and he would soon serve the Fourth Republic. The risks that he had taken ended up furthering his career and were archived for the foreseeable future.

During the rest of the Liberation, Papon served two other regional commissioners in Bordeaux, both of them eminent resisters, Jacques Soustelle and Maurice Bourgès-Manoury. When Cusin left Bordeaux on 26 April 1945 for the Ministry of National Economy, Jacques Soustelle, who had joined the Free

French in London in 1940, became regional commissioner of the Republic in Bordeaux. After the war, Soustelle played a large role in Algeria, first in 1945 as minister of the colonies in de Gaulle's provisional government, but more so as governor-general of Algeria from 1955 to 1956. Papon, newly appointed the prefect of Paris police in March 1958, would have occasion to renew acquaintance with his former superior, since Soustelle was an instigator of the 13 May 1958 putsch that returned de Gaulle to power. Soustelle remained in Bordeaux briefly, until 26 June 1945.[32] In June, he was replaced by Bourgès-Manoury, who had been the CFLN's military delegate in the Occupied Zone from 1943 to 1944, and then assistant chief of staff to the French army until the end of the war in Europe. Papon spent only ten days under the supervision of Bourgès-Manoury, who later served variously as minister of finance, armaments, defense, industry and commerce, and the interior under the Fourth Republic. Like Soustelle, Bourgès-Manoury figured prominently in the Algerian crisis from 1954 through 1958.[33]

Cusin, Soustelle, and Bourgès-Manoury mounted a joint defense of Papon when accusations surfaced against him in 1981.[34] A colonial war defined the postwar restoration for all of these men except Cusin, but the Occupation, which each of them had experienced in a very different fashion, haunted their later encounters.

BEYOND THE LIBERATION: PARIS–CORSICA–FRENCH NORTH AFRICA, 1945–1958

In fall 1945, soon after Papon finished his duties in Bordeaux and returned to Paris, he was put in charge of Algerian affairs in the cabinet of Interior Minister Adrien Tixier. Papon's association with Algeria and the Maghreb region is indirectly related to one of his pre–World War II posts as attaché to the undersecretary of state for foreign affairs in the Chautemps government, 1937–38. There he dealt with issues related to the French protectorates in Morocco and Tunisia.[35] North African expertise would turn out to be an essential, defining line in Papon's career path, although prior to the war this was not a foregone conclusion. Papon, during his trial, claimed that "what most marked me during this period was the discovery of Islam."[36] After his demobilization in 1940, he rejoined the Interior Ministry, now part of the *État français*, in the Bureau for Communal and Departmental Affairs (Direction des affaires départementales et communales). This office was directed—another coincidence—by Maurice

Sabatier, born in Algeria. When Sabatier was promoted to the rank of administrative secretary-general in 1941, his duties also included monitoring correspondence on Algerian affairs.[37] He made Papon, now a subprefect, his cabinet director. The association between Sabatier and Papon lasted until August 1944, when the two went separate ways.

Papon's earlier experience with North African affairs was no doubt one of the reasons for his postwar appointment to the French Interior Ministry's Bureau of Algerian Affairs. Papon began his new duties on 26 October 1945, roughly five months after the end of the war in Europe on 8 May. This day not only marked the end of the war in Europe, it was also marred in the French Algerian cities of Sétif and Guelma by bloody riots pitting the colonial administration (and European colonists, or *pieds noirs*) against Algerian supporters of national independence, especially though not exclusively the supporters of Messali Hadj and his Algerian People's Party (Parti populaire algérien, or PPA). These riots in northeastern Algeria, in the region of Constantine, occasioned a bloody repression by French authorities. European deaths during the confrontations tallied more than 100, but native Algerian deaths were much greater. The official death toll was placed at 1,150 victims, but the U.S. consulate in Algiers as well as the PPA alleged a figure of 40,000–45,000 deaths. An unofficial French estimate made in the region a few days after the incident suggested that deaths might have numbered 15,000.[38] This event played an important role in the eventual foundation of the Committee for Revolutionary Unity and Action (Comité révolutionnaire d'unité et d'action, or CRUA), the forerunner of the National Liberation Front (Front de libération nationale, or FLN), which would eventually lead Algeria to independence in 1962. According to Papon's own version, he joined the Bureau of Algerian Affairs precisely because Tixier, who soon officially absolved him of collaboration during the German occupation, felt that his experienced hand would calm the dangerous situation created by the Sétif-Guelma riots.[39]

The general public's knowledge and understanding of the riots in eastern Algeria was sketchy. As the historian Charles-Robert Ageron says, "the attempt at an insurrection in Algeria, initially quashed in May 1945 by a severe military repression, was not perceived in France in all its gravity. The 'incidents of Sétif' were attributed to the economic crisis, to Nazi propaganda or to a crisis of authority, never to a spontaneous explosion of popular nationalism."[40] Typical in this regard is the left-wing newspaper *Le Franc-Tireur*, press organ for one of the principal internal resistance organizations in the Unoccupied Zone of France during World War II. A front-page headline on 12 May 1945 reads, "Serious situation in Algeria, where disruptive elements are exploiting the unrest caused by economic difficulties." The newspaper was torn between an economic and a conspiratorial interpretation of 8 May 1945. In a continuation on the inside pages, the reporter gave a reasonably accurate rendition of events, though the government's massive repression was considerably downplayed. On 21 June and 4 July 1945, the newspaper reported on Minister of the Interior Tixier's fact-finding mission to Algeria in the wake of the riots. Tixier's direct knowledge of the tense situation undoubtedly influenced his decision, the following October, to assign Papon to the bureau that dealt with such a hotbed. The Constantine region obviously required special administrative talents and experience.[41] A prefect who had successfully negotiated the Occupation and the Liberation in as difficult a post as the Gironde prefecture would have the self-assurance to master postwar Algeria as well. In the week after Tixier's return to the metropolis, the Sétif-Guelma incidents were debated in the French National Assembly, and the true importance of the riots became clear, at least to the reporter for *Le Franc-tireur*, who indicated on page two of the 11 July 1945 issue that the "bloody disturbances of 8 May in the Constantine region were necessary for people to agree to admit, at last, the existence of an Algerian question." Some of the heated debate was synopsized. According to the reporter, the colonialist deputy Cuttoli, who blamed the Algerian nationalist agitators, spoke for those who felt that the best policy in Algeria was to "make the Arabs sweat [*faire suer le burnous*]." Deputy Aboulker for the opposition responded and blamed police for most of the bloodshed, concluding that "the government [should] export some democracy to the other side of the Mediterranean." The incidents in Sétif and Guelma were powerful enough to create echoes more than a year later. On 22 August 1945, the newspaper reported a question on the floor of the National Assembly concerning the Sétif-Guelma riots: the reporter judged that the "situation, after one year has passed, is still dominated by the tragic events that have bloodied Algeria and concerning which worrisome obscurities persist." The Constantine area created headlines in Paris and held them.

Marcel-Edmond Naegelen, a luminary of the French Socialist Party (or SFIO) who also served as governor general of Algeria a few years after the riots, expressed a more conservative view of events: "on 8 May 1945, the very day of the German capitulation, riots suddenly bloodied the Sétif and Guelma regions. Government bureaucrats, farmers, small businessmen, women, and children were savagely assassinated, sometimes after horrible mutilations. What password given and transmitted mysteriously had the assassins obeyed, suddenly attacking Algerians of European descent, for no immediately apparent reason?"[42] Naegelen lays blame for the violence mostly on Algerian independence movements (indigenous nationalist separatists as opposed to the European colonists), and while he castigates the overreaction of government troops as "quick, brutal, and blind," he also downplays the extent of the brutality and insists on the suffering of the European victims. Naegelen asserts that extremists on both sides, both the Algerian independence movements that incited the riots and the colonial ultras who avenged the European victims by "taking target practice" against the Arabs, had succeeded in isolating moderate colonists and those among the Algerians who wanted nothing better than to cooperate with the French Republic.[43] These events certainly were harbingers of the wider war that broke out in November 1954, in precisely the same region of Algeria. More importantly for our purposes, they show the sort of tense circumstances Papon was deemed capable of handling, not only in 1945–46 as a member of the Interior Ministry's Bureau of Algerian Affairs, but later as well, in the higher positions of authority he occupied at one time or another in Algeria from 1949 through 1958.

On 26 June 1946, Papon was named cabinet director for Jean Biondi, undersecretary of state for the interior. (Six months earlier, on 6 December 1944, the purge commission for the Ministry of the Interior had given Papon a clean slate with respect to his work under the Vichy regime.)[44] In his new position in Biondi's cabinet, Papon served as a member of the interministerial commission for the Antilles and helped create the French overseas departments (DOM) of Martinique, Guadeloupe, and Guyana. He was then named prefect of Corsica on 21 January 1947, where he served successfully through fall 1949, and apparently with much local popularity, devoting himself to improving the island's economy.[45] Papon, under orders from the minister of the interior, Jules Moch, apparently allowed the United States to use Corsican air bases to supply Israel during its struggle for independence. Papon's actions as prefect of Corsica helped him regain respectability and solidify his chances for a successful postwar career. He was soon named prefect of Constantine, partly because Moch was very satisfied with his discreet efforts to aid Israel: "Judging by the congratulations from Mr. Tsur, head of the Israeli secret services, and from Mr. Walter Eytan, [Israeli] ambassador to France, . . . we did good work. That was the judgment of Mr. Jules Moch since he appointed me to head the department of Constantine. I made contact once again with Islam, which my hand had already grazed."[46]

Papon, in his trial c.v., passed very quickly over the period from 1949 to early 1956. He served as prefect of the Algerian department of Constantine (1949–51), as secretary-general of the Paris police prefecture (1951–54), as secretary general of the Moroccan protectorate under French premier Pierre Mendès-France (1954–55), and lastly (February 1956) as a technical adviser to the minister of the interior, Champeix, in the Guy Mollet coalition government that escalated the Algerian conflict. In March 1956, Papon was named inspector-general of northeastern Algeria.[47] He also successfully stood for election in 1956 as mayor of his birthplace, Gretz-Armainvilliers in the department of Seine-et-Marne. He was mayor for three years.[48]

Papon's career was now taking a definite turn toward colonial affairs. His service as bureau chief for Algerian affairs in 1946 was certainly linked to the fact that he had held similar positions under Sabatier just before World War II and in the early days of Vichy. His appointment as prefect of Constantine in early 1949 confirmed and amplified his career ties to French North Africa. Papon slips into a literary, quasi-heroic tone whenever the region is mentioned. Whether it is a question of 1936, 1949, or 1956, he always associates the "discovery" of a personified, exotic Islam with turning points in his career. In his 1978 interview in the magazine *Jours de France*, he digressed on "Constantine, where I became aware of Islam, while living an extraordinary experience between two civilizations, two religions, two ways of existing and understanding each other. I really loved that Berber land, which I preferred to Algiers itself." Algeria occasioned some florid prose in Papon's 1988 memoirs too : "Like a lava flow, the setting sun streams down the slopes of the Chettaba. The sky, indifferent to humankind's miseries, colors the first signs of spring with melancholy."[49]

Behind such admiration and ostensible passion lie some harsh, practical realities. Constantine had been volatile ever since the 8 May 1945 riots. The governor-general of Algeria in 1949, when Papon first became prefect of Constantine, was none other than Marcel-Edmond Naegelen, quoted above. Naegelen had been minister of education before being appointed to Algeria in February 1948, where he was expected to supervise elections for the Algerian Assembly, the first such ballot under the Fourth Republic's new statute for Algeria. The campaign was controversial and difficult because of the escalating conflict between Algerian nationalists and European colonists.[50] There were widespread allegations that Naegelen rigged the 1948 elections, allegations that he later denied in his memoirs where he presents himself as a reformer. As he tells the story, however, Algerian nationalists became more and more active under his tenure, and this forced him to adopt a politics of repression and launch police raids against rebel enclaves.[51] The Constantine region borders on Tunisia and was a key for the soon-to-be rebels' arms supply from sympathetic Arab countries, especially Nasser's Egypt. Naegelen characterizes Constantine as "the poorest of the three [Algerian departments], the one where the European population was least dense, the one which pan-Arab propaganda affected most directly, the one which had been the theatre for the horrors of May 1945 in the cities and regions of Sétif and Guelma, the one where the general rebellion would break out in the Aurès [mountains] on 1 November 1954."[52]

According to Naegelen, the department of Constantine in 1948 was ten times as large as the biggest department in metropolitan France, and a prefect "even had he remained there ten years could not pretend to have thoroughly visited the tortuous coast, the harsh plateaus, the first Saharan desert oases, nor to have discovered the entire region's landscapes and human faces." The prefect, "whatever his degree of activity, could not truly get to know, manage, and animate the vast spaces confided to his care, with their multiple characteristics and needs."[53] The prefect's administrative reach and power weakened the farther one got from the departmental capital, a fact that we should bear in mind when Papon later describes the oversight he had over military and civilian affairs when he returned to Constantine as superprefect in 1956, though by then the government had reduced the size of the circumscription. (In 1956 the French government divided the three original Algerian prefectures into twelve.) Prefects had difficulty keeping authority over civilian affairs alone, according to Naegelen, who served as governor-general from 1948 through 1951. Naegelen occasionally characterizes the prefects who served under him, but he does not mention them by name, which clearly shows the expectations the French government had at the time for prefects. The prefect was a pony of power, not a stallion, and he executed policies conceived at higher echelons. A good example is what Governor-General Naegelen said to his three prefects in late 1950: "For these elections to the Algerian Assembly [4–11 February 1951], I gave instructions for absolute neutrality and I asked the prefects to make sure that these instructions were applied rigorously."[54] The prefects, who were the governor-general's agents, typically stayed "two or three years at the most " and aspired above all to return to continental France, according to Naegelen.[55] Algeria was a career step, and in this Papon did not differ from his peers, although he had more success in climbing the ladder.

Naegelen's tenure as governor-general of Algeria ended on 15 April 1951.[56] The final moments were dominated by actions he took to back up one of Papon's actions, though as usual Naegelen maintains the anonymity of his prefect : "I was obliged, at the request of the prefect of Constantine, to sanction a civilian administrator who had rigged a vote and declared as the winner a candidate who had been beaten, adding as well that he 'sh——' upon the prefect, the governor."[57] When Paris brought pressure to bear to relax the sanctions, Naegelen vigorously supported his prefect and refused to revoke the sanctions. (Coincidentally, he also used the interference from Paris as a pretext to resign as governor-general and resume his mainland political life.)[58]

After Naegelen's departure, Papon finished his tour of duty under a new governor-general, Roger Léonard, who ironically had been cabinet director for the prefect of the Gironde in 1939, before he was dismissed by Vichy and joined the Resistance.[59] Léonard presided over Algeria at the outbreak of the war in 1954. It is worth mentioning, and has only recently come to light with the release of government documents on Algeria, that Naegelen and Léonard were informed of torture by police forces and prison guards. Both issued instructions to their prefects forbidding these practices. Naegelen knew of such illegal government practices early in his mission and reacted quickly with a circular (21 October 1949) that promised to hold both torturers and their administrative superiors responsible.[60] Papon spent his last months as prefect combating the effects of disastrous weather on his circumscription.[61] In his December 1988 curriculum vitae for the French courts, he said that his work from 1949 to 1951 was concerned with reforming the economic "infrastructure" and aiding the electoral careers of those among the native Algerian notables who still favored ongoing political association with France.[62]

On 15 December 1951, Papon became secretary-general of the Paris police prefecture, under the orders of Prefect Jean Baylot, whom Papon considered forceful and competent.[63] The journalist and historian Jean-Luc Einaudi paints a different picture of Baylot, however, in his book *La Bataille de Paris: 17 octobre 1961*. According to Einaudi, Baylot was an extreme anti-Communist official who reincorporated into the police force numerous men who, at the Liberation, had been dismissed for collaboration under the German occupation. Einaudi alleges that Baylot and his assistant, police commissioner Jean Dides, availed themselves of the services of a notorious fugitive from justice, Alfred Delarue, who had abetted the Gestapo. Furthermore, under Baylot's purview there was a major case of police brutality in Paris on 14 July 1953, in the context of a peaceful demonstration in favor of Algerian independence. The demonstrators were local supporters of influential Algerian political dissident Messali Hadj. Six of them were killed and forty-four wounded in the police attack. (If we accept Einaudi's implication, this confrontation foreshadowed a similar incident of police violence under Papon's watch as Paris police prefect on 17 October 1961.)[64] Papon served as secretary-general of the Paris police from fall 1951 through summer 1954. During this period, he wrote *L'Ère des responsables*, an essay on modern government administration.[65] Pierre Mendès-France's electoral victory in 1954 brought about the dismissal of Baylot. On 16 July 1954, Papon moved on to become secretary-general of the French protectorate of Morocco, which obtained its independence in 1956.[66] At the time of his appointment, however, the country was still shaken by internal power rivalries among sultans and by tensions that the French had fomented with ill-advised political decisions.

Francis Lacoste was the French resident-general of the protectorate at the moment of Papon's appointment. (France had obtained official control over Morocco in the decade prior to World War I.) Although Papon was involved primarily with socioeconomic reforms, he also witnessed a rising tide of violence in Morocco that included terrorist bombings by Moroccan nationalists, counterterrorist attacks and assassinations by colonialist ultras (with police complicity), and violent clashes between the police and the Moroccan independence movement, Istiqlal. The situation he would inherit later in his career, when he became superprefect in eastern Algeria in 1956, turned out to be very similar. The escalating violence in Morocco induced the French premier, Edgar Faure, to dispatch a new plenipotentiary, Gilbert Grandval, who replaced Secretary-General Papon with his own man, Jacques Fourmon, in July 1955.[67] Violet indicates that Papon returned to France "without any particular assignment." Papon says that he spent this brief period on the sidelines. [68] In January 1956, he worked for the Office of Long-Term Economic Planning (Commissariat général du plan), and then, on 2 February 1956, he became technical adviser to the cabinet of the minister of the interior for Algerian policy, Marcel Champeix.[69]

In the course of spring 1956, Papon returned to Constantine as superprefect of northeastern Algeria, but he arrived under special circumstances. On 19–20 March 1956, the resident minister of Algeria, Robert Lacoste, obtained from the National Assembly special administrative powers to deal with escalating violence. He obtained the right to take emergency measures to maintain order, under a law that has been characterized as "quasi-dictatorial."[70] The newspaper *Le Monde* spoke of the "practically unlimited powers [granted] those responsible for order and security."[71] By April 1956, authorization for a military draft of 200,000 men was impending, and Maurice Papon was being mentioned as a possible successor to the prefect of Constantine, Dupuch, who had "tirelessly confronted since 1 November 1954 not only the rebellion which hit his department particularly hard, but also the incomprehension and agitation of [his] European [constituents]." The only thing delaying Dupuch's replacement was a forthcoming "territorial reorganization."[72] Up to this point, Algeria had only three departments, centered respectively on the cities of Oran, Algiers, and Constantine, going from west to east. Ongoing oil exploration in the Sahara was strong impetus for an administrative restructuring, as was the pressing need to divide the Algerian interior into military zones and sectors.[73] Papon's boss, Minister of the Interior Champeix, had arranged the new territorial map, which subdivided the three original departments into twelve relatively smaller ones. At a meeting of the council of ministers at the Elysée Palace on 24 April 1956, Maurice Papon was named prefect for the department of Constantine, the same position that he had held from 1949 to 1951, with the notable difference that the Interior Ministry now augmented his powers considerably by naming him, in addition to prefect, administrative inspector-general for most of north-eastern Algeria (Inspecteur général de l'administration en mission extraordinaire, or IGAME). Papon was one of three such superprefects appointed in 1956 during the administrative reorganization.

Papon inherited a "nerve center" in the war. Through the spring of 1956, at least, the level of violence in Constantine was much greater than that in Oran and Algiers.[74] Papon's domain, called an *igamie*, was made up of two redrawn yet still vast departments, Constantine and Bône, which stretched along more than one-third of the Algerian coastline. This region was the foyer for the FLN's abrupt military escalation of the war on 19–20 August 1955, in which one historian sees the first "mass uprising" of the Algerian war and a "point of no return": "1 November [1954] was a signal, 20 August [1955] was an insurrection," according to Henri Alleg, Communist militant and historian of the Algerian conflict. Armed attacks, bombings, and arson by the rebels marked Constantine and Bône, and the French military ripostes were massive and costly to the FLN[75] For January 1956, the commanding general of the division stationed in Constantine reported 112 native Algerians killed in his zone, 142 schools, farms, or homes burned, and 259 acts of sabotage directed against railways, bridges, or telephone lines. Near Bône and the Tunisian border, the commanding general counted 304 acts by the insurgents for January and 334 for February.[76] Papon's *igamie* incorporated two and one-half of the six military zones of the FLN's military branch, the National Liberation Army (or ALN).[77] The Paris newspaper *Le Monde* gave a succinct description of Papon's new powers in April 1956, at the moment of his appointment as prefect and IGAME: "Mr. Papon will assume . . . the functions of general administrative inspector on special mission in the departments of Constantine and Bône. His duties will include coordinating and supervising the activities of the civilian and military authorities in the departments of Constantine and Bône, including the civilian and military command of the Aurès region." The Aurès is one of the most difficult and mountainous regions in all Algeria, a situation aggravated by its proximity to the Tunisian border, across which most of the rebels' supply of arms had to pass.[78] The administrative and military reorganization that accompanied the creation of the three *igamies*, or superprefectures, was completed by January 1957 and was intended to lessen divergences and friction between the civil service and the army, to the benefit of the latter, which garnered considerable police powers that it lacked before.[79]

The army was now subject to considerably less civilian supervision, and this opened the door to great abuses of power. Papon did not arrive at his new post until 17–18 May 1956, but it was clear beforehand that the region he was going to govern was very troubled. A story in *Le Monde* of 29–30 April 1956 told of a sudden "outburst of terrorism in the Constantine region," and on 3 May 1956 another story reported on military operations that resulted in the deaths of sixty rebels near Constantine. A week before Papon's arrival in the city of Constantine, a grenade exploded in a crowded café near the Jewish quarter, killing nineteen.[80] The FLN commemorated the events of 8 May 1945 in a crescendo of violence throughout Algeria, but especially in the Constantine region, where insurgents and the French Jewish community exchanged gunfire in the crowded quarters of the city. The upsurge in rebel military activity began immediately before Papon's nomination and lasted well beyond his return to Constantine.[81]

Papon helped implement the new territorial division. Soon after his arrival, eastern Algeria was split into four separate departments, from the coast toward the Saharan interior. Ironically, his new position as IGAME was roughly equivalent to the regional commissionerships of the Republic held by Cusin, Soustelle, and Bourgès-Manoury at the liberation of mainland France in 1944. On 8 October 1956, Papon visited the Sétif area in the company of Generals Noiret and Dufour. They inspected the efforts to recruit native Algerians into a movement of counterdissidence that involved the formation of village self-defense groups, supervised by French personnel.[82] Such groups were distinct from the *harkis*, units of native Algerians enrolled directly in the French army itself. The village self-defense group, or *maghzen*, was part of a special government unit ostensibly directed toward the civilian population and public works. These units, called special administrative sections (*Sections administratives spéciales*, or SAS), were first created in 1955 under then governor-general Jacques Soustelle. In Algeria the special administrative sections were in principle under civilian, not military, authority. On site in the isolated villages, however, they were commanded by military officers who most often belonged to the army's active or reserve officer corps and who were temporarily "detached from their weapon," to use the French military expression.[83] Seven hundred special administrative sections were created during the war,[84] and when Papon was appointed prefect of the Paris police in 1958, he would deploy some of these sections in the French capital in an attempt to control Algerian neighborhoods.[85]

The SAS established medical services, improved food supply, opened schools, and did other civilian tasks in remote villages that were under pressure to support the FLN. The historians Bernard Droz and Évelyne Lever, in contrast to Henri Alleg, characterize the special administrative sections as "the most original and least disputable form of pacification," an evaluation that Henri Le Mire echoes.[86] Droz and Lever, nevertheless, insist that these sections were in fact part of a larger political scheme that had a heavy military finality: "The systematic occupation of the countryside by an army that had grown to over 400,000 men, the multiplication of special administrative sections, and the massive population regroupings, were complementary efforts." The positive accomplishments of the SAS were counterbalanced by "a whole host of repressive measures" which the army and administrators "covered" and for which they "share[d] responsibility."[87] Even the hawkish Le Mire, who tends to take an apologetic attitude toward French military policy in Algeria, admits that the local SAS leader's greatest temptation was to help nearby army operations, while military commanders often used the nearby SAS as reconnaissance troops or tactical reinforcements. The SAS with its local self-defense militia made armed night patrols to ward off FLN incursions. Furthermore, when it was impossible to co-opt local populations, entire villages were evacuated to relocation camps, in order to provide isolation from the FLN.[88] Torture and massive transfer of populations certainly occurred under Papon's tenure, and today these practices inevitably rouse echoes of the German occupation of France. The special administrative sections were ambiguous, to say the least. Papon's October 1956 visit to Sétif, mentioned in the preceding paragraph, shows that he was committed to this and similar strategies.

As prefect and administrative inspector-general, Papon had to maintain public order. In this context, he portrayed himself at his trial as the Jewish population's shield against the FLN: "The Jewish community [*la communauté israélite*], especially in Sétif, had received dire threats from the National Liberation Front. I took special precautions to assure it was protected," including the dispatch of troops.[89] Papon also had to coordinate his civilian administrative duties with those of the military command in a region that was crisscrossed by the FLN's strategic pipeline for arms and personnel. One of the two departments under Papon's supervision bordered on Tunisia, where the rebels had established training camps. The borderlands gave the FLN a channel for the passage of critical aid from sympathetic Arab states.[90] In 1988, an officer of the court transcribed Papon's version of his duties in Algeria, which were threefold: "One of my first missions was going to be the installation of five prefectures, Bône, Bougie, Sétif, Batna, and Constantine. . . . The second task was to bring about the cooperation of civil and military authorities, which was not the easiest thing to do. The third task was to begin, to the greatest extent feasible, the pacification of the rebellious zones, while trying to protect the populace, make contact with the rebel leaders, and put in place as rapidly as possible social, educational, and administrative structures."[91] At his trial in 1997–98, Papon gave a more succinct rendition: "From the cabinet of Mr. Champeix, the secretary of state for the interior, I was called to head the Constantine region, as IGAME, with the mission of putting in place the new departments of Bougie, Bône, Sétif, and Batna, where at the time the prefects were in the process of being appointed. My mission was 'pacification.' . . . Indeed, the IGAME has civilian responsibilities, but also implicit military ones [mais aussi militaires sans le dire], and I took charge of the military problems in the Constantine region."[92]

Minister of the Interior Jules Moch had originally created the position of IGAME in circumstances that had nothing to do with the Algerian conflict. During 1947, at the height of postwar labor unrest, Moch proposed that inspectors-general be appointed for France's mainland military regions. The goal was to assure that prefects and military commanders apply the central government's directives properly and consistently. The position of IGAME as first conceived had a mixed military and civilian orientation. The inspector general's powers were even broader than it seemed. The scope of his office depended on the terms in his internal letters of mission, and though he was attached to the Interior Ministry, other ministries could mandate his tasks, too. The IGAME reported to all parties concerned, and later statutes did not substantially change the job definition.[93]

Jacques Isorni, a lawyer and deputy in the French National Assembly, was part of the parliamentary commission that visited Algeria during summer 1956, and he noted Papon's desire to merge civilian and military affairs in Algeria: "Dinner at Constantine with Prefect Papon. He confirms the excellent morale of the army. . . . He is angry about not having two hundred million francs or two battalions so that he might hasten pacification. He really is enthusiastic about the generals!" More or less positive about the progress against the rebels, Papon suggested that the army "reconvert itself in view of close cooperation between the civilian and military administrations."[94] (Isorni, known for his legal defense of Marshal Pétain, favored maintaining the French Empire by force of arms and reforms.) By the spring of 1958 the military initiative and balance had indeed shifted considerably away from the FLN, due in part perhaps to his own efforts. The electrified fence known as the Morice line, which extended from Bône southward along the Tunisian border, was built mainly within the confines of Papon's igamie, and it had allowed the French army to bring its weight to bear heavily against the FLN's lines of supply. What was called the battle of the frontiers peaked from January through April 1958, a period that culminated Papon's service as IGAME.[95] He was transferred to Paris in mid-March.

The journalists Jean-Luc Einaudi and Bernard Violet, who in their respective books have examined Papon's career in detail, have profiled his actions as coordinator of civilian and military policy in the Constantine *igamie*. Violet notes, among other things, that in September 1956 Papon presided over another meeting of the commanding generals for areas under his purview. The meeting was followed five days later by police and military intervention in Bône, Bougie, and other locales. That same month, Papon's agricultural reforms were announced in the local newspaper, *La Dépêche de Constantine*, in whose columns Papon's name figured regularly from 1956 through early 1958. In spring 1957 Papon presided over a meeting at Sidi-Kamber with the staff of an infantry regiment that was involved in pacification.[96] He supervised an intense campaign of pacification in and around Sétif from summer 1957 through the fall. On 17 September 1957, Papon and the regional commanders, Generals Loth and Desfontaines, held a press conference at Constantine to describe the progress that French civilian and military authorities were making against the rebellion. When questioned by reporters, Papon had to acknowledge that 100,000 Algerians had been displaced in a strategic regrouping of entire village populations that was ostensibly intended to foil FLN pressure and avert its reprisals. (On the other hand, regroupings severed the FLN from its popular base of support and isolated its troops in the countryside, or *bled*, where they became easy targets for the French military.) The sites for the regroupings were often surrounded by barbed wire, and by 1960 a government report estimated that over one million Algerians were living in such concentration camps throughout Algeria.[97]

Massive population regroupings did not reflect Papon's personal initiative so much as French general policy in Algeria, where repressive measures intensified after General Raoul Salan's appointment as commander-in-chief in Algeria (November 1956). The general had acquired a reputation for toughness, innovation, and bravura during the French war in Indochina, which had lasted from 1946 to 1954. Partially on the basis of the French experience in Vietnam, Salan and his officers reoriented the war in Algeria toward "psychological warfare"; that is, toward a war of countersubversion and antiguerrilla tactics.[98] Einaudi, however, who insists on Papon's obvious enthusiasm for the military and police tasks that fell under his sway, quotes public remarks in May 1956 and September 1957 where the prefect of Constantine accepts, and indeed exalts, the blurring of the lines between civilian and military responsibilities. Papon encouraged his constituents to tolerate this abuse of powers, and there is evidence that police in

Constantine did frequently use torture in local prisons, thus emulating the behavior of military forces in the region.[99]

Charles de Gaulle's son-in-law, Alain de Boissieu, served as a lieutenant colonel in one of the sectors under Papon's control. De Boissieu played only a minor role as a character witness at the 1997–98 trial, but Papon dropped hints early in the proceedings that de Boissieu would vouch for the moral correctness of the pacification operations the prefect had supervised in Constantine: "I always protested against torture. . . . I ask you, Mr. Court President, if the deposition of General de Boissieu might be read now. He was there at the time."[100] The judge postponed the reading for procedural reasons, but under further questioning, Papon's lawyer, Jean-Marc Varaut, rejected the implication that his client had approved the use of torture: "General Boissieu (*noise from the audience, lawyer Varaut raises his voice*) has said that Mr. Papon was always actively opposed [*s'est opposé*] to acts of torture once he was told of them."[101] De Boissieu's deposition was eventually read into the record, but it was not as expansive and precise as the defendant might have wished. The unofficial transcript synopsizes de Boissieu's testimony: "the court president reads the deposition of General de Gaulle's son-in-law. [Alain de Boissieu] considers Maurice Papon to be 'of great moral rigor' and a 'great state servant in all circumstances.' Then [the court president] calls a recess."[102]

When trial lawyers for the plaintiffs questioned Papon about the infamous torture centers that were operative in his own region of Constantine, and at Orléansville in the Algiers *igamie*, he first responded indirectly, alleging the respect that native Algerians had for his sense of justice and his efforts to foster peace and reconciliation: "In the Muslim *wilayas* [administrative regions]—and you can find proof of it even now—people called me the *Mâhadi*. That means 'master,' but in the sense of the wise one, the just one, and that title is perhaps the best decoration that I ever had in my career." Pressed to answer whether or not he knew of the torture centers in or around Constantine, he maneuvered around the question by denying that he had ever approved of any illegal practices: "I always protested against torture, against hasty justice, and that is the sense in which I exercised powers of influence over the military units that were stationed to maintain order in Constantine." At the same time, he retreated considerably from his initial description of his duties as inspector general, or IGAME: "Mr. [Gérard] Boulanger [lawyer for the plaintiffs] has misunderstood me. I must have explained myself badly. I thought I had clearly said a few minutes ago that my authority went beyond the strict bounds of civilian operations, but that this was not an authority given to me by law [*une reconnaissance de droit*], instead it was a state of fact [*un état de fait*], since I had been appointed in dramatic circumstances and since Mr. Lacoste had spoken publicly in a way that enthroned me as a sort of tutor of our overall political line, which in turn was based upon the political line of the military men of the hour. I said that I had a certain amount of influence that allowed me to oversee [*contrôler*] the acts of the army and to censure those which went beyond the bounds of human conscience."[103] One of the most infamous of these torture centers, the ferme Ameziane, was in operation as of April 1957 near the city of Constantine, though it was officially designated an interrogation center. In a circular, Governor-General Lacoste, who was Papon's immediate superior, openly praised such centers where the army, the police, and the gendarmerie could coordinate their efforts in the interest of administrative efficiency.[104] In the *igamie* in eastern Algeria, Papon encountered a situation that resembled the Bordeaux prefecture from 1942 to 1944, namely an environment where the lines of command and the flow of power were often conveniently flexible and intentionally vague. Furthermore, it is not clear from Papon's statements at trial whether from 1956 to 1958 the generals had exercised the real power, or whether Papon had appropriated his own share of it. We may surmise, nevertheless, that his personal history had taught him quite well how to maneuver comfortably within situations where power was defined as much by willful participants as by statute.

According to one historian of French overseas law, Arlette Heymann, the distinction between military and civilian powers in Algeria was, in any case, historically very fragile, since the colony had been organized in the nineteenth century by the very military authorities who had conquered and occupied it. Prior to the outbreak of war in November 1954, civilian authorities in the three original departments of Oran, Algiers, and Constantine had tried to maintain separation of military and civilian powers. Heymann attributes these efforts to "French democracy's suspicion of the military," but at best the separation was tenuous.[105] During the war, from 1954 to 1962, the old pattern of military control over police affairs nevertheless reemerged and was even approved officially by the French government decree of 17 March 1956 (made in conjunction with Lacoste's nomination as governor-general) whereby the prefects in Algeria were authorized, within their respective jurisdictions, to delegate police powers to the military. According to Heymann, the French army in fact exercised police powers in Algeria from 1956 until the end of the war in 1962, in its effort to pacify both the cities (where the prefects exercised the bulk of their influence with the help of the gendarmes) and the open countryside (where the military was accustomed to operating independently).[106] The statutory blurring of lines between the civilian and the military is an integral part of the context surrounding Papon's appointment as IGAME of Constantine and Bône.

To what extent then, could a prefect and inspector general like Papon really exert control over the actions of the French troops within his jurisdiction? Was his authority primarily moral in nature, entailing the right to oversee army actions and condemn them, or was he really complicit in the generals' and colonels' suppression of formal liberties, as several lawyers for the plaintiffs implied by their line of questioning at the trial? According to Heymann, the minister in residence, Lacoste, delegated "responsibility for maintaining order to the military authorities in the totality of the departments of Bône and Constantine" by his official decision, or *arrêté*, dated 7 May 1956. We should note, however, that the new departments of Constantine and Bône correspond exactly to Papon's own jurisdiction as administrative inspector-general (IGAME). Lacoste's wording might reflect a simple transfer of powers to Papon in his capacity as supervisor of the military and civilian affairs in the two departments in question. Indeed, Papon arrived in Algeria and assumed his official duties shortly after Lacoste's *arrêté*. Heymann takes note of Lacoste's constant efforts to free French military commanders in Algeria from limitation or constraint by most civilian authorities. Police powers were "exercised by low-ranking military officers in complete independence [from the usual civil authorities]." Heymann also asserts that as of 16 March 1956, the date of the decree on the delegation of police powers, "the negation of judicial rules could not have been more clearly a matter of fact" in Algeria.[107] Lacoste intended to free the French army from the need to respect civil rights.

Papon's career before 1942 and after 1944 was not the main focus of his trial, so it is hardly surprising that in 1997–98 the court, in the relatively brief time it devoted to his c.v., left these postwar colonial episodes unresolved. In response to a lawyer's question, Papon said that in "an organized state, in a state that has self-respect, in a hierarchy that is trained to respect the state, I do believe that every civil servant has the duty to obey. In a revolutionary period, whatever the political orientation of the revolution, in a period when the state no longer is master of its own destiny, as was the case during the German occupation [of France], the situation is entirely different."[108] The problem with Papon's distinction here is that from 1956 through 1958 the French state was master of its own destiny but had also clearly ceased to respect the separation between military powers and civilian ones. The French National Assembly and France's resident minister of Algeria, with the support of conservative former resisters like Jacques Soustelle and Maurice Bourgès-Manoury, intentionally weakened the separation of powers between the army and the civilian administration in Algeria. Under these circumstances, Papon felt no compunction to maintain distinctions that his superiors were willing and eager to abolish, and he did not question the ethics behind the war. His fine distinction between an organized state and a revolutionary context is frivolous. One may easily conclude that wherever there was hierarchy, he obeyed it regardless of circumstance: as in 1942, so too in 1956.

As one of Lacoste's administrative strongmen, Papon had certainly played a role in the *engrenage*, or descent into political and military repression, that freed the French army from democratic civilian control. He was placed in a position of responsibility at the very moment the French political process began to go awry, in spring 1956, days after Lacoste received special powers in Algeria. Papon remained in that position of responsibility until shortly before a French generals' putsch (13 May 1958) brought de Gaulle back to power in a series of events that led to the death of the Fourth Republic and the birth of the Fifth. In order to reach the last episode in Papon's association with Algeria, however, we have to move forward in time beyond 1958, to the terrorist campaign that the ultracolonialist Secret Army Organization (Organisation armée secrète, or OAS) launched in Algeria and Paris in 1961 and 1962, while de Gaulle's new Fifth Republic and the FLN were negotiating the Evian accords on Algerian independence. Papon had not foreseen the last act of this international political drama, but as head of the Paris police he had to try to control it.

1958 AND BEYOND: THE RETURN TO PARIS

Papon served from 17 May 1956 through 15 March 1958 as prefect of Constantine and IGAME for northeastern Algeria. Suddenly he was named prefect of the Paris police. Gunfire in the thirteenth arrondissement between two policemen and an Algerian, which punctuated a major increase in FLN violence, had precipitated a crisis of confidence between the police and their prefect, André Lahillonne.[109] At the police prefecture on the Île de la Cité in the center of town, the conflict spilled into the surrounding streets, and several policemen disrupted traffic to show their displeasure at the lack of support from their superiors. The group then marched to the Palais Bourbon, where the French National Assembly is housed, but dispersed once the protesters had vented their complaints. Some of the dissident policemen nevertheless managed to get into the National Assembly, and this aggravated the public scandal.

The premier, Félix Gaillard, promptly replaced Lahillonne with Papon, whose ability to manage tense, violent situations had been amply proven during his two years as superprefect in Algeria. Experience in an arena like Algeria, where military realities and expediency displaced ethical considerations, had once again enhanced Papon's career rather than impeding it. His appointment as police prefect was also no doubt partly due to yet another old acquaintance from the liberation of Bordeaux, Maurice Bourgès-Manoury, former commissioner of the Republic in 1945 and now minister of the interior under Gaillard. (Echoes of World War II did not stop here: as the journalist Bernard Violet notes, Jean Chapel, who had been Maurice Sabatier's cabinet director in Bordeaux from 1942 to 1944, was also named to replace Papon in Constantine.) Upon the news of his own appointment as prefect of the Paris police, Papon had rushed to swear into office some recently elected Muslim officials for the Constantine region, and, happy that he had taken one last measure to pacify Algeria, he took the plane for Paris with Minister Lacoste. They arrived on 16 March 1958, and Papon began exercising his duties as police prefect. He promptly restored order at the headquarters, but the specter of FLN terrorism was in Paris to stay. French attacks on the FLN-ALN hierarchies had been very successful at the battle of Algiers and during subsequent skirmishes on the borders of Morocco and Tunisia. The FLN coordinating committee, attempting to relieve military pressure in North Africa, decided to export terrorism to mainland France in the summer of 1958, although a drift in this direction was already clearly perceptible as early as the spring of 1957.[110] The turmoil in the Paris prefecture that led to Lahillonne's dismissal and Papon's appointment was a major warning of the upsurge in urban terrorism that the new prefect faced.

Almost immediately upon his return to Paris, however, a different cause of turmoil (but one still related to the war in Algeria), forced Papon to muster all his authority and experience. As of April 1958, another of his former patrons from the days of the Liberation in Bordeaux, former commissioner of the Republic Jacques Soustelle, was in the thick of dissidence against the enfeebled Fourth Republic. He was actively plotting and preparing de Gaulle's return. Soustelle was a primary instigator of the generals' putsch in Algiers on 13 May 1958 that led de Gaulle back to power with the mandate to abolish the Fourth Republic and construct the Fifth.[111] On 10 May 1958, Papon had been approached by Pierre Pflimlin to serve in a new cabinet under the Fourth Republic, as the minister with responsibility for Algeria, an honor that Papon found opportune to refuse.[112] (His service as minister was postponed until 1978 and the presidency of Valéry Giscard d'Estaing.) Papon became a staunch Gaullist from 13 May 1958 onward, less than two months after he first assumed his duties as head of the Paris police.

His earlier enthusiastic support for the generals in charge of pacification in Algeria dissipated very quickly thereafter. As French government policy evolved toward the notion of emancipating the colonies, French army officers in Algeria became progressively more hostile to de Gaulle, as did Soustelle, and in 1962 Prefect Papon was one of those responsible for safeguarding de Gaulle against a series of OAS assassination attempts. This apparent loyalty to de Gaulle could quite plausibly be attributed to the institutional reflexes for survival that Papon had acquired as a veteran prefect, rather than to any deeply held political convictions on his part. If he had not disobeyed Sabatier from 1942 to 1944 under the *État français*, or Lacoste from 1956 to 1958 under the Fourth Republic, why would he behave differently when faced with de Gaulle's surge back into power in May 1958, backed by an army in revolt? As police prefect, he could easily abet the downfall of the Fourth Republic, while currying de Gaulle's favor in the interest of his own career. A prefect's personal enthusiasms, it would seem, cannot allow him to neglect what the government of the next moment may look like, whether it is collaborationist, colonialist, or bent on decolonization.

In the meantime, another violent public incident in 1961 came close to marring Papon's career as de Gaulle's police prefect. The way Papon handled events in this case gives further credence to resister Roger-Samuel Bloch's contention that Papon, despite his usual prefectorial restraint, was on occasion too much of a "fonceur," or risk taker, for the good of his own career. Bloody confrontations took place on 17 October 1961 between the Paris police and Algerians in the wake of a march in favor of independence. Many of the demonstrators were killed or wounded, and this thrust Papon into the newspaper headlines. According to the lawyer and writer Gérard Boulanger, Papon deliberately encouraged his police agents to be vindictive and brutal in their encounters with Algerians and in their "reprisals" against the FLN in Paris.[113] In moments like these, Papon was no longer the ideal, anonymous character in prefect's clothes. He went beyond the boundaries of his role.

Papon's former superior in Algeria, former governor-general Naegelen, was far from being soft on opponents to government policy. Shortly after the 17 October 1961 demonstration, he condemned the FLN agitation and terrorism that preceded it.[114] More significant, perhaps, is his outright attack on government mismanagement of the entire situation: "For lack of timely precautions to assure [the Algerian worker population] a healthy habitat, decent opportunities for professional improvement, good protection [from FLN extortion], it became necessary, in order to try to stop FLN terrorism in the middle of Paris, to use procedures that made the evil worse rather than curing it." The condemnation obviously took aim at Papon, though the former governor-general remained true to habit and refused to name his ex-subordinate. After all, Papon was still just a prefect at the time. As an example of an ill-advised measure, Naegelen cited "the forced closure of cafés patronized by 'North Africans' early in the evening."[115] This is an obvious reference to the police prefect's official circular imposing a curfew on Algerians in the Paris region. The restrictions apparently were approved by Roger Frey, minister of the interior, in early October 1961. Algerian workers were strongly advised not to be out and about town between 8:30 at night and 5:30 in the morning, and this was accompanied by the early closing of cafés.[116] Naegelen rightly protested against these "measures of racial discrimination" that "couldn't do anything but accentuate the Algerian workers' impression that they are not treated in France as if they were French. . . . As soon as a face appears tanned, that individual is suspect. He must show his identification card and his work permit. Right beside him and beside the agents interrogating him, men with white skin pass by unmolested."[117]

At the time, the Paris municipal council questioned Papon about the unexplained deaths of many Algerian demonstrators on 17 October 1961. He responded that the FLN was responsible for the murders and had used the altercation to camouflage its own liquidation of a rival group, the resurgent Algerian People's Party, or PPA.[118] None of this impeded his career as prefect, which lasted until his voluntary retirement in 1967, though the events of fall 1961, to his dismay, did not entirely disappear from his horizon. He had to confront them again at his trial for crimes against humanity in 1997–98. The implication was that his role in the events of 17 October 1961 formed a disturbing pattern when they were compared to the part he played in the deportation of Jews during World War II. Here, some lawyers for the plaintiffs seemed to suggest, was a further instance where Papon's career ambitions outweighed his concern for human lives. In 1997–98, Papon argued that his actions from 1958 through 1962, though beset with difficulties, had been basically conciliatory. He gave as an example his decision to transfer some officers to Paris from the special administrative sections in Algeria. As has been suggested, these special administrative sections were fraught with ambiguity; it was unclear if they were military units or civilian work groups. According to Papon's version, they allowed him to maintain a peaceful presence in areas like Paris's eighteenth arrondissement, which had a large population of Algerians. The SAS officers were "able to penetrate the [Paris] milieus of the FLN" and inhibit its campaign of urban terrorism. When a lawyer insinuated that the special administrative sections were used in France as instruments of repression, Papon angrily asserted that even in Algeria such officers "never were involved in repression."[119]

Whether or not Papon accurately described the role that special administrative sections played in the Algerian brush and later in Paris, his testimony on this sensitive issue implies an uneasy continuity of routines between, on the one hand, his old role as prefect and inspector-general in Constantine from 1956 to

1958, and on the other hand his new role as prefect of Paris police from 1958 to 1967. In his memoirs, which were published in 1988, he inadvertently gave an example of this confusion of roles and boundaries. While discussing his deployment of the (supposedly peaceful) special administrative sections in Paris, he also mentions an organization that he created at the same time, the Service for Coordinatiing Algerian Affairs, or SCAA, an antiterrorist police unit meant to fight FLN fire with fire: "There I was, just like yesterday in Algeria, with the sword in one hand, the olive branch in the other."[120] In the final analysis, the special administrative sections were part and parcel of a paramilitary strategy. The writer Michel Levine describes the SCAA as "an autonomous tactical general staff" of police units whose "task [was] to dismantle" the hierarchy of the FLN's operations in France.[121] The SCAA used a variety of means, including the infiltration of Algerian neighborhoods in France, collection of information on Algerians residing in France, the creation of a file system, or *fichier*, on Algerians who passed through the service's hands, and arrests followed by interrogations at the Vel d'hiv (and later in a detention center at Vincennes). The result for many of those who passed through the SCAA was forced repatriation to Algeria. According to Levine, Papon also condoned the methodical use in Paris, as of January 1960, of *harkis* (native Algerians who had served the French army or police in North Africa) to patrol and pacify Algerian neighborhoods in Paris. Levine suggests that the flow of suspects through Papon's anti-FLN apparatus was in the "hundreds of thousands."[122]

Papon's Algerian and Parisian experiences, in the least, interpenetrate. He seemed at ease from 1949 through 1962 with a variety of tactics that were covertly repressive and at times overtly so, with or without the approval of his government superiors Naegelen, Léonard, Lacoste, and Frey. Papon's public responses and testimony have not dissipated doubts about his attitudes and practices as prefect and inspector-general at the height of the Algerian conflict, from 1956 to 1958, nor have they quieted suspicions that attitudes and practices he carried over from his prefectorial past had a connection with the police brutality directed against Algerian demonstrators on 17 October 1961 in his Paris precinct. At the end of World War II, Papon was a "fonceur," or risk taker, said the resister Roger-Samuel Bloch. Another critic has suggested that Papon seems not to have changed much since then: we seem to be dealing with "the same wily and deceitful functionary" in 1942, in 1956, and in 1961, namely, a bureaucrat "committed to serving the powers that be, no matter what the price in moral terms."[123] In 1981, however, when public accusations were made concerning Papon's role in the deportation of Jews during World War II, flaws began to show, too, in other phases of his prefectorial career. His official uniform suddenly seemed ill-tailored, and he no longer enjoyed the requisite professional anonymity. He had allowed the interests of his career to suppress a higher ethics at several moments on his path from Bordeaux, through Algeria, to Paris. One of the lawyers for the plaintiffs in Papon's trial, Michel Tubiana, stated the argument succinctly for the defendant's benefit: "You understood nothing about your obligations in 1942 in Bordeaux, in 1956 in Constantine, in 1961 in Paris. Those were times where one needed to hate [inhumane policies] and you were only apathetic. It was necessary to balk and you were complacent."[124]

NOTES

1. Charles-Louis Foulon, *Le Pouvoir en province à la libération: Les Commissaires de la République, 1943–1946* (Paris: Armand Colin, 1975), pp. 130–31, see also p. 276 for Cusin's biography. All translations from the French are mine, unless otherwise indicated.

2. See, for example, Henri Alleg et al., *La Guerre d'Algérie*, 3 vols. (Paris: Le Temps Actuel, 1981), and Pierre Miquel, *La Guerre d'Algérie* (Paris: Fayard, 1993). Papon figures by name in Alleg, vol. 3, pp. 365–66, 369, in connection with the police violence in Paris against Algerians on 17 October 1961. The Alleg history refers constantly to the Constantine region, where Papon was prefect and later inspector- general, but not to Papon by name, with the exception noted above. Miquel mentions Papon twice by name: in 1958, concerning refugee camps in the Constantine region (p. 366), and in 1961, relative to police violence in Paris (pp. 497–99), where Papon is portrayed as under the influence of the colonialist and terrorist Secret Army Organization (Organisation armée secrète, or OAS). For a passage in Alleg where Papon appears without being named per se, see *La Guerre d'Algérie*, vol. 2, p. 240, where the prefect of Constantine visits Ben-Daoud in the company of two generals.

3. Jeanne Siwek-Pouydesseau, *Le Corps préfectoral sous la Troisième et la Quatrième République* (Paris: Armand Colin, 1969), p. 113; cf. Pierre Doueil, *L'Administration locale à l'épreuve de la guerre, 1939–1949* (Paris: Sirey, 1950), pp. 295–96; see also Catherine Erhel, Mathieu Aucher, Renaud de La Baume, eds., *Le Procès de Maurice Papon, 8 octobre 1997–8 janvier 1998* (Paris: Albin Michel, 1998), vol. 2, p. 609. This last work is an unofficial transcript of the court proceedings, as per French law. Henceforth, Erhel et al., *Le Procès de Maurice Papon*.

4. See Michael Slitinsky, *L'Affaire Papon* (Paris: Alain Moreau, 1983), pp. 15–16; Léon Zitrone, "Les Hommes du temps présent: Maurice Papon, Ministre du Budget—'Une certain conception de l'état,' " *Jours de France*, no. 1250, 25 November–1 December 1978, p. 50; Maurice Papon, *L'Ère des responsables* (Paris: Arthème Fayard, 1960), inside front cover.

5. Maurice Papon, *Les Chevaux du pouvoir: Le Préfet de police du général de Gaulle ouvre ses dossiers 1958–1967* (Paris: Plon, 1988), outer back cover.

6. These ellipses do not occur in Papon's official c.v., République française, Ministère de l'Intérieur, *Annuaire du corps préfectoral et de l'Administration centrale* (see the editions 1947, 1953, 1957, 1960).

7. Eric Conan, *Le Procès Papon: Un Journal d'audience* (Paris: Gallimard, 1998), p. 224; court summations by Boulanger and Tubiana, as quoted in Conan, *Le Procès Papon*, pp. 240, 261.

8. "Cusin (Gaston)," *Who's Who in France, Dictionnaire biographique 1959–1960* (Paris: J. Lafitte, 1959); Charles-Louis Foulon, "Gaston Cusin, 1903–1993," *Universalia 1993: La Politique, les connaissances, la culture* (Paris: Encyclopaedia Universalis France, 1994); Foulon, *Le Pouvoir en province à la libération*, pp. 276, 293; Gérard Boulanger, *Papon, un intrus dans la République* (Paris: Seuil, 1997), pp. 60–72.

9. "Lacoste (Robert)," *Who's Who in France, Dictionnaire biographique 1959–1960*; Debré, *Trois Républiques pour une France*, vol. 1 (Paris: Albin Michel, 1984), pp. 349–50.

10. Erhel et al, *Le Procès de Maurice Papon*, vol. 2, pp. 606–10; see also Jean Bruno and Frédéric de Monicault, *L'Affaire Papon. Bordeaux: 1942–1944* (Paris: Tallandier, 1997), pp. 144–47, and Gérard Boulanger, *Maurice Papon: Un Technocrate dans la collaboration* (Paris: Seuil, 1994), pp. 19, 213–21.

11. Erhel et al., *Le Procès de Maurice Papon*, vol. 2, pp. 608–9.

12. Erhel et al., *Le Procès de Maurice Papon*, vol. 2, pp. 611–12. See also extracts of Cusin's letter to Minister of the Interior Adrien Tixier, in Bernard Violet, *Le Dossier Papon* (Paris: Flammarion, 1997), pp. 45–46. Boulanger, *Papon, un intrus dans la République*, pp. 76–79 recounts the meeting but asserts it posed little risk for Papon at the time.

13. See Title 2, art. 4, of the ordinance of 10 January 1944, in Foulon, *Le Pouvoir en province à la libération*, pp. 59–60. On the powers conferred, see also Doueil, *L'Administration locale à l'épreuve de la guerre*, pp. 42–51, and François-Louis Closon's recollections, *Commissaire de la République du général de Gaulle* (Paris: Julliard, 1980), pp. 24–30, 48–80.

14. This is notably Boulanger's thesis, in *Papon, un intrus dans la République*, pp. 93–158.

15. Cusin's superior, Emile Laffon, concluded by 1944 that a wholesale purge of the administration was unadvisable. See Foulon, *Le Pouvoir en France à la libération*, pp. 61–84, but especially pp. 61–65. On Vichy administration, see also Marc-Olivier Baruch, *Servir l'État français: L'Administration en France de 1940–1944* (Paris : Fayard, 1997).

16 On decentralization, see Grégoire Madjarian et Aude Bergier, *Conflits, pouvoirs et société à la libération* (Paris: Union générale d'éditions, 1980), pp. 84–102, and

Charles-Louis Foulon, "La Résistance et pouvoir de l'État dans la France libérée," in Fondation Ch. de Gaulle, ed., *Le Rétablissement de la légalité républicaine, (1944)* (Brussels: Complexe, 1996), pp. 189–213. Madjarian, p. 94, concludes that change was imposed as far as possible from on top, with prewar organizations and hierarchies being restored. Ph. Buton and J.-M. Guillon, *Les Pouvoirs en France à la Libération* (Paris: Belin, 1994), take issue with this view. On the Gaullist view of conditions likely to prevail, see Doueil, *L'Administration locale à l'épreuve de la guerre*, p. 62, n. 1.

17. Debré, *Trois Républiques pour une France*, vol. 1, pp. 350–51.

18. Laffon's confidential instructions, quoted in Foulon, *Le Pouvoir en province à la libération*, p. 86. Most commissioners had copies of the instructions.

19. Boulanger, *Papon, un intrus dans la République*, pp. 65–66.

20. Erhel et al, *Le Procès de Maurice Papon*, vol. 2, p. 615–16.

21. Some objections came from the Landes department, others from the Gironde. See Jacques Pélissier, response to Charles-Louis, in Fondation Ch. de Gaulle, *Le Rétablissment de la légalité républicaine (1944)*, p. 208; Erhel et al, *Le Procès de Maurice Papon*, vol. 2, pp. 616–20, 627–28. See also Jean-Luc Einaudi, *La Bataille de Paris* (Paris: Seuil, 1991), pp. 43–44; Boulanger, *Papon, un intrus dans la République*, pp. 128–58.

22. Foulon cites Rennes, where three prefects and ten subprefects were suspended or put on leave. He concludes, however, that overall "the administrative purge was not thorough," with the exception of the police (*Le Pouvoir en province à la libération*, pp. 162–64). The commissioners could suspend personnel, but the minister of the interior and council of state had final say. Cusin referred the Papon case to his minister in November 1944.

23. Quoted in Foulon, *Le Pouvoir en province à la libération*, p. 62.

24. See Foulon, "Gaston Cusin, 1903–1993," *Universalia 1993*; Jean Morin, response to Charles-Louis Foulon, in Fondation Ch. de Gaulle, ed., *Le Rétablissement de la légalité républicaine (1944)*, pp. 206–7. See also a synopsis of Morin's testimony in Erhel et al, *Le Procès de Maurice Papon*, vol. 2, pp. 627–28, and Morin's remarks in Bruno and Monicault, *L'Affaire Papon*, pp. 26–37.

25. On Papon and the deportations, see Einaudi, *La Bataille de Paris*, pp. 40–41; but especially Boulanger, *Maurice Papon: Un Technocrate dans la collaboration*, p. 157–70, for example, on the deportation of 15 July 1942, pp. 176–79 on Déhan, and more generally pp. 129–96, on the French government agencies active in the repression of the Jews in Bordeaux. See also see Conan, *Le Procès Papon*, pp. 161–63, on the arrests of 10 January 1944 and on night arrests.

26. Bruno and Monicault, *L'Affaire Papon*, p. 164.

27. Jean Morin, response to Ch.–L. Foulon, in Fondation Ch. de Gaulle, ed., *Le Rétablissement de la légalité républicaine (1944)*, p. 206. See Conan's record of similar remarks by Morin at trial, *Le Procès Papon*, p. 223. Pierre Bécamps, in his *Libération de*

Bordeaux (Paris: Hachette, 1974), pp. 116–17, 123, 197, echoes local sentiment (at the time of the Liberation) that Sabatier and unspecified subordinates acted humanely. He also notes that, at the Liberation, Mérignac camp director Rousseau, former mayor Marquet, Déhan, and the police were blamed locally for the arrest and deportation of Jews.

28. As quoted in Eric Conan, *Le Procès Papon,* pp. 38–39.

29. Boulanger, *Maurice Papon: Un Technocrate dans la collaboration,* pp. 218–21, alleges that Papon used Bloch to create a resistance record, taking few risks to help Bloch while keeping Sabatier informed.

30. Siwek-Pouydesseau, *Le Corps préfectoral sous la Troisième et la Quatrième République,* pp. 80–81; cf. Doueil's figures for the purge of prefects versus subprefects, *L'administration locale à l'épreuve de la guerre,* pp. 303–4.

31. Violet, *Le Dossier Papon,* pp. 44–46; Erhel et al., *Le Procès de Maurice Papon,* vol. 2, pp. 616–19. The purge commission of the Interior Ministry urged on 6 December 1944 that Papon's appointment be confirmed, and the minister accepted the commission's advice.

32. On Soustelle, see Jean Lacouture, *De Gaulle,* vol. 1 (Paris: Seuil, 1984), pp. 693–95; Foulon, *Le Pouvoir en province à la libération,* p. 276; "Soustelle (Jacques, Emile)," *Who's Who in France, Dictionnaire biographique 1959–1960* ; "Soustelle, Jacques," *Historical Dictionary of the French Fourth and Fifth Republics, 1946–1991* (Westport, Conn.: Greenwood, 1992); Boulanger, *Papon, un intrus dans la République,* p. 231.

33. On Bourgès-Manoury, see "Bourgès-Manoury (Maurice, Jean-Marie)," *Who's Who in France, Dictionnaire biographique 1959–1960*; Jean-Louis Crémieux-Brilhac, *La France Libre de l'appel du 18 juin à la Libération* (Paris: Gallimard, 1996), p. 769; Foulon, *Le Pouvoir en province à la libération,* p. 277; Boulanger, *Papon, un intrus dans la République,* p. 232; "Bourgès-Manoury, Maurice" *Historical Dictionary of the French Fourth and Fifth Republics.*

34. "MM. Bourgès-Manoury, Cusin et Soustelle: Des attaques scandaleuses," *Le Monde,* 8 May 1981, p. 28.

35. See "Papon (Maurice)," *Who's Who in France, Dictionnaire biographique 1959–1960*; République française, Ministère de l'Intérieur, *Annuaire du corps préfectoral et de l'administration central,* 1947, pp. 383–84; État français, Ministère de l'Intérieur, *Annuaire du corps préfectoral et de l'administration centrale,* 1943, p. 400; Erhel et al., *Le Procès de Maurice Papon,* vol. 1, pp. 186–87; Violet, *Le Dossier Papon,* p. 21.

36. Erhel et al., *Le Procès de Maurice Papon,* vol. 1, pp. 186, 188.

37. Conan, *Le Procès Papon,* pp. 56–57. On Sabatier and the bureau of communal and departmental affairs, see Boulanger, *Maurice Papon: Un Technocrate dans la collaboration,* pp. 28–32, 38–40.

38. For the various estimates of the death toll, I rely on Alleg et al., *La Guerre d'Algérie,* vol. 1, pp. 265, 267. This history is generally well documented, but on

Alleg's Communist militancy and revisionism in *La Guerre d'Algérie*, see Bernard Droz and Évelyne Lever, *Histoire de la guerre d'Algérie (1954–1962)* (Paris: Seuil, 1962), pp. 106–7, 156.

39. Erhel et al., *Le Procès*, vol. 1, pp. 193–94.

40. J. Thobie, G. Meynier, C. Coquery-Vidrovitch, C.-R. Ageron, *Histoire de la France coloniale*, vol. 2. (Paris: A. Colin, 1990), p. 358.

41. See Albert Camus's analysis of the Sétif-Guelma riots, in "Crise en Algérie," *Essais*, Pléiade collection (Paris: Gallimard, 1965), pp. 939–59, which contains articles that appeared in *Combat* beginning in May 1945: " . . . the political malaise preceded the famine" (p. 950).

42. Marcel-Edmond Naegelen, *Mission en Algérie* (Paris: Flammarion, 1962), p. 14.

43. Naegelen, *Mission en Algérie*, pp. 14–18.

44. Erhel et al., *Le Procès de Maurice Papon*, vol. 2, p. 618.

45. République française, Ministère de l'Intérieur, *Annuaire du corps préfectoral et de l'administration central, 1947*, pp. 383–84; "Papon," *Who's Who in France, 1959–1960*; Violet, *Le Dossier Papon*, pp. 49–50; Erhel et al, *Le Procès de Maurice Papon*, vol. 1, p. 189.

46. Ibid., p. 190.

47. Erhel et al., *Le Procès de Papon*, vol. 1, pp. 190–91 ; "Papon," *Who's Who in France, 1959–1960*.

48. Violet, *Le Dossier Papon*, p. 75; Erhel et al., *Le Procès de Maurice Papon*, vol. 1, pp. 190–91.

49. Léon Zitrone, "Les Hommes du temps présent: Maurice Papon," *Jours de France*, no. 1250, 25 Nov.–1 Dec. 1978, p. 50; Papon, *Les Chevaux du pouvoir*, p. 17.

50. Violet, *Le Dossier Papon*, p. 53; Naegelen, *Mission en Algérie*, p. 19.

51. For Naegelen's firm denial, see *Mission en Algérie*, pp. 62–68. On the accusations of election fraud, see Einaudi, *La Bataille de Paris*, pp. 44–45. Camus considered the 1948 elections dishonest ("Terrorisme et répression," *Essais*, p. 1868; the essay originally appeared in *L'Express*, 9 July 1955).

52. Naegelen, *Mission en Algérie*, pp. 59–60; see also Violet, *Le Dossier Papon*, pp. 53–4.

53. Naegelen, *Mission en Algérie*, pp. 150–1.

54. Ibid., p. 184.

55. Ibid., p. 151.

56. Ibid., p. 205.

57. Ibid., p. 66.

58. Ibid., pp. 185–204. Naegelen quotes a letter from a constituent in Khenchala, describing the electioneering that caused the prefect of Constantine to seek sanctions against the commune's administrator. Papon is named only by his title.

59. Violet, *Le Dossier Papon*, p. 61.

60. "La Mémoire enfouie de la guerre d'Algérie," *Le Monde*, 5 February 1999, p. 1 and succeeding pages. The story is based on the volume *La Guerre d'Algérie par les documents*, edited by the Service historique de l'armée de terre (SHAT). According to *Le Monde*, Léonard issued a similar circular on 4 March 1952, but after Papon's departure. Droz and Lever, *Histoire de la guerre d'Algérie*, pp. 140−41, indicate that torture was used during the French repression of the 1947 Madagascar rebellion and during the Indochinese conflict preceding the Algerian war. The 1955 Wuillaume and 1956 Mairey reports to the government pointed to French use of torture in Algeria.

61. Violet, *Le Dossier Papon*, p. 63.

62. Maurice Papon, Interrogatoire de *curriculum vitae*, 9 Dec. 1988, conducted by François Braud, conseiller à la chambre d'accusation de la cour d'appel, Bordeaux, quoted in Violet, *Le dossier Papon*, p. 64.

63. Violet, *Le Dossier Papon*, pp. 63−65.

64. Einaudi, *La Bataille de Paris*, pp. 45−47.

65. Einaudi, *La Bataille de Paris*, p. 47; "Papon," *Who's Who in France, 1959−1960*.

66. République française, Ministère de l'Intérieur, *Annuaire du corps préfectoral et de l'administration centrale*, 1957, p. 479.

67. On Papon's service in Morocco, see Violet, *Le Dossier Papon*, pp. 69−74; Boulanger, *Papon, un intrus dans la République*, pp. 234−36.

68. Violet, *Le Dossier Papon*, p. 74; Erhel et al., *Le Procès de Maurice Papon*, vol. 1, pp. 190−91.

69. République française, Ministère de l'Intérieur, *Annuaire du corps préfectoral*, 1957, p. 479; Einaudi, *La Bataille de Paris*, pp. 47−48.

70. "Lacoste (Robert)," *Who's Who in France, Dictionnaire biographique 1959−1960*, for his resistance; Droz and Lever, *Histoire de la guerre d'Algérie*, p. 93, on the extent of his powers as resident minister.

71. "Robert Lacoste et l'armée disposent désormais des plus larges pouvoirs en Algérie," *Le Monde*, no. 3470, 20 March 1956, p. 1.

72. *Le Monde*, no. 3490, 12 April 1956, p. 1.

73. On the need for a military reorganization, see Droz and Lever, *Histoire de la guerre d'Algérie*, p. 96.

74. Alleg et al., *La Guerre d'Algérie*, vol. 1, p. 552; vol. 2, pp. 171−72, 180−81; Droz and Lever, *Histoire de la guerre d'Algérie*, p. 111.

75. Alleg et al., *La Guerre d'Algérie*, vol. 1, pp. 557−59, who asserts that casualties resulting from the French riposte ranged from 2,000 to 12,000. The northern part of the Constantine region, very active militarily, was initially part of the rebels' combat zone 2.

76. Alleg et al., *La Guerre d'Algérie*, vol. 2, pp. 31−32.

77. See Alleg et al., *La Guerre d'Algérie*, vol. 2, p. 214, for a map of the *igamies* and the Algerian *wilayas*.

78. *Le Monde*, no. 3502, 26 April 1956, p. 6. Arlette Heymann, *Les Libertés publiques et la guerre d'Algérie* (Paris: Librairie Générale de Droit et de Jurisprudence, 1972), p. 73, notes that Algeria was divided into twelve departments and the three positions of superprefect were officially appointed by decree on 28 June 1956.

79. Alleg et al, *La Guerre d'Algérie*, vol. 2, pp. 221–22.

80. *Le Monde*, no. 3521, 19 May 1956, p. 5, on Papon's arrival; on the level of violence in the region, no. 3505, 29–30 April 1956, p. 3, and no. 3507, 3 May 1956, p. 5; on the grenade attack, no. 3517, 15 May 1956, p. 7.

81. See Alleg et al., *La Guerre d'Algérie*, vol. 2, pp. 123–26 (on the tension throughout Algeria but especially in Constantine around the time of Papon's nomination and arrival), and vol. 2, pp. 172–73 (on gunfire in Constantine between FLN and Jews); see also Violet, *Le dossier Papon*, pp. 78–80, on the period around Papon's arrival, and more generally pp. 74–90 for his experience as IGAME.

82. Alleg et al., *La Guerre d'Algérie*, vol. 2, p. 240. Papon is mentioned only by title.

83. Henri Le Mire, *Histoire militaire de la guerre d'Algérie* (Paris: Albin Michel, 1982), p. 130.

84. On the SAS, see Le Mire, *Histoire militaire de la guerre d'Algérie*, pp. 129–31; Droz and Lever, *Histoire de la guerre en Algérie*, pp. 138–39. According to Le Mire, by 1959, 250 of the 700 SAS were commanded locally by active army officers, 450 by army reserve officers. Le Mire distinguishes local commanders, on site in the *bled* and living among the villagers in the *douars*, from upper-level command posts attached to the prefects and subprefects. Civilian officers from the government office for indigenous affairs staffed the latter.

85. Erhel et al., *Le Procès de Maurice Papon*, vol. 1, pp. 197, 201–2.

86. Droz and Lever, *Histoire de la guerre en Algérie*, p. 70; Le Mire, *Histoire militaire de la guerre d'Algérie*, pp. 130–31 ("And if the army derived any honor from its action in Algeria, it is first—and foremost—to the SAS personnel that this is due").

87. Droz ad Lever, *Histoire de la guerre d'Algérie*, pp. 111, 139.

88. Le Mire, *Histoire militaire de la guerre d'Algérie*, pp. 130–32; Droz and Lever, *Histoire de la guerre d'Algérie*, p. 139.

89. Erhel et al., *Le procès de Maurice Papon*, vol. 1, p. 196.

90. Droz and Lever, *Histoire de la guerre d'Algérie*, pp. 115–16.

91. Papon, Interrogatoire de *curriculum vitae*, 9 Dec. 1988, as quoted in Violet, *Le Dossier Papon*, p. 76.

92. Erhel et al., *Le Procès de Maurice Papon*, vol. 1, p. 190.

93. I rely here on Doueil, *L'Administration locale à l'épreuve de la guerre*, pp. 69–71, and on the decree of 24 May 1951, which replaced the 4 March 1948 and 26 January 1951 decrees, in République française, *Annuaire du corps préfectoral et de l'administration centrale*, 1957, pp. 980–81.

94. Jacques Isorni, *Mémoires*, vol. 2: *1946–1958* (Paris: Laffont, 1986), pp. 361–62.

95. On the Morice line, see Droz and Lever, *Histoire de la guerre d'Algérie*, pp. 132–33.

96. On all these activities, see Violet, *Le Dossier Papon*, pp. 82–84.

97. On Papon's press conference, see Violet, *Le Dossier Papon*, pp. 88–89; on the regroupings, see Alleg et al., *La Guerre d'Algérie*, vol. 2, pp. 240–43, vol. 3, pp. 209–11, and Droz and Lever, *Histoire de la guerre d'Algérie*, p. 139.

98. On the change in tactics and Salan, see Alleg et al., *La Guerre d'Algérie*, vol. 2, pp. 243–46.

99. Einaudi, *La Bataille de Paris*, pp. 48–51.

100. Erhel et al., *Le Procès de Maurice Papon*, vol. 1, p. 193; see also vol. 1, p. 190.

101. Ibid., vol. 1, p. 201.

102. Ibid., vol. 2, p. 648.

103. For the above quotations, see Erhel et al., *Le Procès de Maurice Papon*, vol. 1, pp. 192, 193, 195.

104. Alleg et al., *La Guerre d'Algérie*, vol. 2, p. 499, quote a Lacoste circular of April 1957 but give no further information on the document. Einaudi, *La Bataille de Paris*, p. 50–51 quotes the circular, dating it 11 April. On torture centers, see Droz and Lever, *Histoire de la guerre d'Algérie*, pp. 139–41.

105. Heymann, *Les Libertés publiques*, pp. 67–68

106. Ibid., pp. 69–75.

107. Ibid., p. 75.

108. Erhel et al., *Le Procès de Maurice Papon*, vol. 1, p. 206.

109. In this paragraph and the next one, I rely for my information on Violet's rendition of Papon's move from Constantine to Paris, *Le Dossier Papon*, pp. 91–98.

110. On the course of the war in Algeria and FLN policy decisions, see Droz and Lever, *Histoire de la guerre d'Algérie*, pp. 124, 130 n. 3, who also indicate, p. 128, that FLN leaders approved terrorism against Europeans in Algeria as early as 1956.

111. See Jacques Soustelle, *L'Espérance trahie* (Paris: Editions de l'Alma, 1961). The English novel *July 14 Assassination* by the pseudonymous Ben Abro (London: Jonathan Cape, 1963) echoes, rightly or wrongly, French left-wing suspicions about Soustelle, whose parliamentary immunity was lifted in 1961 in the context of his vehement opposition to de Gaulle's policy in Algeria. Soustelle, despite deep complicity in French civil unrest from 1958 through 1962, had an untouchable reputation as a resister and, among others, vouchsafed Papon's conversion to legitimacy at the Liberation. This explains perhaps why Papon praises Soustelle in *Les Chevaux du pouvoir*, pp. 32, 66, 282, and 388, for instance.

112. See Papon, *Les Chevaux du pouvoir*, pp. 17–66, for the events surrounding his appointment as police prefect and his own version of the events of 13 May 1958; on

Pflimlin and Papon, see Jean Lacouture, *De Gaulle*, vol. 2: *Le Politique, 1944–1959* (Paris: Seuil, 1985), p. 461.

113. Boulanger, *Papon, un intrus dans la République*, p. 242.

114. Naegelen, *Mission en Algérie*, p. 279.

115. Ibid., p. 289.

116. Violet, *Le Dossier Papon*, pp. 104–5; Michel Levine, *Les Ratonnades d'octobre: Un Meurtre collectif à Paris en 1961* (Paris: Ramsay, 1985), pp. 25–31; Benjamin Stora, *La Gangrène et l'oubli. La Mémoire de la guerre d'Algérie* (Paris: La Découverte, 1991), p. 94.

117. Naegelen, *Mission en Algérie*, p. 289.

118. Violet, *Le Dossier Papon*, pp. 119–21; see similar remarks by Papon in 1997–1998, Erhel et al., *Le procès de Maurice Papon*, vol. 1, p. 198. Stora, *La Gangrène et l'oubli*, p. 93, acknowledges the tension in Paris between the FLN and Messali Hadj's supporters.

119. Erhel et al., *Le Procès de Maurice Papon*, vol. 1, pp. 197, 202. See also Papon, *Les Chevaux du pouvoir*, pp. 103–4, where he describes a meeting with de Gaulle in which the use of the SAS in Paris was first broached.

120. Papon, *Les Chevaux du pouvoir*, pp. 108–9.

121. Levine, *Les Ratonnades d'octobre*, p. 34.

122. Ibid., pp. 34–42; see also Boulanger, *Papon, un intrus dans la République*, pp. 240–41.

123. Richard J. Golsan, "Memory's *bombes à retardement*: Maurice Papon, Crimes against Humanity, and 17 October 1961," *Journal of European Studies* 28.1–2 (March–June 1998), p. 169.

124. As quoted in Conan, *Le Procès Papon*, p. 261.

EXTREME RIGHT-WING

PERSPECTIVES ON THE

TOUVIER AND PAPON TRIALS

Christopher Flood

INTRODUCTION

To members of France's extreme right belonging to or allied with the Front National (FN), the trials of Paul Touvier and Maurice Papon could scarcely be a matter of indifference. Commentators in the mainstream French media expected that in judging the defendants, the courts would also judge the Vichy regime, and in particular the French state's treatment of Jews, including its indirect complicity in the Final Solution. The FN and its ideological allies took issue with these expectations, but recognized the need to tread carefully. The trials gave the party's enemies an excellent opportunity to damage it in the eyes of the public by associating its views with shameful acts perpetrated by servants of the Vichy regime, or even worse still, by the Germans. As one FN writer put it at the start of the Papon trial, "in the final analysis the reference to the past is being used to take aim at Le Pen and nationalism in the present."[1] As the electoral performance of the FN had drawn attention to the party from the mid-1980s onward, hostile observers had often grouped it with earlier manifestations of the extreme right, thereby raising the specter of a revival of fascism. As Mel Cohen has noted, even when explicit connections were absent, the link was frequently reinforced in the popular imagination by cartoon caricatures of the party's president, Jean-Marie Le Pen, and others in fascist-style paramilitary uniform.[2]

The party's publicists, including a number of former members of the New Right who joined in the later 1980s, had attempted to distance the FN from these associations. They claimed to have developed a new ideological synthesis, drawing on the ideas of what they called the "national" right since the time of the Revolution, but rejecting the antidemocratic, authoritarian conception of government, the racist and anti-Semitic elements, and the willingness to resort to political violence characteristic of the extreme right in the past.[3] While claiming to represent the *true* right, as distinct from parties that merely passed for right-wing, the FN rejected the label of *extreme* right for itself. It even fought court cases to force a right of reply when described as extreme right-wing in the press. Its campaigns to portray itself as new and different no doubt contributed to the FN's electoral appeal in some quarters, yet it never disarmed the skepticism of the party's opponents in political, journalistic, or intellectual circles.

Despite the danger of giving ammunition to their enemies, the FN and its ideological allies made direct and indirect public attacks on the Touvier and Papon trials, although these efforts were not based on any great affection for the two defendants as individuals. The old age and frailty of both defendants were evoked during the hearings to highlight claims that the legal proceedings were entirely inappropriate. Neither Touvier nor Papon was an ideal candidate for hagiographic treatment from an extreme right-wing perspective. Touvier had been a man of extreme right-wing views but was far from being an upstanding example for the present day. Regardless of the other charges that had been dropped following earlier proceedings against him, there was no dispute that Touvier had been directly responsible for the execution of Jewish hostages at Rillieux-la-Pape, and some of his actions while on the run after the war had been deeply disreputable.[4] As for Papon, his alleged role in the slaughter of Jews was less direct, and he had been a man of stature until his wartime past was exposed to public attention in 1981. But there was no reason for the extreme right to show particular loyalty toward him. He had never been one of their own. His career as a civil servant, then as a politician, had suggested an opportunistic ability to accommodate himself comfortably to whichever political forces were dominant at a given time. The former Radical of the interwar years had eventually evolved into a tough-minded Gaullist, but he had always remained in the political mainstream, which the FN claimed to despise. The perception was summed up by Le Pen in a speech given on 19 October 1997, when he remarked, "Monsieur Papon is not one of our political friends and we do not feel any particular warmth towards him. He is not from our parish. . . . But what concerns us above all in this affair is the method."[5]

As Le Pen's words implied, what mattered more to extreme right-wing commentators were not the defendants themselves, but the larger issues. These observers challenged the legitimacy of the judicial process itself and questioned the validity of the historical arguments that were adduced in support of the charges. They were also eager to denounce the political motives that they attributed to those who had sought to ensure that the two men were tried and convicted as exemplary figures. The sensitivity of FN writers on the subject was undoubtedly heightened by the party's view of itself as the blameless victim of systematic judicial persecution. Its leading figures had frequently been subjected to punishment by the courts on the basis of what they considered to be bad laws, political manipulation of legal processes, and biased decisions in civil cases brought by antiracist pressure groups such as LICRA or SOS Racisme, which had the vocal support of the liberal media. For example, the Touvier trial coincided with the prosecution of *Présent* (a newspaper catering to the Catholic traditionalist wing of the FN) and its columnist Catherine Parmentier for an article on immigration. The latter stages of the Papon trial coincided with proceedings against Le Pen for having physically assaulted the Socialist politician Annette Peulvast-Bergeal at Mantes-la-Jolie.[6] The Touvier and Papon cases were both illustrations of the familiar processes and forces that the extreme right believed to be dragging French society down. The types of arguments produced by extreme right-wing observers were strikingly similar in relation to both trials.

The passage of time between the two cases, however, shifted the context of these parallel critiques. Touvier was the first Frenchman to be tried for crimes against humanity, whereas Papon was the second, and the trials were separated by a gap of three and a half years. The Touvier trial had followed a period of several years in which issues relating to the Occupation, and especially to the situation of the Jews, had already been the subject of endless debate in political, journalistic, and academic circles amid much public soul-searching in the name of the "duty to memory." By the time Papon came to trial, there had been a great deal more of the same, including President Chirac's official acknowledgment on 16 June 1995 of the responsibility of the French state in persecuting Jews, and an equivalent speech by the new Socialist prime minister, Lionel Jospin, on 20 July 1997. A few days before the start of the Papon trial, and in response to suggestions from Jewish representative groups, thirty French bishops made a formal act of collective repentance for the failure of the French church to protest earlier and more vigorously against the treatment of the Jews under Vichy. One of the police trade unions, subsequently made a similar gesture relating to the actions of their counterparts under the Occupation. The Ordre des médecins, representing doctors, did likewise in recognition of the fact that their predecessors had acquiesced in the exclusion of Jews from the medical profession under Vichy's discriminatory legislation. This climate of collective remorse and the endless delving into tragic events of the wartime period were deeply resented by extreme right-wingers, who viewed them as abject and excessive.[7] Meanwhile, in the years since the Touvier trial, the FN had raised its share of the vote in the presidential and municipal elections of 1995 and the parliamentary election of 1997, giving it a solid national platform of about 15 percent from which to move forward. The message of national preference, national pride, and ethnic homogeneity appeared to be making its way. Although the Papon case elicited many assertions from the extreme right that did little more than reiterate those made at the time of the Touvier trial, some elements of analysis and interpretation were more elaborate, more self-confident, and expressive of a greater degree of irritation at the fact that the process of passing symbolic judgment on the Vichy regime was being repeated amid an orgy of collective self-mortification. More specifically, the comments in extreme right-wing publications conveyed a stronger sense that the writers believed they knew what lay behind it all. The analysis that follows in the remainder of this chapter will draw particularly, though not exclusively, on *National hebdo* and *Présent*, the two newspapers most directly linked to the FN.

THE ILLEGITIMACY OF THE PROCEDURE

The basic challenge to the legitimacy of both trials was the assertion that the fundamental rules of French law were being disregarded. The main lines of argument in this area had already been set out four years before Touvier's trial by his lawyer, Jacques Trémolet de Villers, himself a man of the reactionary right.[8] During Touvier's and Papon's trials, these claims were reiterated in the extreme right-wing press. First, there was the issue of retroactivity: a law that had only been incorporated into French statutes in 1964, and later subjected to a succession of reformulations, was being applied to actions that had been taken by the defendants in the early 1940s. Jean Madiran, editor of *Présent*, repeatedly drew attention to the fact that retroactive application of the law was contrary to article 8 of the Declaration of the Rights of Man, formulated in 1789 and still a fundamental principle enshrined in the constitution of the Fifth Republic.[9]

Likewise, Madiran and others argued that the notion of imprescriptibility (meaning no statute of limitations) was alien to French law, which had traditionally respected the commonsense assumption that distance in time affects the reliability of evidence and testimony. Besides, what higher interest could it serve, asked the lawyer Georges-Paul Wagner during the Touvier trial, and Jean-Marie Le Pen during the Papon trial, to reopen the national divisions of fifty years ago and to judge them in the light of present-day perceptions and preoccupations?[10] A further point made against each of the trials was that in the climate of intense, venomous publicity surrounding the case, the defendant was not presumed innocent until proven guilty. On the contrary, the assumption was that the judgment of the court at the end of the spectacle was merely required to put an official seal on the verdict that was known in advance.[11] The juries could not possibly find the defendants innocent under the circumstances, FN writers asserted. In any event, if the expected verdict had not been reached, there would inevitably have been a retrial.

With regard to Touvier, the claim was made that his actions had already been judged, albeit under a different law, so that the present trial infringed the rule according to which no one should be tried twice for the same offense. Papon's case was obviously different in this respect. He had not been indicted until 1983 as a result of the complaints laid against him following the revelations in *Le Canard enchaîné* on 6 May 1981 (see chronology, p. 260). However, an unsigned article in *National hebdo*, the FN's principal journalistic outlet, repeated Papon's own misleading claim that the Jury of Honor (comprising leading veterans of the Resistance), to which he had submitted his case in 1981, had completely exonerated him. The article also echoed his assertion that the course of the investigation had been constantly distorted by politico-judicial interference to ensure that it produced the intended conclusion.[12]

The tone of the reports in the extreme right-wing press on the conduct of the trials themselves was consistent with the presupposition that they would be dismal travesties of forensic examination. The performance of the lawyers for the civil plaintiffs was singled out for regular expressions of contempt and derision, with Arno Klarsfeld's histrionics figuring largely in both trials. Inconsistent or implausible claims in the testimony of prosecution witnesses were displayed as demonstrations of the inevitable incoherence of trials mounted so long after the events. There were frequent expressions of outrage at alleged instances of illegitimate pressure on the court from within and outside the proceedings. There were shows of anger when the defendants were vilified in the media, or when defense arguments were dismissed as insults to the memory of the six million dead. There was disgust at the behavior of the presiding judge in the Touvier trial. There was revulsion toward the demonstrations outside the court in Bordeaux, the hounding of Papon when he was released from custody, and the demands for instant changes in the law to make it possible to reincarcerate him during the trial. Profound contempt was also shown for the hypocrisy of those whose own activity, or that of one of their parents, under Vichy should have inclined them to greater charity toward the defendants. For example, the eminent columnist Françoise Giroud was cited by Pierre Faillant de Villemarest and François Brigneau as someone who had written for German-controlled publications, with Brigneau supplying the additional information that she had falsely claimed to hold the Médaille de la Résistance when she stood as a candidate in the Paris municipal elections of 1977.[13]

In the end, since the verdicts had been discounted by extreme-right critics long in advance, they did not have much to add during the course of the trials. However, in *Présent*, besides repeating the arguments of legal principle, Jean Madiran pointed out that the Gayssot Law of 1990 made it a criminal offense to deny that a crime against humanity had been committed if that crime was recognized by a French or international court as having occurred. Although Touvier was deemed to have acted directly in pursuit of the German project of genocide, the inference to be drawn from the trial was that the Milice had been implicated through Touvier, and since the Milice was an official organization of the French state, it followed that the Vichy regime had indeed been a party to the extermination of the Jews. To deny this, or even to protest Touvier's innocence, would be to risk being fined or imprisoned. Thus the injustice was compounded to the point of absurdity.[14]

As for Papon's case, Jeanne Smits, a *Présent* journalist, remarked on the fact that the defendant was sentenced only to ten years in prison. She took this relatively light sentence as an indication of the understandable unease felt by judges and jurors in convicting Papon of crimes against humanity. The sentence was either too lenient or too harsh. If his crimes had been of such gravity, and if he had knowingly colluded in the Final Solution, Smits asked, how could ten years possibly be sufficient to mark society's revulsion? But if there was doubt as to whether he had, in fact, committed crimes against humanity, how could he be legitimately convicted at all, since any lesser crimes would have been prescriptible?[15]

QUESTIONS OF HISTORY AND MEMORY

In an article on the Touvier trial, Georges-Paul Wagner had remarked that a court of law is not an appropriate place for producing an overview of the history of a period: its function of conducting detailed examinations of specific episodes in the lives of individuals made it ill fitted to adopt the broader perspective.[16] During the Papon trial *National hebdo* produced a satirical pamphlet, *Téléfatras*, mocking the absurdity of using the trial of one man to judge an entire society and an historical period fifty years after the events. The fear on the extreme right was that, in any case, the alleged historical lessons of the Occupation were already being drawn for the public outside the court by the media and other bodies that offered ideologically driven interpretations of the period. They represented their own approach as a struggle against the historical distortions that were being perpetrated in the name of the supposed "duty to remember" that had become a leitmotif of the present period.

With regard to the two men's own actions, the familiar tactic adopted by extreme right-wing commentators was to attempt to lessen the weight of the allegations by pointing to mitigating factors, extenuating circumstances, or, where feasible, errors in the charges. Much was made of the false claim that Touvier had bargained the number of hostages to be shot down from the figure of one hundred originally demanded by the Germans to seven only.[17] Papon's actions in connection with signing the orders for deportation convoys were set against the fact that his place in the administrative hierarchy had meant that he was merely a signatory of orders relating to the deportations, not a decision maker in that regard. Both Touvier and Papon—more convincingly in the case of Papon—were also said to have given aid to the Resistance. A particularly supportive article accompanied an interview with Papon in *Enquête sur l'histoire*, a magazine edited by Dominique Venner, one of the godfathers of the New Right. The article portrayed the prefect, Sabatier, and his staff as having been reluctant to execute the orders to arrest foreign Jews and having done whatever they could to delay the process. Papon was represented as a junior official who had no involvement in or authority over preparations for the roundups. On the other hand, it was claimed that he had done all he could to reduce the number of arrests—thereby saving many lives—and to improve the conditions of those who were transported in the convoys. It was reported that the Germans had considered him to be an agent for the Americans and that his promotion to the rank of prefect after the war had been a reward for his extensive services to the Resistance.[18]

When focusing on the wider context, extreme right-wing commentators sought to undermine the stereotypical binary image that presented France's wartime experience as a struggle between the forces of salvation (Gaullists, Resistance, the Allies), and the forces of degradation (Pétainists, French Fascists, the Germans). The arguments therefore had both defensive and aggressive aspects consistent with positions that had been set out many times before in extreme right-wing publications. On the defensive side, for fairly obvious reasons, the tactic was to excuse and to contextualize the Vichy regime—and hence the actions of its officials, including Touvier and Papon—rather than to offer a wholeheartedly revisionist apologia for the reactionary political, social, and economic project encapsulated in the *Révolution nationale* or for the principle of collaboration with Germany. In the political climate surrounding the two trials, to have mounted an explicit defense of these aspects of Vichy would merely have given ammunition to enemies, since it would have appeared too clear an acknowledgment of the ideological and historical links between the present-day extreme right and its forerunners during the Occupation.

Thus there was a tendency to insist on the fact that the Vichy regime that Touvier and Papon served had been legitimately established, with full powers voted to Pétain by an overwhelming majority of the National Assembly in July 1940. A number of writers followed the tradition of maintaining Pétain's personal honor and, in effect, of endorsing the sword-and-shield thesis by emphasizing the devastating impact of the German invasion that had made Pétain's governance and personal sacrifice as necessary to the survival of the nation as had Charles de Gaulle's work in organizing the Free French. For example, in an open letter to Robert Paxton purporting to refute the latter's insulting view of Vichy, a retired air force general, Jacques Le Groignec, made the impassioned demand:

> Remember! The country which you reduce to the label of "Vichy" was simply the 40 million French people who, in September 1939, despite being materially ill armed and morally ill prepared, had stood up to a people who were twice as numerous, powerfully armed, and in search of revenge. What you call "Vichy" was a wounded country which was to be watched over for four years by an illustrious soldier who had been called by the Nation and its representatives to sacrifice his glory in order to temper the demands of an inhuman enemy and to prevent the installation of a Gauleiter who would have undertaken the destruction of all the Jews of France, among other crimes.[19]

On the crucial issue of Vichyite treatment of the Jews, the line of defense was more to emphasize the limits of the policy rather than to defend the ideology or the propaganda underpinning the regime's discriminatory measures.[20] Therefore the approach was to stress the distinction between the exclusionary nature of French policy and the exterminatory goals of German policy. Insofar as Vichy defenders accepted that French collaboration with Germany had included an indirect contribution to the Holocaust, they denied that this had occurred with knowledge of the Final Solution. Vichy sympathizers noted that the number of Jews from France (foreign or French Jews) who had died in the Holocaust was small in comparison with that of other occupied countries because Vichyite officials had deliberately slowed the process of roundups and deportations. On two occasions Le Pen himself aired a broader argument that implicitly echoed his notorious claim that the Holocaust had been a "detail" of the Second World War. On the subject of France's wartime experience, he objected to the current historico-judicial debate that had become excessively focused on the sufferings of the Jews at the expense of attention to those of the rest of the population:

> I do not want to rewrite history. However, I would not want judicial or political coercion to force our country to accept a vision of history which does not correspond to the reality experienced by French people. It is true that terrible things happened, there were immense sorrows and heavy losses: 600,000 French people were lost in the Second World War. But they were not all of the same religion, they were from every religion and every background. And how could we say that someone whose relatives were torn to pieces by English or American bombs should have felt less grief and deserve less respect than those who died in other circumstances, including the terrible death camps?[21]

The second major plank of the defense was to assert the extreme right's own role in resistance to the Germans. The FN itself has always had space among its older members for men who had been loyal to Vichy or who had even been members of pro-German Fascist groups during the war—among them François Brigneau, André Dufraisse, Paul Malagutti, Jean Madiran, and Henri Roques, for example. But it has also included former members of the Free French or the Resistance, and has claimed to stand for reconciliation between all those whose motive was to do their patriotic duty as they saw it. In 1993, claiming to answer the need for objective understanding of the past, as opposed to the lies and legends perpetuated through the present cult of historical memory, the FN had illustrated its own version of the Resistance by holding a colloquium on the subject.[22] One of the stated aims of the event had been to challenge the left's pretensions to have been the driving force in the Resistance within France. Above all, the speakers showed particular resentment of the claims made by the Communist Party (PCF). It was pointed out that many of the early resisters in France, like many of the Free French outside France, had been men of the (extreme) right who had committed themselves at a time when the PCF was seeking collaboration with the Germans and leaders of the Social-ist Party (SFIO) were pledging loyalty to Vichy. To validate this claim on behalf of the extreme right, several decorated veterans of the Free French or the Resis-tance who were now FN members—Jean-Baptiste Biaggi, André Figuéras, Robert Hemmerdinger, Jacques Lafay, Marc Mattéi, Raymond Mérentié and Jean Vallette d'Osia—gave personal testimony and also used the occasion to denounce the Communists.

During the trials themselves the part played in the Resistance by extreme right-wingers from the earliest stages was reasserted. For example, writing in the FN-supporting Catholic magazine *Monde et vie* during the Touvier trial, Pierre Faillant de Villemarest cited his own personal experience as a student in Clermont-Ferrand, where, he claimed, General Cochet had circulated an appeal as early as 16 June—not September as the Gaullists claimed after the Libera-tion to preserve their own mythology—to continue the struggle. Faillant de Villemarest and other students had helped to distribute the tract and had sub-sequently set up a somewhat amateurish network to carry out resistance activ-ity. The point of this testimony was not so much to undermine the primacy of the Gaullists as to point out that Cochet, like Frenay, was not hostile to Pétain and intended to use the pause offered by Vichy to set up resistance networks. According to Faillant de Villemarest, supported by anecdotes from his own ex-perience or observation, three out of every four people within the Vichy gov-ernment, the administration, the police, and what remained of the armed forces were plotting in one way or another against the small minority of convinced collaborators, but all of this had been conveniently obscured in the interests of the Gaullists and the Communists.[23]

The aggressive aspect of the historical arguments involved relativizing the charges against Vichy by pointing to the crimes of others and seeking to dis-credit the accusers. The process of denouncing the war crimes of others in-volved familiar echoes of claims made during the Occupation by Vichy's own publicists. The causes of the defeat were taken up, as they had been so often by Pétain and others in the wake of the disaster. François Brigneau in *National hebdo* during the Touvier trial and Jacques Le Groignec in *Présent* during the Papon trial reminded readers that France had, in effect, been abandoned to face Ger-many alone, given the failure of Britain to provide adequate military support for France during the German invasion and the failure of the United States to intervene at all at that stage.[24] Brigneau also focused on the actions of the Al-lies in the later stages of the war in order to demand that if there was indeed a duty to remember, it should equally include the victims of the bombing of French towns before and during the Normandy landings. He likewise reminded readers of other actions, such as the destruction of Dresden and Hiroshima, as illustrations of his claim that the Allies' hands had scarcely been clean.

The domestic causes of the defeat were revisited with the traditional claim that the politicians of the Third Republic, and more particularly of the Popular Front, had been responsible for an appalling crime against the nation by precipitating France into the war without adequate preparation. Most writers did not go further in the direction of reviving Vichyite charges against the supposed vices and decay of the Third Republic. A predictable exception in this regard was François Brigneau, himself a veteran of the antiparliamentary, anti-Semitic, antimasonic, anti-Communist ultra-right and former member of the Milice who had shared a cell with Robert Brasillach at Fresnes before the latter's execution. At the start of the Papon trial, in one of his regular columns for *National hebdo*, Brigneau mounted an impassioned defense of Vichy, coupled with a diatribe against the forces that had brought France to a state of chronic debilitation during the interwar years:

> Before judging Papon, people should start by rediscovering the emotional climate of the summer of 1940, when France was crushed by defeat, eaten up by despair, seething with anger and yearning for hope.
>
> People would need to explain what a large section of the nation held against the Jews and Freemasons who had pushed us into the war, and against the communists who were now Hitler's allies, and the Popular Front, with its law on the forty-hour week when everyone should have been working sixty, and the Third Republic, a dying regime, with its repeated ministerial crises, its repeated devaluations and its succession of financial scandals.[25]

The issues of collaboration and resistance also provided grounds for attack. On the one hand, it was pointed out that the small minority of enthusiastic collaborationists based in Paris had included many men whose ideological origins had been on the left: the ex-Socialist Marcel Déat and the ex-Communist Jacques Doriot were among the notorious cases in point.[26] This line of attack fitted conveniently with the FN's usual disclaimer of any links between itself and fascism or nazism. For example, at the FN's colloquium on the Resistance in 1993, Yvan Blot had argued that although fascism and nazism had been a synthesis of elements drawn from the right as well as the left, they were fundamentally distinct from the true right, not only because of their socialist components, but also because they incorporated a strong element of the gnostic, revolutionary, totalitarian aspiration to mold society in order to create a new human type, whereas the right respected the traditions, the basic freedoms, and the cultural heritage of the nation.[27] Conversely, without denying that the Communists had played an important part in the Resistance, it was possible to draw attention to the equivocal, semi-collaborationist stance of the PCF during the period of the Nazi-Soviet pact, on the one hand, or their brutality during the Liberation and purges, on the other.[28]

Before Papon's trial, both he and his lawyer, Jean-Marc Varaut, had given the impression that since the case was supposedly a judgment on the whole Vichy regime, reference should be made to the activity of members of the Union générale des Israélites de France (UGIF), the organization established in November 1941 by Xavier Vallat during his time as commissioner-general of Jewish affairs to group together representatives of the Jewish community with a view to coordinating philanthropic and social action. This matter provided material for an article in *Enquête sur l'histoire* by Jean-Claude Valla, one of the founders of the New Right think tank GRECE (Groupement de recherches et d'études pour une civilisation europeénne), and more recently author of a revisionist account of the Touvier case. Valla pointed out that the UGIF had played a part in organizing the recruitment of foreign Jews for agricultural work under appalling conditions in the Ardennes, in the manning of the transit camp at Drancy by Jewish guards under Jewish commandants, in providing names for updating the register of Jews in Paris even when the roundups of foreign Jews were already taking place, and in directly helping to round up Jewish children for transportation to Drancy. Valla did not draw out an explicit conclusion for Papon's trial, but his closing remarks carried a clear implication. Having observed that leaders of UGIF had been exonerated by a Jury of Honor after the war on the grounds that they had had no choice, he continued:

> All of the Jews implicated in these matters defended themselves by explaining that they had been obliged to compromise in order to try to prevent the worst. They had chosen the lesser of two evils. And what is more, they were completely unaware of the fate which awaited the Jews who were deported. These are precisely the arguments which were put forward by French senior civil servants who were accused of having given way to German demands. It is the explanation that René Bousquet used and the one which Maurice Papon is using today.[29]

In the event, Varaut did not use the case of UGIF in Papon's defense. This provoked a sour article in *National hebdo* by the veteran Holocaust denialist Robert Faurisson, who made a scathing attack on Varaut. Besides criticizing him for making far too many concessions to the general condemnation of Vichy, Faurisson accused Varaut of failing to point out the extent to which Vichyite officials had intervened as a buffer between the Germans and the Jews or of showing the excellent relations between the government and leaders of the Rabbinate, the Central Consistory, and other Jewish organizations. He argued that Varaut should have demanded access to the archives of the Central Consistory for the Hauts-de-Seine (where Drancy was located) or the records of the Juries of Honor, composed entirely of Jews, who had exonerated UGIF officials. In Faurisson's view, this would have highlighted the injustice of putting Papon on trial now for lesser crimes than those for which Jews had pardoned members of their own community immediately after the events. The conclusion of the article made it clear that Faurisson himself had sent a file of evidence to Varaut for use in the defense but Varaut had ignored it.[30]

The extreme right's attempts to relativize the actions of the defendants and of Vichy sometimes offered reminders of the Historians' Debate in Germany. They drew an explicit or implicit comparison between the Holocaust and other historical acts, which they equated with genocide. A few weeks before the Touvier trial an article by Pierre de Meuse in *Identité*, the FN's theoretical magazine, returned to one of the historical episodes that had been the object of considerable attention from the extreme right during the recent upsurge of historical debate concerning the French Revolution. The article did not allude directly to the Touvier case. It did not attack the claim that the extermination of the Jews had been unique. It did not state that historical denialism was by no means exclusive to those who rejected orthodox accounts of the Final Solution. Nevertheless, those issues formed part of the historiographical-ideological context of the writing. This much was suggested by the abstract that preceded the article, as it opened with the words: "At a time when the necessity of preserving 'memory' is being invoked in relation to certain events during the last war, and this memory is becoming increasingly selective, it would be unjust not to recall the drama of the Vendée which was commemorated very discreetly last year."[31] De Meuse defined the massacres carried out by the armies of the Republic in the Vendée after the defeat of the royalist insurrection there in 1793 as "a crime against humanity in the name of humanity."[32] The core of the argument was that this had been a prototype of systematic, premeditated extermination in pursuit of a totalitarian project of ideological hegemony by the ancestors of today's left in France.

Some months before the Papon trial, *Identité* took up the issue of crimes against humanity again. This time it produced a dossier of five articles under the overall title of "Communism: A Crime against Humanity," in which direct comparisons were drawn between the Nazis' extermination of Jews and the atrocities carried out under Communist regimes against alleged class enemies. Following a line of argument already anticipated by Bernard Antony in an article for *Présent* during the Touvier trial, the introduction to the collection described the Communist record as a "monstrous balance sheet, a thousand times worse than the one left by Nazism."[33] Statistics were produced to show the vast numbers of people killed in pursuit of the Communist project in the USSR and other countries, amounting to a claimed total of some two hundred million dead. The argument was that the West had shown passive acquiescence, and sometimes active complicity, in these crimes because its dominant ideology of political and economic liberalism shared ideological roots with socialism and communism in the rationalistic dream of progress fostered during the Enlightenment. The particular case of the Frenchman Pierre Boudarel, who had served as an ideological commissar in the Viet Minh death camps in Indochina before returning to France and being protected for many years by the PCF while he worked as a university professor, was taken as an example of the inequity and hypocrisy of France's elites, since it had not been found expedient to bring him to trial for crimes against humanity once his former activities had been exposed. To ram the point home, the FN-linked Catholic fundamentalist organization Chrétienté-Solidarité mounted a mock show trial of Boudarel at the Palais de la Mutualité during the Papon proceedings and used the whole of the back page of *Présent* as an advertisement for the occasion.[34]

POLITICAL MANIPULATION

What did the extreme right see lying behind the trials? Who stood to gain from them, and why? It is characteristic of the extreme right to assume the existence of conspiracies or at least collusion between individuals or groups working to promote their own interests at the expense of the interests of the nation. The fact that the two trials were conducted in a highly charged political atmosphere of recriminations and exhortations to acknowledge collective guilt lent itself to being interpreted in this way. Some rather vague remarks in Trémolet de Villers's book in 1990 had pointed the finger at two sets of enemies, the Communists and the Jews. He maintained that the Communists wanted to use the case to revenge themselves on their political enemies, to undermine the authority of the state, and to discredit the church, while the Jews shared the Communists' desire to use Touvier's links with Catholic clergy to defame the church.[35] However, although there were expressions of dark curiosity as to the motives behind the trial, there was little sign of this interpretation being taken up more widely by the extreme right during the trial itself. There was, of course, a sense that it was a show trial, but extreme right-wing commentators tended to refer vaguely to "those who" had wanted the trial, without specifying clearly who "they" were. For some, the media were certainly part of it.[36] Or there were the "memory militias," as *National hebdo* journalist Béatrice Péreire called them.[37] Or there were "those who endlessly proclaim that 'France is the home of human rights,'" as Jean Madiran put it.[38] And, according to Martin Peltier, editor of *National hebdo*, there were those who wanted to replace the Christian message to the young with an ersatz Heaven of rights and the Shoah as a vision of Hell.[39]

During the Papon trial the focus sharpened. The two forces most often cited as responsible for the endless agitation concerning the supposed duty to remember and to procure exemplary convictions were those familiar targets of extreme right-wing hostility, the Communist Party and Jewish pressure groups—each with international connections. One or both of these groups were taken by a number of extreme right-wing commentators to be acting to manipulate the general public for their own ends with the complicity of the political establishment, the media, and France's "moral authorities" (the church, civil rights groups, etc.). Papon himself had claimed that several political interest groups were in league against him: the Communists wanted to settle old scores dating from his time as prefect of police in Paris under de Gaulle's presidency, the ultra-left in the media and the judiciary hated everything he represented, and "the international pressure group" (read Jews) wanted to use him to implicate France in genocide, though he did not say why.[40]

It might have been expected that after the collapse of the Soviet bloc and the long-term decline of the PCF as an electoral force within France, anticommunism would have appeared less relevant even to the extreme right than it had in the past. However, that was not the case. Extreme right-wing publicists claimed that the PCF still enjoyed enormous influence through its networks of support and its role as part of the political establishment. Far from being proscribed, as the extreme right believed it should have been, the PCF remained relatively respectable and was allowed to posture as a guardian of civil and human rights. Its past and present members were not subjected to prosecutions or even treated as outcasts. From this perspective, the Touvier and Papon trials, as well as the loud participation of the PCF in campaigns around the supposed duty to remember the war, were viewed as being aimed to divert attention from the party's own disgrace and from the crimes committed by communism across the world. At all costs, therefore, the Communists had to prevent the relativization of the Holocaust and to hold up the specters of fascism and racism, which in turn sought to discredit the FN by association, hence "the demonizing problematic: nationalism = fascism," as Pierre de Meuse put it.[41]

Right-wing commentators perceived these efforts as the other side of the Communist Party's attempt to hijack the memory and mythology of the Resistance in order to present itself as the guardian of France's honor and to attack the nationalist right as traitors. The collusion of the mainstream parties of the moderate left and right (the Socialists, the center-right UDF, and the Gaullist RPR, which Le Pen and his colleagues habitually grouped together with the PCF under the label of "the Gang of Four") with their many allies in the media, the trade unions, civic bodies, and other dependent groups was assumed to be a further element in the picture. They were all components of a network of power in which interdependence overrode apparent ideological differences and political disagreements. That was why Le Pen, in his end-of-1997 interview for *National hebdo*, replied to a question about the trials and the recent work on historical memory by stating that if the real truth were established, it would destroy the myths supporting the whole network. It would thus cause "a fantastic acceleration of the disintegration of our political system and of the Gang of Four whose only cement is their shared, counterfeit vision of twentieth-century history."[42] If that happened, he claimed, then he would cease to be demonized and the PCF would be put in its proper place at last.

Like the Communists, and sometimes represented as being linked to them, the Jews were regarded as the other set of principal beneficiaries and manipulators of the agitation surrounding the trials. Of course, the FN claimed to have abandoned the anti-Semitism of its forebears — and in any case needed to contend with the Pleven and Gayssot laws against incitement to racial or ethnic hatred. It was no longer a case of unabashed biological or cultural determinism representing Jews as inherently parasitic, debased, destructive, and driven to pursue domination by manipulating whatever forces of division and exploitation of Gentiles were most expedient at a given time. The distaste and the suggestions of conspiracy were more subtle and complex. Martin Peltier accepted that Jews could be assimilated to national society and were capable of national ideals but suggested that the understandable anxieties of ordinary Jews in the light of previous persecution were being exploited by those whom Peltier provocatively christened the "Judapo" (emblazoning the word in massive letters across the front page in white on red above a star of David), or "politically organized Judaism," meaning both Jewish representative organizations and antiracist organizations in which Jews played a prominent part, as well as politicians, journalists, and campaigners linked to the PCF or other left-wing parties.[43]

The themes were echoed in other far-right articles. The old association of Jews with subversion and the pursuit of domination was thus still present in a slightly attenuated form. The Jewish lawyers for the civil plaintiffs received biographical coverage emphasizing that most of them had left-wing connections. The fact that several of them acted for the plaintiffs in both cases reinforced the impression that there were disreputable objectives in play. Lawyer Joë Nordmann was an object of particular loathing on the part of the extreme right. At the time of the Touvier trial he had been denounced as an unreconstructed Stalinist, and an article in *Minute* had dwelled on the tactics he had used in the 1951 trial of David Rousset, during which Nordmann had denied the existence of the Soviet forced labor camps and had sought to discredit the testimony of survivors by accusing them of playing the same game as the Nazi propagandists.[44] His participation in the Papon trial invited a further list of distasteful details of his application of Stalinist politics in his legal career.[45] Other Jews who were connected with the cases received similar treatment: the historians Denis Peschanski and Pierre Vidal-Naquet, the civil servant/historian Marc-Olivier Baruch, and the lawyers Yves Jouffa and Arno Klarsfeld (again) were among the men whom Gabriel Lindon described as "those who have been given responsibility for stirring the intellectuals, the press, the lawyers, the power groups and other lobbies to go in for the kill."[46] Besides implying the Jewish link with the international revolutionary left, another article by Peltier further suggested that the Jewish pressure groups were promoting a climate of collective guilt and remorse in France and other countries to ensure a privileged status for Jews, not only within those countries themselves, but also for Israel as it benefited from exceptional treatment by other states and was thus able to promote its interests in ways that other countries were not.[47]

CONCLUSION

It is essential to keep a sense of perspective. Because something is said by the extreme right, whom we all love to hate, it is not necessarily a product of paranoid delusion or a cynical lie. In any case, although extreme right-wing commentators were highly critical of both trials, they were not obsessed by them. The Touvier and Papon cases did not often receive front-page coverage in the extreme right-wing press and excited far less protest than issues such as immigration, urban violence, or the general misdirection of government. There was no sign that the FN and its ideological allies were eager to attach themselves so closely to the defendants that they could be dragged down with them.

The attacks on the trials were ideologically driven and polemical in tone, but not all of the criticisms were themselves ideologically specific. Many of the objections to the legal and judicial aspects of the cases were similar to points made by other observers who were far from sharing the political viewpoint of the extreme right. For example, writing with the historical journalist Éric Conan, Henry Rousso, director of the Institut d'histoire du temps présent, aired comparable reservations on the subject of the Touvier trial in the book *Vichy, un passé qui ne passe pas* (Vichy: An Ever-Present Past) and spoke extensively on the problematic aspects of the Papon trial in the interviews with Philippe Petit collected in *La Hantise du passé.*[48] Indeed, Conan and Rousso also argued that the constant public preoccupation with the crimes of Vichy, the collaboration with Germany, and above all the persecution of Jews had continued for so long and with such intensity that it could be considered pathological and damaging, especially since the supposed deficiencies of the postwar purges were being judged in the light of perceptions that were anachronistic and sometimes excessively reductive. In this respect too they shared common ground with extreme right-wing commentators.

Whatever their motives, writers in *National hebdo, Présent,* and other extreme right-wing publications were not making absurd claims when they argued to the effect that many of the historical issues raised by the trials were in shades of gray, rather than black and white. For instance, the distinction of degree between Vichy's repressive, exclusionary anti-Semitic policy and Germany's exterminatory policy cannot simply be dismissed out of hand, however repugnant Vichy's own policy was. Even the question of precisely who knew how much in France about the ultimate destination of the Jews transported out of the country via Drancy was less straightforward than the impression given by Papon's accusers, even if the extreme right-wing claim that no one knew anything appears disingenuous. Conversely, it is true that in popular memory extreme right-wing participation in the Free French forces or the internal Resistance has been overshadowed by the memory of Vichy or of the fascist collaborationists. As for the Allied bombing of civilian populations of towns and cities, including those in France, it is true that the side that won the war has a better opportunity than the defeated to ensure that its justifications of ends and means gain wide acceptance. Furthermore, while numerical comparisons are obscene when considering systematic, mass murder, it was not absurd to draw attention to massacres committed in the USSR, Cambodia, and elsewhere under Communist regimes (though a truer comparison would equally have included all of the other similar crimes of extermination committed under Fascist regimes before, during, and since the Second World War).

Even the charges of political manipulation leveled by extreme right-wingers against the Communists, the left more generally, and Jewish or other antiracist pressure groups during the Papon trial cannot simply be dismissed as paranoid ranting or deliberate distortions. Naturally these sections of French political opinion revile the memory of Vichy and of nazism. Why would many of their members not wish to see those who carried out or abetted atrocities punished, even fifty years after the events? And obviously these sets of people did want to see the FN damaged by association because they do see affinities between today's extreme right and its forerunners. They also see the revival of the extreme right as dangerous for the future and they have attempted to fight it at every opportunity.

However, none of this alters the fact that extreme right-wing commentators were operating in a specific ideological and political context which meant that the trials offered opportunities for reiterating habitual accusations against the mainstream political parties, the media, and other interest groups that they accused of undermining the strength of the nation. Furthermore, while a number of the arguments put forward by extreme right-wing commentators refer to real difficulties of juridical or historical interpretation, and while their indignation may have been more or less genuine, the fact remains that Le Pen and others have regularly courted the role of victim by provoking scandal in relation to the wartime past, including the Holocaust, and by playing on their own links with the old extreme right when it suited them to do so. In this sense their protests concerning the trials were merely matters of business as usual.

NOTES

1. Unsigned, "Questions pour un Papon," *National hebdo*, 9–15 October 1997. At the time of the Touvier trial, see Martin Peltier, "Touvier chez les picaros," ibid., 21–27 April 1994: "Up to now I had remained very discreet about this business, which I consider to be a trap, regardless of its judicial outcome." And Pierre de Meuse, "Le Procès interdit," *Identité* 24 (spring 1997), p. 23, caption to photo of Georges Boudarel, listing among the aims of both trials, "to counter the rise of national currents by means of the demonizing problematic: nationalism = fascism."

2. Mel Cohen, "The National Front and the Burden of History," paper presented to the 93rd Annual Convention of the American Political Science Association, 28 August–1 September 1997, p. 3. Cohen offers a particularly valuable analysis of many issues that are relevant to the present chapter.

3. For detailed discussion of the FN's ideological stance, see Christopher Flood, "National Populism," in Christopher Flood and Laurence Bell, eds., *Political Ideologies in Contemporary France* (London: Cassell/Pinter, 1997), pp. 103–39.

4. On the Touvier case, see Richard J. Golsan, ed., *Memory, the Holocaust, and French Justice: The Bousquet and Touvier Affairs* (Hanover, N.H.: University Press of New England, 1996).

5. Speech to FN regional councilors, Nice, 19 Oct. 1997, http://www.frontnat.fr/nice2.htm. There was an interesting parallel between the two defendants and their respective lawyers. Touvier was defended by Jacques Trémolet de Villers, an extremely combative man associated with the Catholic, reactionary wing of the extreme right. Papon was defended by Jean-Marc Varaut, himself a former activist on the neomonarchist extreme right but latterly passing for a more moderate, flexible figure who was given a fairly sympathetic profile in *Libération*. For a lucid and dispassionate anticipatory discussion of the Papon case, see Bertram Gordon, "Afterword: Who Were the Guilty and Should They Be Tried?" in Golsan, *Memory, the Holocaust, and French Justice*, pp. 179–98.

6. On the Parmentier case, see editorial statements, messages of support, and appeals for "protest subscriptions" in *Présent*, 15, 16, 17 March 1994 and thereafter. On the Le Pen case and its implications in the eyes of the FN, see, for example, Marie-Claire Roy, "Ce qu'ils reprochent au FN," and Le Pen, "Chirac piétine la Constitution et casse l'unité française," interview with Muriel Plat, both in *National hebdo*, 2–8 April 1998; Le Pen, "Défendons la France et la République française," and Gabriel Lindon, "À Versailles, une justice grand orientée," both in *National hebdo*, 9–15 April 1998.

7. See for example Béatrice Péreire, "Pardon M'sieu-dames. Tous à genoux. Inventez vos péchés," *National hebdo*, 9–15 October 1997; Unsigned, "Le Grand Pardon: Les Médecins aussi . . . ,' ibid., 30 October–5 November 1997; Jean Madiran, "La Grande Samba des menteurs," and Alain Sanders, "Maintenant la police! Bientôt les cheminots?" both in *Présent*, 9 October 1997.

8. Jacques Trémolet de Villers, *Paul Touvier est innocent* (Bouère: Dominique Martin Morin, 1990).

9. See for example Madiran, "Le Procès Touvier: Sous la contrainte," *Présent*, 18 March 1994; "Une France sous l'influence s'est condamnée elle-même," ibid., 21 April 1994; "La Rétroactivité de la loi pénale nous a été imposée. La France n'a capitulé qu'après avoir résisté pendant 34 ans," ibid., 10 October 1997, and repeated as a poster on the back page at intervals throughout the trial.

10. Georges-Paul Wagner, "Le Procès Touvier et "l'État de droit,'" *Présent*, 22 March 1994; Le Pen, speech in Nice, 19 October 1997.

11. See, for example, Georges-Paul Wagner, "Comment on s'asseoit sur la chose jugée," *Présent*, 14 October 1997; Mathilde Cruz (pseud. François Brigneau), "Papon," *National hebdo*, 9–15 October 1997.

12. See unsigned article "Questions pour un Papon," and François Brigneau, "Ne parlons pas de Papon," both in *National hebdo*, 9–15 October 1997. Papon makes the claims in "Une Nouvelle Affaire Dreyfus?" interview with Dominique Venner and Eric Vatré, *Enquête sur l'histoire* 23 (October–November 1997), pp. 10–14.

13. Pierre Faillant de Villemarest, "Lettre ouverte aux dépeceurs de cadavres," *Monde et Vie*, 7–27 April 1994, pp. 6–7; François Brigneau, "Le Journal d'un homme libre," *National hebdo*, 31 March–6 April 1994. See also for example Béatrice Péreire, "Nach Casablanca," ibid., 23–29 October 1997, for sarcastic comments on other figures.

14. Madiran, "Une France sous l'influence. . . ."

15. Jeanne Smits, "Le Procès Papon: L'Affaire qui n'aurait pas dû avoir lieu," *Présent*, 4 April 1998.

16. Wagner, "Le Procès Touvier et 'l'État de droit.' "

17. See for example Jean Madiran, "Le Procès Touvier s'ouvre ce jeudi 17 mars à Versailles," *Présent*, 17 March 1994; François Brigneau, "Le Journal d'un homme libre," *National hebdo*, 17–23 March 1994.

18. Unsigned, "Maurice Papon à Bordeaux," *Enquête sur l'histoire* 23 (October–November 1997), p. 14. The magazine is not exclusively a vehicle for extreme right-wing historiography, but its contributors are drawn predominantly from the extreme right. For a brief reference to Touvier's alleged resistance activity, see Philippe Lambert, "Touvier: Les Faux Procès," *National hebdo*, 31 March–6 April 1994.

19. Jacques Le Groignec, "Lettre ouverte sur la France à Monsieur Robert Paxton," *Présent*, 10 October 1997; and see for example Le Pen, "La Complaisance de la société pour le crime est pire que le crime lui-même," interview with Martin Peltier, *National hebdo*, 23–29 October 1997; Brigneau, "Ne parlons pas de Papon"; and his "Grâce au procès Papon," *National hebdo*, 27 November–3 December 1997. This line of argument was traditional on the extreme right: see for example the dossier "Pétain devant l'histoire" *Enquête sur l'histoire* 4 (autumn 1992).

20. See for example Le Groignec, "Lettre ouverte sur la France . . ."; unsigned, "Questions pour un Papon"; Madiran, "La Grande Samba des menteurs"; and the brief, unsigned piece, "L'Amitié avec Xavier Vallat est-elle possible?" *National hebdo*, 9–15 October 1997, which emphasizes the deliberate restraint of his action, drawing on François Brigneau's *Xavier Vallat et la question juive* (Paris: Publications F.B., 1997).

21. Le Pen, speech at Nice; and see his "La Complaisance de la société . . ." for remarks in a similar vein.

22. Published as Conseil scientifique du Front national, *D'une résistance à l'autre; l'histoire en question de 1940 à 1993* (Paris: Editions Nationales, 1994).

23. Faillant de Villemarest, "Lettre ouverte. . . ." Dominique Venner, whose *Histoire critique de la Résistance* (Paris: Pygmalion, 1995) makes much of the contribution

of the extreme right to the Resistance, nevertheless retains 6 September as the date of the written appeal (p. 151).

24. Brigneau, "Le Journal d'un homme libre," *National hebdo*, 21–27 April 1994; Le Groignec, "Lettre ouverte. . . ."

25. Brigneau, "Ne parlons pas de Papon"; and see his "Regarder l'histoire en face," *National hebdo*, 11–17 December 1997.

26. See Henri Landemer, "Déat, Doriot, Luchaire et les autres," *Enquête sur l'histoire* 23 (October–November 1997), 45–48.

27. Yvan Blot, "Fascisme et socialisme, une même famille?" in *D'une résistance à l'autre*, pp. 39–42.

28. See Patrick Jansen, "La Cocollaboration," *Enquête sur l'histoire* 23 (October–November 1997), pp. 18–20; Brigneau, "Le Journal d'un homme libre," 17–23 March 1994.

29. Jean-Claude Valla, "Une collaboration juive," *Enquête sur l'histoire* 23 (October–November 1997), p. 55; and for Valla's interest in Touvier, see his *L'Affaire Touvier, la contre-enquête* (Paris: Editions du Camelot, 1997).

30. Robert Faurisson, "Histoire: La Reculade de Bordeaux," *National hebdo*, 9–15 April 1998. Faurisson remains unchanged: see his earlier article, "Aveux méritoires," ibid., 19–25 February 1998, welcoming recent research by Éric Conan and by two Jewish Canadian historians into significant inaccuracies in the postwar reconstruction of the crematorium and gas chamber at Auschwitz I.

31. Pierre de Meuse, "Un Crime contre l'humanité au nom de l'humanité," *Identité* 21 (January–February 1994), p. 21.

32. id. (title of the article). For another example of extreme right-wing interest in the Vendée, see the extensive dossier "1793: La Vendée et la Terreur" in *Enquête sur l'histoire* 5 (winter 1993), pp. 4–73.

33. Unsigned, "Le Communisme, crime contre l'humanité," *Identité* 24 (spring 1997), p. 4; and see Bernard Antony, "Le Procès Touvier," *Présent*, 24 March 1994.

34. *Présent*, 18 October 1997; and see Bernard Antony, "En Indo, à Alger, à Paris, le même nihilisme falsifie l'Histoire," interview with Martin Peltier, *National hebdo*, 30 October–5 November 1997.

35. Trémolet de Villers, *Paul Touvier est innocent*, pp. 46–48.

36. See for example Faillant de Villemarest, "Lettre ouverte . . ."; Madiran, "Le Procès Touvier s'ouvre ce jeudi 17 mars à Versailles," *Présent*, 17 March 1994.

37. Béatrice Péreire, "Engagez-vous dans la milice," *National hebdo*, 24–30 March 1994.

38. Madiran, "Une France sous l'influence. . . ."

39. Peltier, "La Négation de Pâques," *National hebdo*, 7–13 April 1994.

40. Papon, "Une Nouvelle Affaire Dreyfus?" p. 14.

41. Pierre de Meuse, "Le Procès interdit," p. 23, caption to photo. For echoes of papon's charges against the Communists, see, for example, Georges-Paul Wagner, "Papon: Le Harcèlement communiste," *Présent*, 16 October 1997; Prudence Tan, "Le Procès communiste," ibid., 17 October 1997.

42. Le Pen, "Les Temps sont proches," interview with Martin Peltier, *National hebdo*, 25–31 December 1997.

43. *National hebdo*, 9–15 October 1997.

44. See unsigned article, "Il est beau, l'infatigable défenseur des droits de l'homme!" *Minute*, 20 April 1994; Jean Madiran, "Les Aveux du stalinien Joë Nordmann," *Présent*, 14 April 1994.

45. On Nordmann and the other lawyers for the plaintiffs, see Gabriel Lindon, "Le Barreau rouge," *National hebdo*, 16–22 October 1997.

46. Gabriel Lindon, "Procès Papon; les picadors de l'histoire," *National hebdo*, 9–15 October 1997.

47. Martin Peltier, "L'Exception juive," *National hebdo*, 9–15 October 1997.

48. Conan and Rousso, *Vichy, un passé qui ne passe pas* (Paris: Fayard, 1994); Rousso, *La Hantise du passé* (Paris: Textuel, 1998).

THE PAPON TRIAL

IN AN

"ERA OF TESTIMONY"

Nancy Wood

PART I: THE VICTIM-AS-WITNESS

" . . . Watching this haunting figure so devastated by her life, and recalling the arguments against the trial, I came to the view that if the trial could offer even slight relief to Esther Fogiel, it would not be in vain, and that even should this be the case for just a single victim, it would justify the proceedings—indeed make of them a sacred obligation."[1]

Amid all the controversy generated by the trial of Maurice Papon, few took issue with Bertrand Poirot-Delpech's estimation of the therapeutic value that it potentially represented for those victims, or relatives of victims, who testified to the tragedies that they and their loved ones endured during the years when Maurice Papon was secretary-general of the Gironde prefecture. The figure of Esther Fogiel inspired particularly poignant commentaries by a number of the trial's observers.[2] Fogiel, the daughter of migrants from Eastern Europe,[3] recounted, in a voice that seemed to issue from an entombed childlike self, how at the war's outset her mother had placed her in the care of a couple living in the Unoccupied Zone who proceeded to maltreat and sexually abuse her. Convinced she had been willfully abandoned by her parents, she remained ignorant of their deportation and subsequent deaths in Auschwitz until 1945. She told the court she had spent her entire life "making that journey to Auschwitz." She also related that she had attempted suicide at the age of thirty. Following her request, photographs of her parents, and her brother and grandmother, who were also rounded up and deported, were projected in the courtroom. After giving her testimony, Esther Fogiel slipped away, evading the gaze of waiting cameras.

Esther Fogiel had nothing to say about Maurice Papon and made no attempt to explicitly draw a link between the fate of her family and the actions and responsibilities of the former secretary-general. But no one questioned that her testimony was entirely relevant to the proceedings under way. Indeed, Éric Conan described this phase of the proceedings as a kind of "sacred ceremony," observed in a silence that seemed to temporarily suspend the trial's relentless juridical progression.[4] Even Papon, who intervened frequently to challenge other witness statements, to demand proof of their accusations, or to deny personal implication in the events and actions they recounted, listened respectfully to many testimonies from family members of victims. The very fact that photographs of victims were projected onto a large screen of the courtroom, and their names read out, indicated the extent to which the trial exceeded its strictly legal parameters and took on the trappings of a commemorative ritual. Although Judge Castagnède did not always accede to this request on the part of witnesses, he was clearly under pressure to do so, especially when testimonies inspired in the courtroom audience the pathos that Esther Fogiel's heart-rending account elicited.[5]

As Annette Wieviorka has shown in her book published after the Papon verdict, L'Ère du témoin, the deference and esteem which greeted Fogiel's testimony in the Bordeaux Assizes Court represented a distinct moment in postwar attitudes toward the Holocaust witness. Wieviorka demarcates several distinct phases in the attempt to bear witness to the Holocaust. In the immediate postwar period, for many Holocaust survivors the desire to reintegrate into the national community prevailed over their need to narrate an experience whose underlying logic would only confirm how they had been progressively excluded from that very community.[6] And even for those in whom a desire to bear immediate witness existed—a desire which for the likes of a Primo Levi, for example, was so urgent that it constituted a basic physiological need[7]—there was a perception that the wider society was not disposed to listen to the ensuing accounts. To be sure, individual testimonials were both contemporaneous with the Holocaust and were proffered in its aftermath in many different fora, but Wieviorka maintains that these did not "penetrate the social field."[8] Nor did individual survivors perceive their testimonial acts as a potentially binding force in a larger collectivity. Only with the trial of Adolph Eichmann in 1961, according to Wieviorka, does this testimonial voice gain a proper public hearing and the memories of Holocaust victims "become constitutive of a certain Jewish identity."[9]

That this trial should be the inaugural forum for a public hearing of Holocaust testimonials did not convince all of its observers at the time. In *Eichmann in Jerusalem*, Hannah Arendt betrays her impatience with the hundred testimonial accounts—the "endless sessions"—that occupied half the court's agenda. Her objections ranged from the fact that the majority of witnesses did not establish definitive connections between the horrendous events they had witnessed and the personal responsibility of Adolph Eichmann,[10] to the apparent revision of memories with the passage of time, to the prosecution's selection of witnesses for their demonstrated rhetorical powers and "human interest" dimension. At the same time, a certain side of Arendt was clearly sympathetic to Yad Vashem's appeal on behalf of "the right of the witnesses to be irrelevant" with respect to Eichmann's implication in the specific crimes against humanity they related. Indeed, Arendt was so transported by the testimony of one "background witness," Zindel Grynszpan, who related his family's brutal deportation from Germany to Poland in 1938, that she admitted she had been tempted to conclude, "foolishly," that "everyone should have his day in court." More germane to Arendt's restiveness during these testimonials was her view that without recourse to the "transforming realm of poetry," few stories of such unprecedently harrowing events could be effectively told. And to this she added the troubling addendum that only survivors with "a purity of soul, an unmirrored, unreflected innocence of heart and mind that only the righteous possess" could aspire to this aesthetic enterprise.[11] One is led to conclude that in the view of Arendt, victims of lesser moral integrity should have had the good grace to forfeit their day in court.

Following Arendt, Wieviorka treats the Eichmann trial as a site of memory's performativity, tracing the emergence of this dramaturgical impetus in the historically evolving function of Holocaust testimony. She cites the aim professed explicitly by Attorney General Gideon Hausner, of using first-person testimonial narration to act "like a spark in the frigid chamber which we know as history."[12] Intent on avoiding the "cold" appeal to documentation that had characterized the Nuremberg proceedings, Hausner took care to ensure that the witnesses called were those who had already rehearsed their testimonies in prior writing. Wieviorka shows how the selection and "filtering" of testimonies was not only inspired by Hausner's concern to draw from his dramatis personae the most emotionally effective performance, but from a distrust of memory itself. Memories "refreshed" by previous depositions would, Hausner believed, minimize the risk of faulty recollection.

For her part, Wieviorka singles out from the "cast" of the Eichmann trial Ada Lichtman, who testified on 28 April 1961. Lichtman, a Polish Jew, witnessed as a child in the years 1939–41 the roundup and massacre by German soldiers of entire communities in her region and recounted memories of atrocities so shocking that the prosecutor was compelled to ask her whether she had witnessed these sights "with her own eyes."[13] Absent from most memoirs or accounts of the trial, to Wieviorka Lichtman's testimony represented nonetheless "a rupture in the structure and nature of testimony itself" because of the direct manner in which it chronicled details of who had died, how they had died, and how their narrator had managed to survive. In other words, the significance of Lichtman's testimony lay in a recitation whose pared-down nature performed a pedagogical and commemorative function in its own right. The Eichmann trial, according to Wieviorka, marked the "arrival of the witness" (*avènement du témoin*) in this expanded sense and signaled the advent of an "era of testimony" that continues to this day.[14]

While Wieviorka believes that the respect—even reverence—in which many testimonies at the Papon trial were held, despite their evidential shortcomings, confirms the ongoing pedagogical and commemorative value attributed to Holocaust testimony, she also surmises that the trial marked the "transmutation of the witness" (*passage du témoin*) in an important respect. With the passing of the generation who directly experienced the events of the Holocaust, the key testimonial figures are now those, like Esther Fogiel, who evoke not so much the events themselves but the irreparable effects (*la secousse irrémédiable*) these had on young lives.[15] As Éric Conan was to remark, such testimonies functioned less as proof of Papon's personal responsibility for the losses witnesses had suffered than as a "quest for the origin of their sorrows," less as a lesson in history than as a "distraught search for a causality" that would explain once and for all the desolation of their subsequent lives.[16] The testimony of the adult Esther Fogiel, which so moved the audience at the Bordeaux Assizes Court, incarnated in its very mode of transmission—her childlike enunciation—the inconsolable loss suffered by a young Esther Fogiel. And in this respect, one might speculate that the particular emotional salience of Esther Fogiel's testimony resonated not only with child survivors, and with a generation who grew up during the war, but with a postwar generation in France who now seek consolation for their own sense of malaise about a national shame that cannot be made good in commemorative rituals that trials like these have become. For this generation, testimony has become, in the words of Shoshana Felman, a "privileged contemporary mode of transmission and communication about the past."[17] To this extent, the pedagogical value attributed to testimony has, arguably, eclipsed that of history—and the productive tension that has existed between them settled in testimony's favor.

But can a juridical forum like the Papon trial be trusted to "bear witness" in another sense to the ineffable experience that victims have undergone or the losses their family members have endured? Levi's comparison of the compulsion to bear witness with an elementary physiological need conceives of testimony not only as an act of narration—a trajectory of cause and effect—but as a form of survivorship itself. In this respect, child survivor and psychoanalyst Dori Laub has remarked, "The survivors did not only need to survive so that they could tell their story; they also needed to tell their story in order to survive. There is, in each survivor, an imperative need to *tell* and thus to come to *know* one's story."[18] In Laub's view, this comprehension could not take place coincidental with the event precisely because "the inherently incomprehensible *and* deceptive psychological structure of [the Holocaust] precluded its own witnessing, even by its very victims."[19] The assimilation of what victims saw and experienced is therefore necessarily a belated process, whose achievement is dependent not only on the integration of knowledge and insight gained over time, but on a *listener*—on the one hand an external listener who confirms the reality of the victim's lived experience, and on the other an internal listener, an agency of the self that finally grasps the meaning of one's own experience. Testimony is therefore a dialogic process since it requires an external listener in order for the victim to create an "internal witness" to his or her own loss and pain. Testimony in Laub's sense entails this more elaborate and complex psychical process of transmission by which the survivor "comes to know" his or her own story of survival and by so doing is able to ideally achieve the therapeutic goal of "repossessing the act of witnessing."[20]

Can this specific testimonial aim be achieved in a court of law? Is the act of bearing witness in order "to come to know one's story" compatible with the pedagogical, commemorative, or juridical functions of testimony? More precisely, did the trial of Maurice Papon, however flawed as a lesson in history, and as a process by which, in the words of Jean Améry, the "criminal is nailed to his deed,"[21] not only render the verdict needed by survivors and victims' families, but also facilitate a process that allowed them to "repossess the act of witnessing"? One lawyer contended that the simple fact of holding the trial had an "assuaging value" for the civil parties. And one survivor testified in court, "We have been survivors, we hope to become living people"[22]—voicing in vivid terms the hope that transmission would eventually achieve a selfhood released from the singular identity of the survivor. Finally, testimony after testimony regarding individual victims confirmed the role of the local Bordeaux administration and its ancillary services in the implementation of the Final Solution. Surely, establishing this historical truth in a court of law—a truth fudged in the Paul Touvier trial[23]—was a symbolic precondition of that renewal process. Could not these goals and achievements be acknowledged in their own right without jeopardizing the legal task of establishing the accused's personal responsibility for the crimes cited in the indictment?

One possible response is to cite the different kinds of truth that such a trial might yield. The testimonies of survivors and victims' families given at the Papon trial certainly spoke to a truth—the truth of their experience of the Holocaust—and these truths were of a moral, ethical, or even historical order rather than those that lent themselves to juridical certainties. These were testimonies of traumatic separations of family members, of unspeakably tragic losses, of lives shattered and never fully repaired. Called by the civil parties to pay tribute to three functionaries of Papon's rank who had saved Jewish children, Samuel Pisar used the occasion to recount his own memory of the last days with his family before the evacuation of the Polish ghetto where they were living. His mother, he recalled, anguished over whether he should wear short pants or long trousers when the moment came to depart, since in the first case he might be allowed to stay with the women but in the latter he would join the men.[24] In this "image intime," as he called it—a mother calculating her son's life chances on the basis of an item of clothing—Samuel Pisar certainly testified to the truth of the event: the arbitrariness of survival for most Holocaust victims. Or consider a case read to the court from a civil party deposition—that of Irma Reinsberg, a young woman deported from Bordeaux in the convoy of 26 August 1942 who threw herself off the train. She was arrested and, suffering from head injuries, was taken to the hospital in Orléans. A telegram was sent to the Gironde prefecture asking to which camp she should be sent. The reply, signed by "adviser to the prefecture," was: "To Drancy."[25] Here was the irrefutable truth of collaboration and cold indifference on the part of a Bordeaux functionary—even though it was not the former functionary who was sitting in the dock.

In elaborating how the process of repossessing the act of witnessing occurs for Holocaust survivors in the therapeutic context, Dori Laub made the following observation:

> In the process of the testimony to a trauma . . . you often do not want to
> know anything except what the patient tells you, because what is important

is the situation of *discovery* of knowledge—its evolution, and its very *happening*. Knowledge in the testimony is, in other words, not simply a factual given that is reproduced and replicated by the testifier, but a genuine advent, an event in its own right.[26]

This is not to suggest for a moment that the witnesses appearing at the Papon trial confused the courtroom with a therapeutic setting, but merely that it often appeared that the process of repossessing the act of witnessing was contingent upon fulfilling the juridical function that the court was otherwise concerned not to impose as the sole aim of the testimony. In fact, in several instances the failure to fulfill this specific function must have severely hampered that passage from survivorship to "living people" that the above-mentioned survivor so fervently hoped for. Of course, ultimately that judgment is for survivors and victims' families alone to render. However, if one accepts Wieviorka's claim that such trials are increasingly driven by the combined forces of the survivor's internal necessity to "bear witness" in Laub's therapeutic sense and the social demands of a wider public that in this case demanded Papon's conviction, it became difficult for anyone following the trial's reporting to overlook the apparent tensions and contradictions that surfaced between these two imperatives.

Perhaps the most well-known case the court heard was that of the Slitinsky family, represented at the trial by Michel Slitinsky, a civil plaintiff, author of two books on Papon, and the first person to initiate the process of bringing Papon to trial in the immediate postwar period. His father and sister were rounded up in Bordeaux in October 1942; Michel, seventeen at the time, escaped arrest. His father was deported to Drancy and then to Auschwitz, where he was gassed. His sister protested against her internment at Mérignac, the local internment camp, on the basis that she had French nationality. She was released in December 1942. Papon had always claimed he was responsible for saving Alice Slitinsky; the family had always contested this claim and had accused the Service des questions juives, over which Papon allegedly had authority, of delaying her release. The court dossier indeed contained documents addressed to Alice's mother and signed by Papon, relating his interventions with the Germans on Alice's behalf. Judge Castagnède examined these, as well as a letter by SS officer Doberschutz (submitted for the first time by the defense and thus presumably unknown to Michel Slitinsky), making explicit reference to Papon's intervention. Judge Castagnède then confirmed publicly and for the court record the veracity of Papon's claim. As a journalist observed at the time of the hearing, here was irrefutable evidence of "an intervention of the accused on behalf of the sister of his principal accuser."[27] Slitinsky's own testimony on the following day, clearly under the effect of these devastating revelations, crumbled into a meandering testimony that was criticized by Judge Castagnède—solicitously but with evident impatience—for saying so little about the facts concerning the convoy of his father that was under examination. Moreover, it became apparent during questioning by the defense that over the many years he campaigned to bring Papon to justice, Slitinsky had resorted to willful inaccuracies, tampering with documents, and political machinations within the Mitterrandian camp that threatened to bring his personal crusade into disrepute.[28]

The original indictment cited Papon's complicity in the arrest, illegal sequestration, and murder of a doctor of Egyptian origin, Sabatino Schinazi, in November 1943. Father of nine children, son of a Catholic mother and with a Catholic wife, Schinazi was arrested on German orders by French police, interned at Mérignac, and deported to Auschwitz. He died at Dachau in 1945.[29] According to the terms of the Bousquet-Oberg accords of July 1942, because he was married to an Aryan, Schinazi should have been exempted from the arrest list. In any event, faced with lack of evidence to substantiate Papon's complicity in Schinazi's fate—notably Papon's signature on the deportation order for Schinazi's convoy—the questioning of Papon by the civil lawyers focused on his failure to save the doctor from this illegal sequestration and his inaction during the period when Schinazi was interned at Mérignac. This *inaction*, the civil lawyers maintained, could on occasion be qualified as a crime against humanity. Papon invoked the defense that at the time of Schinazi's internment, not only had prefects had no power over those interned on German orders but the Germans, suspicious of prefectural sabotage of the roundups, had been dealing directly with the regional police. But the details of his defense aside, Papon demanded that the court prove his culpability for the convoy that had deported Dr. Schinazi by producing the signature referred to by the indictment. The civil parties were unable to satisfy the accused's demand. Moreover, when Sabatino Schinazi's sons Samuel and Moise Schinazi took the stand, they both concurred that their mother, now deceased, had always accused Papon of being responsible for their father's arrest and refusal to liberate him once his status was clarified. Judge Castagnède, however, read to the court long declarations that the mother had made in 1947 which explicitly accused not Papon but the chief of the Police des questions juives, Lucien Déhan, of orchestrating her husband's arrest. Watching the stunned reaction of the brothers to the judge's rectification of their long-held convictions, which they had recited to the court "like a lesson learned by heart," Éric Conan castigated a prosecutionary zeal that in its eagerness to use testimonies by victims' families had so evidently courted the resulting debacle: "These two testimonies are distressing because they are typical of the judicial manipulation of the victims, of a reorientation of their sorrows."[30]

If the issue of Papon's responsibility for crimes against humanity was subsequently reconfigured by the prosecution in terms of his *passive* criminal agency, there was one case that clearly did not fit this designation. Léon Librach was a twenty-six-year-old French Jew who had been imprisoned in the military prison of Fort-du-Ha in Bordeaux in spring 1942 (for reasons which remain unclear, since at that time French Jews were not by and large the target of German measures). In June 1942 the Germans ordered him transferred to Drancy. Papon had issued an order to transfer Librach to Mérignac even though the Germans had not ordered this intermediary measure (the court saw Papon's order, bearing his signature, projected onto a large screen in the courtroom). Librach was duly transferred from Mérignac to Drancy and then to Auschwitz in September 1942, where he was exterminated. Papon excused himself for his actions on the basis that he had only just arrived in Bordeaux to take up his prefectural duties and was inexperienced and that his reasons for initiating this order were now "lost in the densest fog."[31] However, despite the fact that this one case appeared to prove beyond a doubt Papon's complicity in a crime against humanity, the jury ultimately decided that Papon was not guilty of complicity in Léon Librach's death.

Without knowing the jury's deliberations, it is hard to account for their decision, but the temporality of the proceedings might have played some role. This case took place at the very outset of the examination of the convoys, when the judicial climate was very much to Papon's disadvantage. And it was not followed—as the case led one to anticipate—by further evidence from the civil plaintiffs showing Papon's signature on arrest, deportation, or requisition orders. Moreover, as the prosecution increasingly turned its attention to the issue of Papon's passive criminal agency, the solitary figure of Léon Librach tended to fade from view. In fact, in the summing-up phase of the last few weeks of the trial, the singularity of Léon Librach's dossier played a lesser role than would have been expected in light of its probative status. The defense case that this was an "exception" to Papon's otherwise judicious efforts on behalf of wrongly detained individuals seemed to hold some sway.[32] Meanwhile, the most influential civil lawyers recalibrated their original accusations to focus on the responsibility and criminal culpability attendant upon the fact that Papon had remained in his prefectural post. To have done so knowing that crimes against humanity were being committed superseded the earlier charge of direct and active complicity. One civil lawyer, Michel Zaoui, contended that "it wasn't the signature which demonstrated responsibility" but Papon's implication "in the chain of responsibility of the crime's implementation," and Zaoni spoke of "an administrative crime," an "office crime."[33] This meant, as many commentators have pointed out, asking the court to judge Papon not so much for his individual acts against the victims represented by the civil plaintiffs but for his representative and culpable *function*. And the jury, exercising its "intimate conviction," appears to have complied with this injunction.

But the understandable satisfaction and jubilation among all the civil parties following the verdict's announcement does not erase completely from view the figure of Michel Slitinsky, who, after over fifty years of seeking juridical redress for the arrest and deportation of his father *by French functionaries*, was reduced to silence by an impatient court. It may well be that Slitinsky brought the court's disapproval upon himself by his irresponsible behavior. But this judgment should not overshadow the fact that Slitinsky, too, was entitled to hope that the court might fulfill its paramount legal function of personalizing responsibility for his father's fate, thus allowing him to finally "repossess the act of witnessing" that traumatic moment in his childhood when his father was led away. That in his distracted state Michel Slitinsky was precisely testifying to the *failure* of the judicial process to fulfill this specific legal function at least raises the doubt as to whether the trial of Maurice Papon facilitated — *or could have facilitated* — for many witnesses the therapeutic function of repossessing the act of witnessing. And if for many observers the image of Esther Fogiel will remain etched in their memories of the trial, the disturbing image of Michel Slitinsky's day in court should not be lost from view.

PART II: THE HISTORIAN-AS-WITNESS

The Papon trial also represented the "transmutation of the witness" (*passage du témoin*) in another important sense: historians of Vichy, a number of whom had given testimony in previous war crimes trials, were again summoned to appear as witnesses. And the exalted status that a national public with a seemingly endless appetite for revelations about *les années noirs* had bestowed on Vichy historiography over the past decade ensured these witnesses the devout attention of the media, public, and court alike.

The obvious difference between historians and the witnesses I've discussed in the previous section is that these historians did not, for the most part, live through the times and events of which they spoke. As François Hartog noted, "If, etymologically speaking, the witness is someone who saw what happened, the historian, in this case, obviously did not."[34] Nor were they "experts" in the usual judicial sense, who might be called upon to give opinions of a technical kind on the status of various kinds of evidence submitted. But if that only left to the historian-witness the remaining role of speaking "to the acts attributed to the accused, which might pertain to his personality or his morality,"[35] then it was not clear in what manner historians of Vichy could speak to these dimensions of the Papon case. On the one hand, the law stipulated that only if the witness was personally known to the accused could the former speak about the latter's morality—which was manifestly not the case for the historians with respect to Papon; on the other hand, the "facts" of the case were bound to be conceived by historians very differently than by their legal counterparts.

In the aftermath of the Touvier trial, Henry Rousso and Éric Conan posed the question of whether it was even possible for "historical truth" to find proper expression in a courtroom, given the necessary differences between juridical discourse (the law), judiciary discourse (the court), the historian's discourse, and testimony. They maintained that the historian could not describe "what had happened," but only attempt, on the basis of available traces and navigating "between islands of established truths in an ocean of uncertainty," to reconstitute a plausible account of events. By contrast, justice demanded to know exactly "what had happened" in order to make judgments based on the balance of evidence. The hypotheses developed by historians, they argued, are not of the same nature nor do they have the same consequences as the "intimate convictions" of a jury. Thus in Touvier's case, historians could speculate about whether he was likely to have acted alone or only on German orders according to a range of plausible historiographical interpretations of the degree of agency of a high-ranking *milicien*. But the prosecution needed to convince the jury that despite the evidentiary absence of such an order, its material existence at the time was the incontrovertible reason for Touvier's actions. Without this, Touvier could not be convicted within the terms of the existing law on crimes against humanity: complicity in the criminal acts of an Axis power.[36]

Le Monde's interview with Henry Rousso contained in this volume confirms not only that the Papon trial has strengthened his skepticism regarding the testimonial role historians might play in such trials, but also that the range of his objections has broadened, embracing issues of a procedural, political, and ethico-philosophical nature.[37] Rousso has also expanded on his reservations in a small book published before the Papon verdict, *La Hantise du passé*,[38] and key aspects of this critique were subsequently taken up in the journal *Le Débat*. These cannot be covered exhaustively here, but I would like to focus on the role of one historian who testified at the Papon trial in order to highlight some of the central issues that seem to be at stake.

Marc-Olivier Baruch, a renowned historian of the Vichy administration, was summoned to appear for the civil parties. Indeed, in the lead-up to the trial, media analyses bestowed wide attention on Baruch's central claims regarding the civil service culture (*la culture fonctionnaire*) that prevailed during the final years of the Third Republic and into the Vichy period. In its main outline, Baruch's work cautions against any sweeping generalizations concerning the administrative attitudes or conduct of Vichy officialdom. His studies show that on the eve of the war the French administration was by no means a monolithic entity but embraced a wide range of professions—munitions workers, teachers, ministerial employees, prefects, and so on. Moreover, he highlights that in the late years of the Third Republic, the political inclinations of the majority of functionaries tended to be moderate or even Radical-Socialist, and manifested a high trade-union consciousness. With the defeat of 1940, a large number of these civil servants resigned; with the armistice many, especially among the young, became German prisoners of war. Others were replaced in the specific purge of Jewish functionaries in late 1940 and in the general purge of the administration that continued into 1941. The aging, right-wing composition of the Vichy regime reflected this early upheaval.

Despite this change of personnel and retrenchment of political perspective, Baruch locates the element of continuity between the late Third Republic and Vichy in the insular "culture of obedience" that prevailed notwithstanding the administration's structural overhaul during the Occupation years. It was this culture that survived the defeat, the armistice, and the subsequent purges intact and which would be decisively manipulated by Pierre Laval upon his return to power in April 1942. Laval sought to secure the obedience and loyalty of Vichy functionaries not by issuing ideological appeals on behalf of the National Revolution but by using the system of professional rewards and punishments as a veritable "currency of exchange." The disaffection and dissent toward the regime that did surface was the product of internal divisions caused by these maneuvers and by government interference in a world traditionally protective of its autonomy. Such was the case, for example, with the regime's creation of new departments like the Commissariat général aux questions juives, which provoked discontent within the administrative ranks not primarily on ideological grounds but among those who felt bypassed either in decision making or in the more favorable professional advances this ministry offered its employees. Ultimately, however, such dissent as did exist—and Baruch's own research reveals isolated acts of bureaucratic revolt—did not inhibit the administration's efficiency nor provoke significant rebellion from within.[39]

Clearly this historiographical perspective has an enticing relevance to Papon's specific circumstances. It suggests that Vichy functionaries were inclined to implement rather than resist orders of a morally reprehensible or even criminal kind, not because they were driven by anti-Semitic hatred but because they were already immersed in a long-standing culture of obedience.[40] The fact that more resolute forms of revolt—resignation, and anti-German or pro-Resistance activity within the administration—were extremely limited only reinforces how easily this quiescent administrative culture adapted to collaborationist imperatives.

Reflecting in Le Débat upon his participation at the trial, Baruch explained that although he realized that he had been called to testify in a "pedagogical capacity" in a juridical setting that was very different from the usual venues for such dissertations, he had decided that it was legitimate for the historian to paint for the court and the jury a larger picture of "factual elements which had bearing on the wider debates." Historians could offer explanatory frameworks, "elements of comprehension," without yielding to the temptation to persuade the jury or judge the accused. Moreover, the protocol of questioning such witnesses safeguarded their liberty of speech, allowing nuances, the admission of doubt, or the suspension of conclusions.[41] The particular temporal location of such testimony in the trial's chronology further reinforced its distinctiveness from the kind of questioning and argumentation that characterized the opening and closing phases. Finally, while recognizing that he was not a witness of Papon's morality, not having known the accused personally, Baruch noted that he could speak about the evolving moral climate of the administrative culture in which Papon had been immersed.[42] This was highly relevant to the proceedings insofar as both the prosecution and defense cases lent conflicting significance to the fact that Papon remained in his prefectural post until early 1944— the prosecution citing this as proof of Papon's complicity with a policy of ideological hegemony, the defense as a tribute to Papon's attempt to subvert this from within. Baruch recalled the testimony of one character witness, called by the defense, who had claimed that by remaining in his post, Papon had probably forestalled the installation of more extremist functionaries loyal to the Milice. The force of Baruch's testimony, by contrast, had underscored that this eventuality was by no means inevitable, that by the period in question competing political logics traversed the Vichy regime and significant elements within the government and administration were intent on preventing this hard-line entrism.

These cavils aside, Baruch's own testimony had been primarily devoted to considering the duress under which the ordinary functionary might have operated or, alternatively, the scope for disobedience that Vichy's administrative structures may have provided. "There was always a way," he had maintained, but the scope for independence that did exist was not by and large exploited by the majority of functionaries.[43] Baruch said that he now realized that by broaching the issue of the "margin of maneuver" of Vichy functionaries in this manner he had inflamed certain "politico-journalistic" sentiments, who saw in his testimony an imputation that lack of political will had influenced Papon's decision to remain in post. However, Baruch pointed out that determining the reasons for any functionary's behavior was a more complex manner given that their margins of maneuver evolved over time and according to the specific bureaucratic role. At a factual level, research could be aided by archival sources, which contained reports, scrupulously completed by the occupying Germans, concerning the administrative bodies and personnel responsible for police matters and the responsibilities delegated to functionaries like a secretary-general. However, at a more interpretative level, it was also necessary to ascertain to what extent these possibilities were perceived and sought out by this cadre in the face of more obvious constraints. By citing at the trial examples of several functionaries who had retired from their duties either at the outset of the Occupation or later on, Baruch maintained that he had only tried to establish that a form of conscientious objection had occasionally been exercised. Thus the reasons attributed to perseverance on Papon's part could at least be considered—if not confidently assumed—in the light of such examples.[44] But he acknowledged that perhaps it was "inevitable," in light of the "social demand" that generates any reckoning with the Vichy past, that the historian's discourse would be instrumentalized—even as he/she attempted to resist such manipulations.[45]

Rousso is at pains to emphasize that while he chose not to testify, he respected the decisions of those of his colleagues, like Baruch, who did, and that whatever disagreements the trial had generated, these had been less among historians of Vichy than between the latter and a number of journalists who consider themselves specialists of Vichy and its memorial legacy.[46] The critical thrust of Rousso's objections to the historian's role at the trial, however, addresses issues raised directly by Baruch's testimony.

Rousso contests the central argument that the role of historians was merely to illuminate for the judge and jury the wider historical context of the Papon case by pointing out that in a judicial setting, because the overriding priority is to determine the culpability of the accused, even questioning that seems directed to pedagogical ends will ultimately be framed by, and harnessed to, these legal imperatives. Precisely for these reasons, any attempt to conjecture about, for example, the evolving moral ambience of the Vichy administration will be imprisoned by a mode of questioning whose risks far outweigh whatever elucidation of context might be achieved. This is because however careful the historical expert may be to couch his/her suppositions in the language of the "conditional rather than the indicative" (in the words of François Hartog),[47] in a juridical setting that is intent on reaching a verdict, there is an inherent tendency to apply the general to the specific case at hand. According to Rousso,

> [e]ven if almost all the historians avoided speaking directly about Maurice Papon, the goal of their presence on the witness stand, from the vantage point of the court, was to effect this translation from the more general level to the specificity of the Bordeaux context. This is to forget that the context thus reconstituted is itself the consequence of a generalization derived from singular situations.

Finally, contrary to the claim that judicial procedure safeguarded this instrumentalization of the historian's discourse, Rousso pointed out that the very fact that historians gave testimony at the same time as survivors and family members of victims made them appear, whatever their own precautions, as "testifiers of morality."[48]

The issue of *Le Débat* devoted to the trial weighs in precisely on this question of whether the two modes of reasoning in play—historical and juridical—can, or indeed ought to be, so starkly separated. Thus the juridical temptation to "succumb to metonymy," to derive the specific from the general, which Rousso posits as inevitable, is disputed by Yann Thomas, partly on the basis that it is precisely the vocation of the judge to draw this distinction between culpable act and the broader context in which it is executed. But Thomas also believes that the historical context that the historians were asked to elucidate at the Papon trial, far from being "a pure object of speculative knowledge," was one whose purported character was integral to the definition of a crime against humanity in French law. Insofar as a crime against humanity was composed of inhumane acts and persecutions "committed in the name of a State practicing a politics of ideological hegemony," only by depicting in some manner the political context within which the state and its attendant institutions functioned could criminal signification be conferred on the actions of individuals. Thus acts such as those reputedly committed by Maurice Papon only gained their juridical significance as a crime against humanity when they were inscribed within the larger framework of Vichy's collaboration with the German implementation of the Final Solution. Historians, as "specialists of collective contexts," had a legitimate role to play in delimiting questions concerning the nature of state collaboration and ideology, Thomas contended; the difficulty remained the legal one of establishing the extent to which a given individual became a voluntary agent "of a history fully and self-consciously lived by them." To arrive at this judgment, Thomas maintained, not only bore on questions of evidence but required an interpretative and methodological effort similar to that of the historian, obliging juridical minds "to interpret the collective action of an individual" or, to put it another way, "to integrate the context in the act."[49]

Both sides of this debate, it seems to me, are convincing in their own right, and in any event this is a discussion that one hopes will gather momentum and garner more participants. But it is perhaps significant to note that Thomas concludes his rejoinder to Rousso's critique by defending the necessary collaboration of judges and historians faced with the ongoing criminality that states exhort from individuals acting as their agents. This is a message that is especially compelling in these times when every television viewer was "witness" to an ethnic cleansing in Kosovo of still undisclosed proportions and whose planners and executors one would hope to see sooner rather than later before the Hague Tribunal on charges of crimes against humanity. However, as examples like the Papon trial have shown, and indeed the circumstances surrounding the founding of the Hague Tribunal itself, such legal reckonings with a genocidal past are not primarily the result of juridical initiatives but of political will. This is why I would want to temper Thomas's optimism concerning historico-juridical collaboration with Rousso's basic reminder that those who participate in such trials, historians included, can never be in full mastery of the testimonies they may in good faith deliver.

NOTES

1. Bertrand Poirot-Delpech, *Papon: Un Crime de bureau* (Paris: Stock, 1998), p. 116, cited by Annette Wieviorka, *L'Ère du témoin* (Paris: Plon, 1998), p. 184.

2. See also Éric Conan, *Le Procès Papon* (Paris: Gallimard, 1998), pp. 102–3, and Jean-Michel Dumay's report in *Le Monde*, 21–22 December 1997.

3. As Annette Wieviorka pointed out, though Fogiel claimed her parents had fled pogroms in Latvia in the 1930s, there were no pogroms during those years and emigration was primarily for economic reasons. However, in Wieviorka's view, the inaccuracy of this claim was easily overlooked by a collective memory that readily conjured a flight from anti-Semitism to account for this migratory wave.

4. Éric Conan, "Cérémonies sacrées," *L'Express*, 25 December 1997, and *Le Procès Papon*, p. 104.

5. Conan relates several instances when Judge Castagnède refused such requests, on one occasion remarking, "I can't accede to a roll call of the dead; we are not before a cenotaph." *Le Procès Papon*, p. 102.

6. *L'Ère du témoin*, pp. 99–100. This is a theme developed at length in her previous book, *Déportation et Génocide: Entre la mémoire et l'oubli* (Paris: Plon, 1992).

7. See Primo Levi, *If This Is a Man/The Truce* (London: Abacus, 1987), p. 15.

8. *L'Ère du témoin*, p. 79.

9. Ibid., p. 81.

10. Victims like Lichtman were from the East, where Eichmann's competence and authority were considerably reduced compared to his manifest role in the administration of the Final Solution in the West. See Hannah Arendt, *Eichmann in Jerusalem: A Report on the Banality of Evil* (New York: Penguin, 1992), p. 225.

11. See ibid., pp. 223–29. For an illuminating discussion of other dimensions of Arendt's analysis of the trial as a site of "performativity," see Leora Y. Bilsky, "When Actor and Spectator Meet in the Courtroom," *History and Memory* 8:2 (fall–winter 1996).

12. *L'Ère du témoin*, p. 97.

13. Ibid., p. 105.

14. Ibid., pp. 16, 81.

15. Ibid., p. 181.

16. *Le Procès Papon*, pp. 104–5.

17. Shoshana Felman, "Education and Crisis" in her book, co-authored with Dori Laub, *Testimony: Crisis of Witnessing in Literature, Psychoanalysis, and History* (London: Routledge, 1992), p. 6.

18. Laub, "An Event without a Witness" in *Testimony*, p. 78.

19. Ibid., p. 80.

20. Ibid., p. 85.

21. See Jean Améry, "Resentments," *At the Mind's Limits: Contemplations by a Survivor of Auschwitz and Its Realities*, trans. Sidney Rosenfeld and Stella Rosenfeld (New York: Schocken Books, 1990).

22. Cited in Éric Conan, "Cérémonies sacrées," *L'Express*, 25 December 1997, and *Le Procès Papon*, p. 105.

23. See Richard J. Golsan, ed., *Memory, the Holocaust and French Justice: The Bousquet and Touvier Affairs* (Hanover, N.H.: University Press of New England, 1996). See also Henry Rousso and Éric Conan, "Touvier: Le Dernier Procès d' l'épuration?" in *Vichy, un passé qui ne passe pas* (Paris: Fayard, 1994), for a full analysis of how the price of Touvier's conviction turned out to be a disavowal of a specifically French responsibility for the crimes of which he was accused.

24. *Le Monde*, 5 March 1998.

25. Ibid., 22 January 1998.

26. Felman and Laub, *Testimony*, p. 62.

27. *Le Monde*, 23 January 1998. Despite this intervention on Papon's part, he had not "saved" 130 Jews as he had alleged during the trial. A *Libération* exposé published in the week following Papon's claim showed that he had merely struck off the "Jewish file" (*fichier des israelites*) those who were not Jews according to the *Statut des juifs*. According to *Libération*'s investigation: "He only applied conscientiously Vichy's racial laws, dividing 'Aryans' from Jews, thus condemning the latter to deportation but 'saving' Catholics whom the Germans never had the intention of deporting— or killing" (3 December 1997). Papon maintained later in the trial that by "the simple application of the *Statut des juifs* then in force," letters to the German authorities, warnings to families, and other similar measures he had saved hundreds of persons. *Le Monde*, 18 February 1998.

28. See *Le Procès Papon*, pp. 138–43.

29. *Le Monde*, 29 January 1998.

30. *Le Procès Papon*, p. 150.

31. *Le Monde*, 11 December 1997.

32. See *Le Procès Papon*, p. 86.

33. *Le Monde*, 18 March 1998.

34. François Hartog, "L'Historien et la conjoncture historiographique," *Le Débat* 102 (November–December 1998), p. 8.

35. Ibid.

36. See Conan and Rousso, "Touvier: Le Dernier Procès de l'épuration?," p. 159.

37. See my earlier discussion of these in "Memory on Trial in Contemporary France," *History and Memory* 11: 1 (spring 1999).

38. *La Hantise du passé, entretien avec Philippe Petit* (Paris: Les éditions Textuel, 1998).

39. See especially Marc-Olivier Baruch, *Servir l'État français: L'Administration en France de 1940 à 1944* (Paris: Fayard, 1997), and the interview in *Le Monde*, 1 October 1997. See also Denis Pechanski's article written at the time of the Touvier trial, "Was There Massive Collaboration of Top Administrative Officials?" in Golsan, ed., *Memory, the Holocaust and French Justice*, pp. 87-90. Pechanski notes that altogether "there were 36 prefects and assistant prefects who died because of deportation or their participation in the Resistance. Thirty-five others who were deported returned" (p. 89).

40. See also Éric Conan's summary of Baruch's testimony in *Le Procès Papon*, p. 66, and the report in *Le Monde*, 7 November 1977.

41. This is a point made explicitly by Ann Thomas in "La Vérité, le temps, le juge et l'historien," *Le Débat* 102 (November–December 1998) but alluded to by Baruch.

42. See Marc-Olivier Baruch, "Procès Papon: Impressions d'audience," *Le Débat* 102 (November–December 1998). See also the elaboration and defense of the historian's role in this and other trials in Jean-Noël Jeanneney's *Le Passé dans le prétoire: L'Historien, le juge et le journaliste* (Paris: Seuil, 1998). Jeanneney speaks of "the superiority of historians over witnesses when it is a question not of throwing light on a specific event, but of reconstituting an epoch, its climate, its scope, and its particular logic" (p. 71).

43. *Le Monde*, 7 November 1997.

44. In *Le Passé dans le prétoire*, Jeanneney describes Baruch's testimony as "a rigorous enquiry which leaves permanently open, even after the general and severe considerations of the conclusion, the moral lesson which the reader-cum-citizen is to draw," pp. 86–87.

45. Baruch, "Procès Papon," p. 15. Conan refers to the questioning of Baruch by the civil parties as a "dialogue of the deaf" during which the civil lawyers tried to get him to admit the primacy of anti-Semitic motivations among Vichy functionaries whereas Baruch continued to insist on the logic of collaboration. In his turn, defense lawyer Maître Jean-Marc Varaut asked Baruch to explain the discrepancy between his testimony, which had enumerated the responsibilities delegated to Papon by the regional prefect, and his book published only weeks before the trial began, which only mentions Papon in a footnote. See *Le Procès Papon*, pp. 66, 67.

46. See *La Hantise du passé*, p. 98.

47. "L'Historien et la conjoncture historiographique," p. 7.

48. *La Hantise du passé*, p. 108.

49. Thomas, "La Vérité, le temps, le juge et l'historien." Mine is a very distilled version of an argument that is developed by Thomas with great care and finesse.

THE TRIAL OF PAPON

AND THE TRIBULATIONS

OF GAULLISM

Nathan Bracher

The French media and advocates of the "duty to memory" heralded the trial of Maurice Papon as a great moment in historical pedagogy. The proceedings and Papon's conviction for complicity in crimes against humanity were, both in the formal courtroom proceedings and in the virtual trial staged by the French press, accompanied by an indictment of the moral legacy of Gaullism. The charges leveled at Charles de Gaulle and his postwar institutional policies were several and severe. First and foremost among them was the notion that the General had willfully dismissed Vichy's crimes and knowingly protected collaborators and criminals such as Papon from prosecution. It was indeed in this context that the phrase "Vichy null and void" (to which we shall turn to shortly) became the touchstone of a whole series of alleged lies and moral failures. For once having wiped Vichy off the slate, suggested de Gaulle's accusers, the General supposedly ignored the Holocaust and the suffering of the Jews, rehabilitated prominent Vichy officials, and in sum built his entire political career on lies.

Moreover, prominent commentators both inside and outside the courtroom hailed this presumed destruction of the Gaullist myth as one of the most importance outcomes of the six-month legal marathon, the longest trial of the postwar era in the French criminal court system. In his plea for the prosecution,

Attorney Alain Jakubowicz thus expressed his satisfaction that "the trial had exploded the myth created by General de Gaulle at the time of the Liberation" when, "placing the era of the French State when the Vichy regime had abolished the Republic in a straitjacket," he had "declared this shameful parenthesis null and void." De Gaulle's declaration had not nullified the victims of Vichy, added Jakubowicz, "even if people had pretended to know nothing about them or even deny that they existed for decades."[1] Similarly, in his assessment of the Papon trial's achievements, Le Monde's chief editor saluted the consummation of a "critical and dispassionate reading which was the exact opposite of the fiction of a Vichy 'null and void' maintained by the predecessors of Jacques Chirac."[2]

This essay seeks to explain why, instead of marking any progress in historical knowledge of the German occupation, the entire set of charges launched against the Gaullist legacy are in fact symptomatic of the demise of a political tradition largely completed before the trial and attributable to other forces. Furthermore, this essay argues that both the polemics directed against de Gaulle and the virtual verdicts cited above contain major historical distortions and thus constitute a regression of memory.

The expression "Vichy null and void" served as a lightning rod for the whole panoply of moral thunderbolts. If one were to believe pronouncements of the press, one would think, first, that all of France's reluctance, inability, or refusal to confront Vichy's collaboration and crimes was due to what, thanks largely to Henry Rousso's now classic Le Syndrome de Vichy, has become commonly referred to as the "Gaullist myth" of resistance; second, that up until the Papon trial this "myth" had undergone little scrutiny; and third, that it had consequently still held the majority of French people under its sway throughout all this time. In an editorial written only a few days after the trial opened, for example, the New York Times asserted that

> For years, French leaders maintained the fiction established by Charles de Gaulle that the Vichy Government was the creation of the Germans and a small group of French extremists, while the French people actively or passively supported the Resistance.[3]

Accordingly, the editorialist welcomed the trial as a long overdue occasion for "more exploration of the French role in Vichy." Even more telling were the terms used by Le Monde. The very title of Jean-Michel Dumay's article, "Olivier Guichard Returns to the Subject of the 'Gaullist Myth' of the Inexistence of Vichy" (Olivier Guichard revient sur le "mythe gaulliste" de l'inexistence de Vichy), which covered the testimony of de Gaulle's former chief of staff, suggested that the

General had denied the reality of collaboration and repression. Dumay's subsequent commentary presented Guichard's remarks as an important breakthrough; "Olivier Guichard, a baron of historical Gaullism, made a breakthrough (*a ouvert une brèche*) in returning to the question of the 'Gaullist myth' of the inexistence of Vichy."[4] As commonplace as it may be, the metaphor implicit in the expression *ouvrir une brèche* comes from the language of siege warfare and thus presents the Gaullist legacy as a previously intact bulwark of falsehood valiantly attacked in the battle for truth and memory. The titles of other articles devoted to the various personalities on the side of the prosecution make use of the same register. *Le Monde* depicted Arno and Serge Klarsfeld as having led "sixteen years of *combat*," Michel Slitinsky as a courageous loner who "*has been fighting* since 1945," and Marc Robert as a "bulldozer."[5]

Since some fifty years of presumed obfuscation and denial are thus attributed to de Gaulle's declaration that Vichy was null and void, it would be instructive to return briefly to the concrete circumstances in which this crucial pronouncement was first made. In doing so, one discovers a major discrepancy between the specific ramifications of this fateful phrase for the war era and the moral overtones now ascribed to it. De Gaulle's first public use of the expression dates from 25 August 1944, at the Hôtel de Ville in Paris, the city's traditional locus of the rule of the Republic. Indeed, his visit to the Hôtel de Ville marked not only the return of France's capital to full French control but also the recognition of Charles de Gaulle as the official head of the French government: hence his exchange of greetings with the leaders of the mainland and Parisian Resistance, as represented by the "National Council of the Resistance" and the "Parisian Liberation Committee," and with the prefect of the district of the Seine and his administration. It was at this very moment, after Georges Bidault had asked him to proclaim the Republic, that de Gaulle issued his now famous rejoinder:

> As I [de Gaulle] was about to leave, Georges Bidault cried out: "General! Here you have assembled around you the National Council of the Resistance and the Parisian Liberation Committee. We ask you to formally proclaim the Republic before the French people gathered here." I replied: "The Republic has never ceased to be. The Free French, the Fighting French, and the French Committee for National Liberation have embodied it each in their turn. Vichy was always and remains null and void. I myself am President of the Republic. Why should I take the trouble to proclaim it?"[6]

This precise historical context clearly shows that de Gaulle was primarily concerned with the questions of political legitimacy and legal continuity, not with any historical assessment of the Occupation. Moreover, the elliptical form ("Vichy null and void") now commonly cited obscures another important dimension of this affirmation: de Gaulle's coupling of a *passé simple* and the present tense (*fut toujours et demeure*) in one short sentence stressed that Vichy had been illegitimate and without authority from the very outset, marked by the signing of the armistice and the subsequent scuttling of democratic institutions in June and July 1940. It is even more important to recall that, as Éric Conan and Henry Rousso point out, far from resorting to any expedient invention, de Gaulle was in fact merely reiterating a position contained in the Free French's earliest declarations dating from 1940:

> On October 27, 1940, in his famous Brazzaville manifesto, General de Gaulle had indeed clearly stated that "there no longer exists a truly French government." He added: "The entity located at Vichy and which claims to bear this name is unconstitutional and subservient to the invaders."[7]

De Gaulle had this adamant refusal to grant any legitimacy whatsoever to the "French State" at Vichy inscribed into law by an ordinance issued on 9 August 1944 by the Provisional French Government of the French Republic at Algiers and entered in the *Journal officiel* on the following day.[8] It was urgent to have both the Allies and the French people reject Vichy as illegal and accept Charles de Gaulle as the rightful representative of the French Republic, and not as the leader of some sort of putsch or revolution. And it was also precisely because declaring the Republic at the Hôtel de Ville in Paris would have been strongly reminiscent of previous governmental overthrows that de Gaulle refrained from the gesture.[9] With this detailed examination of de Gaulle's memorable (if now truncated and often distorted) dismissal of Vichy as "null and void," we can measure the disparity between its vital importance as a political doctrine and legal instrument for the Liberation period and its current condemnation as a historical assessment the "Dark Years" in France. This is another case in which fundamental facts have been obscured if not totally forgotten for the sake of a "duty to memory."

Nevertheless, the accusations remain that, in restoring the rule of the legitimate French Republic, de Gaulle displayed a callous indifference not only to the suffering of the Jews but also to the shady past of former Vichy administrators such as Papon who participated in crimes against them. In this light, some commentators eager to settle their political scores with Gaullism presented the trial of the former secretary-general of the prefectorate of the Gironde as merely the most immediate and painful symptom of a sort of general "Papon syndrome." It was Attorney Gérard Boulanger who led the charge on this front, advancing in his *Papon, un intrus dans la République* (Papon, an Intruder in the Republic). In his clearly laudautory summary of the book, Nicolas Weill focuses on the idea that the Papon case resulted from

> a wider confrontation of the Liberation period opposing a nation of *résistants* and State Gaullism more concerned with public order than anything else. The end of the century here in France still bows under the weight of this internal conflict, and the Papon trial is as much a consequence of that strife as it is of Vichy.[10]

The wording here is noteworthy. First, it implies that the issue of "State Gaullism" in the Papon trial is just as important as that of Vichy's collaboration. Second, it conveys a vision of the Liberation that has been filtered through the strongly tinted lenses of May '68, since the caricature scenario of "a nation of *résistants*" (which in itself would merit a lengthy commentary) pitted against "State Gaullism more concerned with public order than anything else" immediately conjures up memories of confrontations between leftist student masses and the forces commanded by de Gaulle and the bourgeoisie. Boulanger's and Weill's preoccupation with "this little internal war of France," however, completely distorts the context of the Liberation, dominated indeed for de Gaulle and his government by a very real need to restore the rule of law and order. This meant not only protecting the Republic against eventual power grabs by Communist factions of the Resistance, but even more urgently putting an end to extrajudicial executions and reprisals and reestablishing a functional, autonomous French administrative infrastructure in face of the Americans who had planned to govern France as an occupied country. What we have here is a textbook example of an ideologically motivated anachronism so rightly decried by Conan and Rousso.

Similar vestiges of the left's complaints against de Gaulle in the late 1960s appear even more clearly in the oft-repeated charge that the General had remained arrogantly indifferent to the plight of the Jews. In their final arguments in favor of condemning Papon for crimes against humanity, two prosecution lawyers thus characterized the accused as "self-assured and overbearing."[11] With this ironic use of a most infelicitous expression that the French chief of state had let slip in reference to the Israelis in the context of the Six-Day War in 1967,[12] the lawyers painted the accused criminal in the image of de Gaulle. Thus we see that even in the formal courtroom proceedings, lawyers for the prosecution did not hesitate to use rhetoric tending to assimilate de Gaulle to

Papon, as do the following lines penned by another "May '68er" with political scores to settle, Serge July:

> The General himself in his *War Memoirs* nowhere mentions the crimes committed against the Jews in France by French people. The crime of Maurice Papon is that of absolute indifference having become a whole mind-set and a system of defense.[13]

July's juxtaposition of "the General himself" and Papon is another obvious indictment of "State Gaullism" decried both in the courtroom and in *Libération* and *Le Monde* from the beginning to the end of the long trial. This entire set of accusations couched in polemical language stemming from more recent ideological conflicts corroborates one of the major criticisms of the Papon trial voiced by Conan and Rousso: in the name of "the duty to memory," partisan politics were influencing the judicial treatment of crimes against humanity and evincing historical sensibility in favor of foregone moral conclusions.

This essay has, in another context, already shown why charges of de Gaulle's supposed indifference to the Jews are unwarranted.[14] However, one specific courtroom example is particularly emblematic of the historical confusion operative in these reproaches. Not surprisingly, it occurred during the testimony of Maurice Druon, currently "perpetual secretary of L'Académie française," and formerly a member of the Resistance with de Gaulle in London (where he composed the famous Resistance song "Le Chant des Partisans" with Joseph Kessel) and minister of cultural affairs under Pompidou, who voiced the opinions one would expect from such a long-standing monument of Gaullism. Objecting to the very principle of the trial, which in his view could only disgrace France to the benefit of the Germans, Druon expressed his fear that postwar unity was being torn apart by the opposition of one category against another. And it was on this score that Attorney Michel Zaoui took exception.

> But Attorney Zaoui returned to the subject of the ceremony of 11 November 1945, in which fourteen coffins were laid out in tribute to the victims of the war. "All categories were to be represented there. Do you know that only one category was not? Those deported because of their race." "In the hearts of some people, there was clearly a coffin missing," added presiding magistrate Castagnède.[15]

While it is true on a general level that there was no specific commemoration or tribute for Jewish victims in the immediate postwar period, Attorney Zaoui's reference to the ceremonies held under the authority of General de Gaulle at the Mont Valérien in early November 1945 is historically inaccurate. For the record, there were in fact not fourteen but fifteen coffins. More importantly, however, we must point out that these ceremonies were not at all designed as a tribute to "victims of the war" as such but rather to honor those who had given their lives in service of French forces that never gave up the combat, as historians Serge Barcellini and Annette Wieviorka explain in their detailed account of the Mémorial de la France Combattante at Mont Valérien:

> Highly symbolical, these fifteen bodies were to represent the France that had kept up the fight from 1940 to 1945. . . . On this 11 November 1945, there was no place for those who were simply victims: prisoners of war, those sent to do forced labor in Germany, civilian victims, Alsatians forced into the German army, Jews who died in the extermination centers.[16]

Contrary to what *Le Monde* and Zaoui would lead one to believe, these ceremonies in no way represented a snub to Jewish victims, simply because they were intended not only to celebrate war heroes but also to illustrate the central Gaullist political doctrine of the uninterrupted combat of the French Republic that was behind the pronouncement "Vichy was always and still remains null and void." That is why the crypt where these fifteen coffins lie in state bears the inscription "We are here to testify to posterity that from 1939 to 1945, its sons fought so that France may live free" (*Nous sommes ici pour témoigner devant l'histoire que de 1939 à 1945, ses fils ont lutté pour que la France vive libre*).[17] While the crypt does contain the coffin of a certain Renée Lévy as well as those of Boutie Diasso Kal, Hedhili Ben Salem Ben Hadj Mohamed Amar, and Berthie Albrecht, the quintessentially Gaullist Mémorial de la France Combattante makes no reference to the religion, ethnicity, or race of any of these martyrs. The choice of individuals to be buried there was indeed carefully made and highly symbolic, but of something quite different. Eleven of the fifteen honored were military men killed on the battlefield. On this level, the intention was to represent several aspects of the struggle: the different phases of the war, including Germany's initial invasion of France in May 1940, the fight to drive the Germans out of France after the Allied landing, and the intermediate battles in North Africa; the various branches of the French armed forces, including the army, the air force, and the navy; the many battlefields where French soldiers had fought and died, including mainland France, Germany, Italy, and North Africa; the various parts of the French Empire having sent soldiers to fight (four of the soldiers buried there are from the colonies); and finally, various branches of the Resistance. With the ceremony held at the Mont Valérien on 11 November 1945 and the memorial subsequently constructed between 1960 and 1962, de Gaulle sought to honor those who had served as combatants in one capacity or another, and who had died as a result of their active opposition to the enemy. First and foremost in this context was to have the *résistants* appear as regular army soldiers (and not as factional revolutionaries) who have done their duty, to present the Resistance in general as emanating from "La France Éternelle" (and not from marginal splinter groups), and to inscribe their combat into the legal continuity of the French Republic. In this light, the most heavy-handed aspect of both the ceremony and the monument in discussion is that they pay no tribute to the tragic events marking the Mont Valérien itself, where some 1,000 victims were shot by the Germans. (I say "victims" because some were hostages selected among Communists and Jews both French and foreign who had been arrested and detained as such, and not for any oppositional activity.[18]) The historical specificity of the Mont Valérien has been completely overlaid by the Gaullist epic, which, although not unrelated to the tragedy of those who died there, makes no reference to the site itself.

As Barcellini and Wieviorka observe, the Mont Valérien was indeed, between de Gaulle's departure from the government in January 1946 and his return to power in May 1958, the object of a struggle over memory between three groups: de Gaulle and his followers, who used it to honor the legacy of "the call of 18 June"; the Communist Party, who commemorated those sent before German firing squads; and the governments of the Fourth Republic, which tried to find common ground.

Presented as a concrete historical example to prove their case against de Gaulle's alleged indifference to the Holocaust, Zaoui and *Le Monde*'s reference to the ceremonies of 11 November 1945 totally obscures the real battle for memory that took place over the Mont Valérien. In the place of history, they have substituted the moral imperatives of "memory," which, as Conan has pointed out, now only recognize the categories of executioners (*bourreaux*) and victims.[19]

This particular courtroom exchange is just one example of the historical confusion that appeared throughout the trial, and which, more than a willful attempt to distort the record of the past, simply underscores the incompatibility of the contemporary generation's values and sensibility with those of the Liberation and postwar era in France. Or to state the point more succinctly, the contortions illustrate a fundamental conflict of *memory* more than a conflict of history. For memory, as Rousso convincingly has defined it, is the way the past is made present, or actualized; since memory is highly charged with affectivity and is related to a particular experience of events, it tends to be partial and partisan. Moreover, memory is the faculty that enables us to insert both past and present into one continuum forming the basis of identity and of future projects.[20] It is hardly surprising to find clashes of memory between different groups separated by completely different experiences and sharply contrasting values.

Such was indeed the case in the Papon trial when those seeking justice for the victims of the Holocaust accused not only de Gaulle and his institutional legacy but also many of the prestigious *résistants* testifying in the courtroom of indifference toward the Jews. For as Pierre Nora has pointed out, our current insistence on individual ethics, personal responsibility, and human rights in assessing the historical events of World War II and the German occupation of France reflects a major evolution of memory involving several factors that were not on the scene in the immediate postwar era. The first such development was the perception of the Holocaust as a unique, unprecedented event central to the understanding of the war, which in itself took some twenty years after the war to achieve. From that point, further shifts took place:

> The Shoah tended to create a twofold demand for historical clarification and moral rigor. It historicized Judaism in a powerful way while at the same time becoming sacred. It emphasized the ethical dimension, which goes along with the contemporary generalization of human rights, a post–May '68 ideology that has itself been becoming more and more powerful since the 1970s and 80s. Now, this ideology of human rights is important for the understanding of the current fixation on Vichy.[21]

And as Nora goes on to explain, the current generation's insistent focus on Vichy and its crimes stems largely from the fact that Vichy now appears as the exact opposite of contemporary values.

At the same time, the current demands of the "duty to memory" are far removed from the imperatives compelling de Gaulle to remember first and foremost the heroic struggle of "La France Combattante" while dismissing Vichy as "null and void." For de Gaulle was determined not only to affirm the continuity of the French Republic, but also to celebrate France as a nation united by suffering and the battle against the Nazis. Although it may at first glance seem ludicrous even to speak of unity in a era marked by virtual civil war between the Resistance and the Milice as well as by considerable squabbling and tensions between the various movements of the Resistance, de Gaulle's "myth" of a nation united in Resistance was not a lie designed to protect Vichy criminals (as was so often suggested throughout the Papon trial), but rather the expression of a political doctrine aimed at mending the fabric of the nation and securing an honorable place for France among the victorious Allied countries.

The speech de Gaulle delivered in Lyon after its liberation provides a perfect example of this myth in action and of its sharp contrast with our present perceptions. After the trials of Klaus Barbie and Paul Touvier, one now commonly associates Lyon with the Nazi criminal responsible for unspeakable acts of torture and the deportation of some forty Jewish children to Auschwitz and with the viscerally anti-Semitic member of the Milice responsible for murdering a number of Jews. In September 1944, however, de Gaulle began his speech by acclaiming "Lyon, capital of the Gauls! Lyon, capital of the Resistance!" thus linking the heroism of the present to the prestige of the past in the historical continuity emphasized by his affirmation that "as a people, we have lived for two thousand years." While acknowledging in a grantedly abstract way all the hardship, suffering, and ordeals of the war, France's chief of state nevertheless affirmed that "this tremendous people never accepted defeat" and that France was "grand, noble, and pure *in spite of everything*." Reminding the crowd that the war was not yet over, de Gaulle saluted "the great army [that] covers us with glory" and promised that " all of France in its entirety" would find itself soon "standing with the victors . . . for the good of humanity."[22] Although such a speech is obviously ill-suited to satisfy our current (and legitimate) demand for a thorough scrutiny of French behavior under the Occupation, it translates not any desire to exonerate Vichy but rather de Gaulle's project for rallying the French people back under the flag of the Republic.

Furthermore, de Gaulle was keen on honoring the Resistance on a collective, abstract level while at the same time refusing to celebrate individual heroes and specific groups.[23] In the context of this unanimist exaltation of the nation at last victorious over the Nazi oppressor, no one was at the time shocked by the absence of separate commemorative ceremonies for Jewish victims. Not only did French Jews adamantly refuse to be set apart (after all, it had been the Germans and Vichy that had isolated them and tried to portray them as irremediably different from their fellow citizens), they even saw themselves as a part of an entire "community of suffering" within the nation, as Pierre Nora reminds us:

> But as they returned to the classic social contract between the French nation and the Jews, French Jews themselves considered in a rather habitual way their sufferings and persecutions as a contribution to a national and patriotic sacrifice.[24]

After the reaffirmation of a specifically Jewish identity in the wake of a general awareness of the Shoah and the emergence of a general mistrust of the state with an accompanying emphasis on individual human rights, such an attitude is now difficult to comprehend.

And that is why such intransigently Gaullist *résistants* of Jewish descent such as Maurice Druon and Jean Jaudel were misunderstood and hooted in the witness stand.[25] As related by Éric Conan, the appearance of Jaudel was particularly poignant and equally revealing. His ardent defense of de Gaulle and his pathetic plea for Papon's dismissal (which in itself shows a total inability or refusal to understand the gravity of Papon's deeds) ended with an incongruous and totally inappropriate "Vive Papon! Vive de Gaulle! Vive la France!" The predictable guffaws spouting from the young lycée students attending the trial in order to learn the lessons of history were emblematic of the chasm separating their generation from that of the *résistants*. For as was the case with other prominent followers of the General, it was as if this former participant in the Gaullist epic had remained frozen in time, still caught up in the vision of grandeur and heroism in service of the nation that had guided him through the harrowing events of the war. One of the key elements of this vision is an idealistic celebration of the nation rallied together in one common cause, which stirs individuals to service and self-sacrifice. De Gaulle himself alluded to this élan in a telling way in relating his famous speech at the Hôtel de Ville in Paris, which, as Rousso observed, can be considered one of the first expressions of the "Gaullist myth of Resistance":

> As I surveyed the vibrantly enthusiastic, affectionate, and curious group of people gathered there, I sensed right away that we had recognized each other, that there existed between us, as combatants in the same fight, an incomparable bond, and that, even though there were watchful divisions and active ambitions among this audience, all it took for our unity to prevail over everything else was for me to be in contact with the crowd. . . .
>
> . . . In the response [to Georges Bidault's address] that I gave extemporaneously, I expressed "the sacred emotion that grips us all, both men and women, in these minutes that transcend each one of our own poor individual lives."[26]

What indeed could be more foreign to the current postconsumerist demand for immediate individual gratification on all levels and for recognition of specific ethnic, racial, or sexual identity than such a "sacred emotion" inspired by "a certain idea of France"? Notwithstanding the exuberant flag-waving and repeated strains of "La Marseillaise" that accompanied the French soccer team's victory in July 1998 and that, as all observers noted, drew tremendous crowds to the Champs-Élysées in a collective outpouring of collective joy reminiscent of the scenes of the liberation of Paris, we can point to several important signs that such ardent devotion to the nation is, if not totally dead politically, rapidly fading into oblivion. In a survey conducted by *Le Figaro* two weeks after the Gaullist RPR's embarrassingly weak showing in the European elections held on 13 June 1999, almost two-thirds of *voters for the right* indicated that they considered Gaullism to be a thing of the past:

> Clearly identified, Gaullism nevertheless appears as a vestige of the past in that 63 percent of those surveyed declare it to be "a notion that no longer means much today."[27]

In an interview published in *Libération*, one of the most prominent advocates of the right, economist Guy Sorman, bluntly declared that the ideal of French grandeur and its attendant nationalism were dead and should be scuttled if the right hoped to regain political power.

> The right must first get rid of Gaullism. It must break with unanimism. General de Gaulle was part of that political philosophy, inherited from Péguy or Maurras, which wants there to be something transcending national divisions. However, this mystique of the people rallied together, so typical of Gaullism, has no meaning.[28]

Along with the poll published by *Le Figaro*, these words seem to announce the repudiation of the Gaullist legacy by moderate, centrist factions of the right in France, leaving only Charles Pasqua and Philippe de Villier's new party— whose name, the RPF (Rassemblement du peuple français), is curiously reminiscent of de Gaulle's failed political formation of the late 1940s — along with Le Pen and Megret to hoist the banner of their own nationalism heavily tainted with intolerance and xenophobia.

Viewed from this perspective, the attacks on the Gaullist legacy that occurred during the Papon trial appear as just another sign of the general demise of "a certain idea of France" brought about mainly by the rapid evolution of French culture and society over the past thirty years, and not by any of the supposed "breakthoughs" touted by *Le Monde* as a positive outcome of Papon's conviction. A poll conducted by Henry Rousso *before* the trial showed clearly that the Gaullist epic held little importance in French young people's perception of World War II, in spite of the fact that they were very concerned and well informed about questions of the war and the Occupation. When asked what came to mind whenever they thought of the war, they first listed—on their *own initiative*, since prephrased responses were *not* provided—"the deaths, the human losses" (19 percent) along with "anti-Semitism, the extermination of the Jews" (18 percent). Only 6 percent of those questioned mentioned "the action of de Gaulle, the call of 18 June," which was thus relegated to twelfth place.

It is as if the present generation, informed by almost thirty years of historiographical lucidity about the true nature of Vichy and its crimes, mobilized primarily by concerns for human rights and ethnic specificity, and unable to understand the "Gaullist myth of Resistance" as anything but an historical lie (rather than a political ideal), has proclaimed "de Gaulle null and void," seeing now a nation united in collaboration and moral turpitude as the true image of France under the Occupation, while leaving only a marginal role for de Gaulle and the Resistance. In an editorial underscoring the supposed benefits of the trial and conviction of Papon for complicity in crimes against humanity, *Le Monde*'s director, Jean-Marie Colombiani, was satisfied that the proceedings had once more shown "the true face of France in the Dark Years: an authoritarian, reactionary regime tempted by Fascism." Alluding specifically to de Gaulle's famous words, Colombiani insisted that the sad truth was the exact opposite: "No: Vichy, alas, was France and its State, supported by a majority, while a small group of rebels organized the Resistance."[29] This is a rather astounding statement, particularly from someone trumpeting the urgent necessity of historical lucidity. For Colombiani seems to be completely ignorant of the most recent assessments of public opinion under Vichy, which, as Philippe Burrin explains, never really supported the Vichy regime beyond the year 1940 and was always hostile (in spite of general passivity) to collaboration and persecution of the Jews.[30] Other prominent historians have pointed out that while those active in the Resistance did indeed form a tiny minority, they were nevertheless able to function like fish in water because of widespread support. Similarly, Serge Klarsfeld has himself proclaimed on several occasions that while Vichy bears the responsibility for the deportation of some 76,000 Jews, the some 275,000 Jews who managed to survive depended on the support of the French people.

At the very apogee of Gaullism marked by the transferal of the ashes of Jean Moulin to the Panthéon, André Malraux had appealed to French youth of the 1960s to remember the sacrifice of the man appointed by de Gaulle to unite all Resistance movements under one leadership but arrested and tortured to death by Klaus Barbie as the true image of France in the war:

May you young people of today think of this man as you would have stretched your hands out toward his poor featureless face on that last day, toward his lips that had not talked; on that day, this was the face of France.[31]

In terms of history, of course, such an idealistic vision proves to be hopelessly inadequate, since there were obviously several faces of France under the Occupation, some of them far from heroic. Nevertheless, in expressions of collective memory that can be found in the controversies over the legacy of Gaullism surrounding the Papon trial, many commentators have proved themselves incapable of escaping the binary logic driving them to hold up one facet of the "Dark Years" as the one truth exclusive of all other possibilities. *Le Monde*'s frank antithesis of Malraux's exhortation in effect completely wipes the legacy of de Gaulle and his Free France off the historical slate. Whatever the fortunes of such a political doctrine may turn out to be, it is a sign both of the demise of the Gaullist legacy in the wake of rapid social change and of the historical confusions occasioned by the Papon trial.

NOTES

1. Jakubowicz's plea on behalf of the private parties in the case was thus quoted and paraphrased by Éric Conan, *Le Procès Papon: Un Journal d'audience* (Paris: Gallimard, 1998), p. 256. All translations from the original French are mine throughout.

2. Jean-Marie Colombiani, "Savoir désobéir," *Le Monde*, 4 April 1998, p. 1.

3. "France's Bishops Confess," *New York Times*, 12 October 1997. (editorial page).

4. Jean-Michel Dumay, "Les Audiences de la cour d'assises de la Gironde reprendront avec l'étude du contexte historique des faits," *Le Monde*, 28 October 1997, p. 8.

5. Laurent Greilsamer, "La Révolte des Klarsfeld après seize ans de combat," *Le Monde*, 14 October 1997; Nicolas Weill, "Michel Slitinsky se bat depuis 1945, contre ceux qui ont déporté sa famille," *Le Monde*, 21 January 1998, p. 10; José-Alain Fralon, "Marc Robert, un bulldozer face aux esquives d'un danseur," *Le Monde*, 27 February 1998, p. 10. And while Papon proved to be particularly pugnacious, nowhere do we find such terms in reference to him: the terms have been clearly reserved for combatants leading the battle for memory.

6. Charles de Gaulle, *Mémoires de guerre* (Paris: Plon, 1980), cited by Christine Levisse-Touzé, *Paris libéré, Paris retrouvé* (Paris: Découvertes-Gallimard/Paris Musées, 1994), p. 91.

7. Éric Conan and Henry Rousso, *Vichy: An Ever-Present Past*, translated and annotated by Nathan Bracher (Hanover, N.H.: University Press of New England, 1998), p. 27.

8. Ibid.

9. See Jean-Pierre Azéma, *De Munich à la Libération, 1938–1944* (Paris: Seuil, 1979), p. 351.

10. Nicolas Weill, "Mouvement éditorial autour de l'affaire Maurice Papon," *Le Monde*, 3 October 1997.

11. See Éric Conan's notes on the plea of Jean-Serge Librach, p. 253, and Michel Tubiana, p. 260.

12. See Henry Rousso, *The Vichy Syndrome: History and Memory in France since 1944*, translated by Arthur Goldhammer (Cambridge: Harvard University Press, 1991), pp. 135–36.

13. July's editorial in *Libération* was cited in "La France en jugement," *Le Monde*, 9 October 1997, p. 30. Relating similar accusations made in the courtroom by Gérard Boulanger, Éric Conan notes that they were pointedly refuted by Jean-Marc Varaut with a few precise references to the very writings of de Gaulle that were being incriminated. See *Le Procès Papon: Un Journal d'audience*, p. 37.

14. For an explanation of why such forays against de Gaulle are unfounded, see my article "Memory Null and Void? The Broken Record of Vichy Polemics in the Papon Case," *Contemporary French Civilization*, 23:1 (winter–spring 1999), p. 73-74.

15. Jean-Michel Dumay, "Les Derniers Témoignages des partisans de Maurice Papon," *Le Monde*, 24 October 1997, p. 10.

16. Serge Barcellini and Annette Wieviorka, *Passant, souviens-toi! Les Lieux du souvenir de la Seconde Guerre mondiale en France* (Paris: Plon, 1995), pp. 168–69.

17. I am grateful to Monsieur Bertrand-Baride Yamoun with the Secrétariat d'État aux anciens combattants et victimes de guerre, who has made it possible for me to visit the Mont Valérien on several occasions. Cf. Barcellini and Wieviorka, p. 172.

18. See Renée Poznanski, *Les Juifs en France pendant la Seconde Guerre mondiale* (Paris: Hachette, 1997), pp. 260, 273.

19. Éric Conan, *Le Procès Papon*, p. 42. Cf. Alain Finkielkraut's analysis of the modern tendency to focus on faceless victims in *L'Humanité perdue* (Paris: Éditions du Seuil, 1996), pp. 123–31.

20. Cf. Henry Rousso, *La Hantise du passé* (Paris: Textuel, 1998), pp. 16, 19.

21. Pierre Nora, "Tout concourt aujourd'hui au souvenir obsédant de Vichy" (interview), *Le Monde*, "Le Procès Papon" (supplément), 1 October 1997, p. viii.

22. The passages quoted are from my personal notes taken while visiting the Centre d'Histoire de la Résistance et de la Déportation in Lyon in the context of the NEH Institute on 26 June 1999.

23. I gleaned much of the material for this paragraph from the lectures of Henry Rousso given in Paris on 22 and 23 June under the auspices of the 1999

NEH Summer Institute on "Memory, History, and Dictatorship: The Legacy of World War II in France, Germany, and Italy."

24. Pierre Nora, "Tout concourt aujourd' hui," p. viii.

25. See Éric Conan, Le Procès Papon, pp. 44–47, 209–11.

26. Charles de Gaulle, *Mémoires du guerre,* cited by Christine Levisse-Touzé, Paris libéré, Paris retouve, pp. 90–91.

27. "Les Valeurs de l'électorat de droite," *Le Figaro,* 2 July 1999, p. 8.

28. "'La Droite doit se débarrasser du gaullisme," *Libération,* 11 July 1999, p. 10.

29. Jean-Marie Colombiani, "Savoir désobéir," p. 1.

30. Philippe Burrin, *La France à l'heure allemande, 1940–1944* (Paris: Seuil, 1995), pp. 185–97.

31. André Malraux, "Transfert des cendres de Jean Moulin au Panthéon," *Oeuvres Complètes* (Paris: Gallimard, 1989), p. 997.

THE LEGAL

LEGACY OF

MAURICE PAPON

Leila Nadya Sadat

I. INTRODUCTION

During the last fifteen years, France has used the definition of crimes against humanity developed at Nuremberg to try three persons accused of committing crimes against humanity in France during the Second World War. The first was the notorious Klaus Barbie, who was sentenced to life imprisonment in 1987. Barbie's trial, although extraordinary from a *legal* point of view, did not raise significant *political* problems for the French and their government. Rather, to most Frenchmen, Barbie's capture, indictment, trial, and conviction represented a fitting end to a Nazi enemy.

The next two cases were quite different, however, for they involved the prosecution of Frenchmen accused of committing crimes against humanity in the course of their duties serving the Vichy regime. That is, the actions of the accused, Paul Touvier in the first case and Maurice Papon in the second, were *lawful* under French domestic law at the time they were committed even though they were (arguably) later criminalized (at Nuremberg) as a matter of *international* law.[1] Thus, from a political perspective, Papon's and Touvier's cases are much more troubling, for they necessarily call into question the entire Vichy regime. On an international level, that is exactly what crimes against humanity do; they were incorporated into the Nuremberg charter for the express purpose of criminalizing (many would argue ex post facto) the Nazis' horrendous mistreatment of their own population. But it is unlikely that the French, one of the four prosecuting countries at Nuremberg, ever thought the charter applied to the actions of the Vichy government, and the incorporation of the crime into French municipal law posed substantial practical, as well as conceptual, difficulties.

It is thus unsurprising that the Touvier and Papon prosecutions wound their way through the French courts inordinately slowly, due to the legal obstacles involved as well as the political pressure exerted to prevent the cases from coming to trial.[2] In Touvier's case, as will be discussed below, the courts were able to proceed only by adopting the view that his actions were directly ordered by the Gestapo, rather than by Vichy. But Papon's case was much more difficult, for the deportations of which he was accused were ordered by him in his capacity as a high-ranking civil servant of the Vichy regime, even though they were carried out in part as a contribution to the Nazis' Final Solution. Indeed, even though it ordinarily takes only a few months for an appeal to be decided, during which time the accused generally remains at liberty, Papon's appeal was not scheduled to be heard until 21 October 1999, one and a half years after he was convicted.

This essay focuses on the legal elements of the Barbie, Touvier, and Papon cases. Part II examines the Touvier and Barbie cases, which developed the legal framework necessary to Papon's prosecution, and part III discusses the application of this law to Maurice Papon. Part IV examines some of the larger questions raised by the prosecutions. In particular, the discussion will focus on two aspects of the French cases. First, what is a crime against humanity under French law, and how does it compare to its international counterpart? Second, what has been the legal import of the cases, both for the French and internationally, now that Yugoslavia and Rwanda ad hoc tribunals exist and are prosecuting individuals for crimes against humanity as a matter of international law?

II. THE PROSECUTIONS OF KLAUS BARBIE AND PAUL TOUVIER FOR CRIMES AGAINST HUMANITY

The Punishment of Collaborators and Enemy Soldiers following World War II

Any study of crimes against humanity necessarily begins with Nuremberg, for it was at Nuremberg that the crime was articulated as a matter of "positive law." Pursuant to article 6 of the Nuremberg charter, the International Military Tribunal (IMT) had jurisdiction to try and punish the "major war criminals of the European Axis countries" for three offenses: crimes against peace, war crimes, and crimes against humanity. Article 6(c) defined crimes against humanity as follows:

[N]amely murder, extermination, enslavement, deportation, and other inhumane acts committed against any civilian population, before or during the war, or persecutions on political, racial or religious grounds in execution of or in connection with any crimes within the jurisdiction whether or not in violation of the domestic law of the country where perpetrated.

The French played an active part in drafting the London accord that established the Nuremberg Tribunal and the charter of the tribunal annexed thereto.[3] They also took part in prosecuting the major war criminals at Nuremberg.[4] At the same time, the French enacted laws to punish "lesser" war criminals—a category that included both suspected French collaborators and non-French enemy agents who committed war crimes either on French soil or against French nationals.[5] The period after the Liberation was marked by purges (*l'épuration*), including summary executions and trials of both French collaborators and German agents captured in France.[6] While Frenchmen were punished for "collaboration" or treason,[7] non-Frenchmen were punished for war crimes.[8] No one was punished by a French court for "crimes against humanity," strictly speaking.[9]

The 1964 Law

Crimes against humanity as defined in the IMT charter were incorporated into French municipal law through a curious bit of legislation adopted in 1964. Designed to remedy a gap in the London accord and charter, which did not mention what statute of limitations[10] applied to the crimes listed therein,[11] the 1964 law provided:

Law No. 64-1326 declaring the imprescriptibility of crimes against humanity.

Sole article. Crimes against humanity, as defined in the United Nations' Resolution of February 13, 1946, taking account of the definition of crimes against humanity figuring in the Charter of the International Tribunal of August 8, 1945, are imprescriptible by their nature.[12]

This law was adopted unanimously by the French legislature to honor the victims of the war. The intention was that any remaining Nazis would be punished, no matter when or where they were found. By this law, the French legislature apparently intended two things. First, that crimes against humanity (as defined in the IMT charter) would become an indictable offense under French municipal law; second, that any defense of prescription[13] would be abolished. In their haste, however, the drafters of the 1964 law overlooked the difference between punishing crimes against humanity as *international* offenses at Nuremberg and punishing them under French law. The resulting text was both ambiguous and incomplete.[14]

Evolution of a Definition

The Early Years of the Touvier Case: 1973–1983

Paul Touvier's case was the first to be brought in reliance on the 1964 law. Although a relatively minor figure in the hierarchy of Vichy officialdom, Touvier nevertheless used his position as Lyon's head of information services in the Milice[15] to inflict substantial harm on those he deemed to be enemies of either himself or the Vichy regime.[16] Sentenced to death during the Purge, he went into hiding until he received a pardon from President Pompidou in 1971 for his wartime actions. Touvier's pardon would ultimately be his downfall, however, for when it was revealed to the public, he came to the attention of victims who remembered him. On 27 June 1973 one such victim, Rosa Eisner Vogel, filed a complaint with the public prosecutor's office (*procureur de la République*) of the Lyon *Tribunal de grande instance*[17] to the effect that she believed Touvier had directed a grenade attack against the synagogue at Quai Tilsitt, Lyon, during the Second World War.[18] Shortly thereafter, Georges Glaeser brought an action implicating Touvier in the massacre of seven Jews (including his father) by the Milice at Rillieux-la-Pape.[19] Finally, on 23 March 1974, other individuals filed charges against Touvier with the prosecutor's office at Chambéry,[20] alleging that Touvier had tortured Robert Nant, a leader of the Resistance, and had arrested and deported other members of the Resistance, many of whom did not survive the experience.[21] All three complainants—Vogel, Glaeser, and Nant—asserted that Paul Touvier was guilty of crimes against humanity.

Several interesting issues were raised by the case. Most importantly for our purposes here were three fundamental questions. First, could the 1964 law apply to crimes committed prior to its passage? (This question posed a significant hurdle for the court due to the very strict notion in French law that penal laws must not be retroactive.) Second, could it apply to Frenchmen? (After all, article 6 of the IMT charter referred only to "Axis" war criminals.) Third, were the acts complained of by the parties "crimes against humanity" within the meaning of the IMT charter?

For three years the case navigated the French judicial system.[22] It was dismissed twice and appealed twice,[23] and even though the Criminal Chamber of the French Court of Cassation (the supreme court of France for criminal matters) heard the second appeal, the court never reached the issues presented.[24] Instead, on the basis of alleged ambiguities in the London accord and charter, among other things, it referred the case to the minister of foreign affairs for a ministerial interpretative response on the application of the IMT charter to Touvier's case.[25] Having thus neatly shifted the problem from the courts to the executive branch, the Court of Cassation avoided the political problems inherent in the case, and the 1964 law (not to mention the Touvier prosecution) was to stagnate for some time.[26] It was only revived when the French courts were faced with another case—the prosecution of Klaus Barbie.

The Prosecution of Klaus Barbie for Crimes against Humanity: 1983–1988

On 15 July 1979 the minister of foreign affairs rendered the long-awaited interpretation of the London accord and charter in the Touvier case.[27] According to the report from the Quai d'Orsay, "the only principle in matters of the prescription of crimes against humanity that one may derive from the IMT charter is the principle of imprescriptibility."[28] This decision paved the way not only for the Touvier case to advance, but also for other cases,[29] including Klaus Barbie's.

Born on 25 October 1913 in Bad Godesberg, Germany,[30] Nikolaus "Klaus" Barbie rose rapidly through the ranks of the Nazi hierarchy to become head of the SIPO-S.D. (section IV), the intelligence branch of the Gestapo, at Lyon.[31] He was posted there after the Germans recaptured Lyon in November of 1942, and was assigned the task of destroying the French Resistance that had come to use Lyon as a base of operations during its time as part of Free France.[32] Following an inquiry that began in 1980, on 12 February 1982 the public prosecutor of Lyon filed charges of crimes against humanity against Barbie, who was then living in Bolivia.[33]

Freed of many of the difficulties that had troubled the Touvier prosecution, notably the still unanswered question of whether Frenchmen and not just citizens of Axis nations could be prosecuted under the 1964 law, and armed with the response of the Ministry of Foreign Affairs as to the problem of prescription, the High Court had no trouble this time in addressing the thornier issues of what constitutes a crime against humanity in French (international) criminal law. This the court did through a series of several opinions, two of which concern us here.[34]

As an initial matter, the Court of Cassation rejected the argument that the crimes had prescribed.[35] Following the interpretation of the Ministry of Foreign Affairs,[36] the court held that Barbie, charged with crimes against humanity, could not benefit from the prescription of the public action,[37] no matter when the crimes had been committed.[38] Thus, almost twenty years after the adoption of the 1964 law, and more than ten years subsequent to the filing of the complaints in the Touvier case, the Court of Cassation finally ruled that the 1964 law meant what it said: crimes against humanity could be prosecuted in France "whatever the date and place of their commission."

Yet now that the procedural problem of prescription had been resolved, the substance of the 1964 law was at issue. One of the thorniest problems was differentiating crimes against humanity from war crimes. This was important for a critical reason: unless the crimes could be characterized as crimes against humanity, the 1964 law could not apply and the public action would prescribe. The difficulty in Barbie's case, however, was that many of the charges against him involved his actions against members of the French Resistance. In particular, he was charged with torturing and murdering Jean Moulin, who had been able to unify the various branches of the Resistance under one command. Barbie cleverly argued that since article 6(c) required the acts to be committed against a "civilian population," the allegations, even if true, could not constitute crimes against humanity because the French Resistance amounted to an armed force. Thus, at worst his actions could only be properly charged as war crimes, which would have prescribed.

Barbie's argument prevailed in the lower courts. On 4 October 1985, the Indicting Chamber of the Court of Appeals of Lyon affirmed the decision of the *juge d'instruction* indicting Barbie on several of the counts against him,[39] but, following the lead of the *juge d'instruction*, held that "only persecutions against *innocent* Jews,[40] carried out for racial or religious reasons, in view of the final solution conspiracy, that is, [the Jews'] extermination, constitute imprescriptible crimes against humanity for which Barbie must answer."[41] Thus the public action had expired with respect to:

> the detention without judgment, the torture, the deportation and the death of members of the Resistance, or those persons that Barbie supposed to be members of the Resistance, even if they were Jewish, [as] those acts, even if atrocious and committed in contempt of the human person and the laws of war, can only constitute war crimes which have already prescribed.[42]

The court added that acts of the defendant, or the organizations to which he belonged, were war crimes (and not crimes against humanity) so long as one could characterize them as having been carried out in furtherance of a military aim: if *"ils se veulent utiles à la conduite de la guerre."*[43]

The illogic (not to mention the insensitivity) of the lower courts' analysis[44] became patently obvious when applied to the situation of Professor Marcel Gompel. Professor Gompel was a Jewish member of the Resistance. He had been arrested and tortured to death by Barbie. The court found that because it was not clear whether Professor Gompel had been arrested in his "capacity as a Jew," or as a member of the Resistance, Barbie could not be charged with this offense, as it had prescribed.[45]

Counselor Le Gunehec, reporting to the Criminal Chamber on the case,[46] criticized the lower courts. In particular, he concluded that article 6(c) never meant to categorically exclude individuals who organized themselves against racial, religious, or political persecutions from the category of victims against whom a crime against humanity could be committed.[47] What article 6(c) did require, however, was a specific *élément moral*, or required finding of intent: first, "the *author* [must] act in application of a governmental or state policy (*politique*), of which he had knowledge, and with which he collaborated";[48] second, the *victim* must belong to a community or particular group—national, ethnic, racial, linguistic, religious, ideological, or political—and must be a victim *because* he is a member of the group against whom the perpetrators have directed their crimes.[49]

The Court of Cassation essentially followed Le Gunehec's report. In the opinion of the court, the crime against humanity was, above all, characterized by the intent of the perpetrator to deny the humanity of his victim, a crime in which the perpetrator wishes to injure the group to which the victim belongs by attacking the victim as an individual.[50] The victim's status, however, whether "innocent" bystander or active opponent, is irrelevant. This particular view of crimes against humanity, it should be noted, was positive insofar as it permitted the court to hear all the counts in the Barbie case. It was deeply problematic, however, in another sense, for it excludes, *ex ante*, many other situations involving massive human rights abuses by governments. For example, if a government attacks its citizenry randomly, in order to terrorize them into submission, but does not single out particular groups for the attack, the French version of crimes against humanity would not apply.[51]

In addition to the court's focus on the discriminatory nature of the crime, the opinion added a further requirement: the perpetrator must carry out his crime on behalf of a "State practicing a hegemonic political ideology." This innovation[52] was without foundation in the text of article 6(c) or French law. Indeed, as was

observed at the time, any state (or any group) not practicing a hegemonic political ideology (whatever that means) cannot ever, as a matter of law, commit a
crime against humanity under French law. In so holding, the Court of Cassation largely insulated French defendants from criminal liability.[53] One need not
be a cynic to believe that the court probably had Touvier, and other similarly
situated individuals, in mind.

Following this decision, the Indicting Chamber of the Court of Appeals of
Paris added two more counts to the indictment against Barbie.[54] Barbie was
tried by the Court of Assizes of the department of the Rhône and was convicted, on 4 July 1987, of crimes against humanity. He was sentenced to life imprisonment[55] and died in prison on 25 September 1991.[56]

The 13 April 1992 Decision of the Paris Court of Appeals
in the Touvier case

Following the decision of the minister of foreign affairs that the 1964 law
should be interpreted to find that Touvier's crimes had not prescribed, the Indicting Chamber of the Paris Court of Appeals held, on 27 July 1979, that an
investigation (*information*) should be opened with respect to Touvier.[57] Touvier
was finally arrested on 24 May 1989, and on 29 October 1991 the investigating
magistrate, Judge Getti, held that Touvier could be indicted on five of the
eleven charges then lodged against him, including the massacre of seven Jews at
Rillieux-la-Pape, a suburb of Lyon.[58]

On review, in a controversial 215-page decision[59] the Indicting Chamber of
the Paris Court of Appeals reversed Judge Getti and threw out the indictment.
According to the upper court's reading of the file, the evidence with respect to
ten of the eleven counts was insufficient. With respect to the one crime for
which Touvier's involvement was undeniable (the massacre at Rillieux), one of
the requisite elements of a "crime against humanity" was missing: the prosecution had not proven that the accused intended to take part in a common plan
by systematically committing inhumane acts and illegal persecutions *in the name
of a State practicing a hegemonic political ideology.*[60]

To reach this conclusion, the Paris Court of Appeals considered the "historical" record of the Vichy government: its policies toward the Jews and its relationship with the Germans then occupying France. Although agreeing that the
Milice and the Vichy government exhibited certain anti-Semitic tendencies, the
court concluded that Vichy France, unlike Nazi Germany, was not a hegemonic
state.[61] Thus, Touvier could not, *as a matter of law*, have committed a crime against
humanity in carrying out Vichy's orders. The court also rejected the idea that
Touvier could be guilty as an accomplice of the Gestapo, finding that Touvier

was not carrying out any German plan at Rillieux—it was entirely *"une affaire entre Français"* (a French affair).[62]

The decision of the Paris court was widely criticized as replete with errors, omissions, and even untruths.[63] The historical record showed that the Milice specifically excluded Jews from their number and repeatedly targeted them for abuse.[64] Moreover, as the civil parties pointed out in their appeal, the court's own words led to the conclusion that the Vichy state practiced an ideology of exclusion, hate, and collaboration with the Germans (i.e., was a "hegemonic" state). Finally, Touvier himself admitted that the Milice carried out the Rillieux massacre under German orders. Indeed, this was his principal defense.

Touvier Is Convicted

On 27 November 1992 the Court of Cassation reversed the Paris Court of Appeals in part.[65] As for the charges that had been dismissed by the lower court due to insufficient evidence, the Court of Cassation affirmed without much discussion,[66] summarily rejecting the appellants' contention that the Court of Appeals had infected its evaluation of the evidence by systematically discrediting all the witnesses except Touvier.[67] Turning to the massacre at Rillieux, the court reviewed without editorial comment the "historical" analysis of the Court of Appeals. It then reversed on very narrow grounds: because the criminal acts committed at Rillieux had been accomplished at the instigation of the Gestapo, and because, under article 6 of the IMT charter, only those acting "in the interests of the European Axis countries" could be tried under article 6(c), the Court of Appeals had contradicted itself by finding that Touvier could not have committed a crime against humanity, while at the same time conceding that he acted at the instigation of the Gestapo.[68]

The case was remanded to the indicting chamber of the Court of Appeals of Versailles, which indicted Touvier for the massacre at Rillieux.[69] The case was set for trial some twenty years and dozens of court decisions after the original complaints were filed. The trial lasted five and a half weeks, during which more than fifty witnesses and experts, the civil parties themselves, and Touvier were heard.[70]

The defense availed itself of essentially four tactics. First, Touvier's attorney, Jacques Trémolet de Villers, attacked various aspects of the procedure by making numerous evidentiary motions and objections. Second, Trémolet de Villers attempted what came to be characterized in the press as a sort of "Schindler defense."[71] Touvier's argument had always been that he ordered the murder of the seven men at Rillieux in self-defense because the Gestapo forced him to after the execution of Philippe Henriot, a high-ranking Vichy official, by the Resistance. But Touvier also claimed that Commandant Knab of the

Gestapo had ordered the killing of a hundred hostages; that Touvier's chief reduced that number to thirty; and that only through Touvier's intervention was the number reduced to seven. Thus, according to his reckoning, he had saved the lives of twenty-three men.

Third, the defense relied on Touvier's advancing age and the press's use of him as a scapegoat to portray him as a defenseless old man who had already suffered enough. His obvious illness and his family's favorable testimony might have allowed this strategy to succeed had Touvier not been his own worst enemy. Evasive and unrepentant when questioned, he often appeared to be lying on the stand, particularly when he denied that he was in any way anti-Semitic.[72] Moreover, in what was one of the most dramatic moments of the trial, the court brought in as exhibits six enormous boxes containing files belonging to Touvier which had been hidden in the Nicean Abbey where he was arrested in 1989. Among the contents, which were spread out in front of the jury, was a collection of Nazi paraphernalia, including swastikas. When queried as to why he had such objects in his possession, Touvier claimed he had accumulated them to sell to collectors. Also present was a notebook that Touvier had used as a diary covering the period between 1985 and 1988, which contained numerous anti-Semitic references.[73]

Finally, Trémolet de Villers attempted to appeal to the jury's sense of justice by pointing to the artificial legal construct on which Touvier's trial was based. One prong of this argument promoted the idea that Touvier was being prosecuted selectively and that many others who were guilty of crimes against humanity over the years had not been punished. This tactic did not appear to impress either the judges or the jury. More significant was the second prong of this argument, which relied on the flaw in the Criminal Chamber's decision of 1992 and which engendered unexpected support from one of the civil party lawyers.

When Judge Getti originally indicted Touvier for the massacre at Rillieux, he rejected Touvier's claim that he was acting under orders from the Gestapo. Indeed, the *dossier d'instruction* tended to support the idea that the execution of the seven men at Rillieux was undertaken on the initiative of the Milice. This was corroborated by the report of Commissioner Delarue and was one of the bases on which the Paris Court of Appeals had thrown out the indictment in 1992. When the High Court reversed the Paris Court of Appeals, however, it refused to hold squarely that French collaborators could be prosecuted under the 1964 law. Instead, it held that they could be prosecuted under the 1964 law only if they were working "in the interests of the European Axis countries." Thus Touvier's somewhat spurious defense became the linchpin of the prosecution's case: Touvier could be tried for the massacre at Rillieux *because* the Gestapo had given the orders to execute hostages in reprisal for Henriot's execution. Of course, Touvier could not deny his earlier claims at his trial without completely destroying his already weak credibility. As it turned out, however, Maître Arno Klarsfeld, a lawyer for one of the civil parties intent on proving Vichy's responsibility, did this for him. Much to the consternation of his colleagues, Maître Klarsfeld announced to the tribunal in questioning Commissioner Delarue:

> They are attempting to make the jury believe that Touvier acted under German orders, when in fact he acted on his own initiative.[74]

If Klarsfeld was right (as he seemed clearly to be), he could win the point of principle (that the Milice executed Jews on its own initiative) but lose the case by destroying the link to the Gestapo that the High Court had found required by the 1964 law. The advocate-general countered:

> The plan was Nazi, but the complicity was French.[75]

On Wednesday, 20 April 1994, after five and a half hours of deliberation, the verdict was delivered. Touvier was pronounced guilty and sentenced to life imprisonment, and the symbolic one franc requested by the civil parties was granted.

III. THE PROSECUTION OF MAURICE PAPON

The Indictment

On 20 October 1942, four armed law enforcement officers, two French and two Germans, arrived at the home of the Slitinsky family in Bordeaux, France. They had come to arrest the Slitinskys as part of a larger operation in which the Jews of the Bordeaux region were to be arrested, interned, and their property confiscated.[76] Michel Slitinsky, then seventeen years old, escaped. His father, Abraham, and sister, Alice, were less fortunate. They were arrested, and Abraham was sent to Auschwitz, where he was killed.[77]

Nearly forty years later, archives were discovered that revealed the role of Maurice Papon, a high-ranking civil servant who was the secretary-general for the Gironde prefecture, in the arrest of the Slitinskys. Indeed, the twenty-six volumes of evidence collected by the investigating magistrates implicated Papon in the deportation of almost 1,600 Jews from Bordeaux. Although not a policy maker himself, Papon was apparently a highly efficient bureaucrat with authority over "Jewish questions" in the Gironde, among other things. He supervised the compilation and maintenance of lists of Jews (which were periodically forwarded to the Germans); organized roundups of Jews; and procured transportation and police surveillance for the convoys.

Numerous victims of the mistreatment, or their surviving relations, filed criminal charges against Papon and others. Since the statute of limitations had already run, the only charge available to the civil parties was to accuse Papon, like Touvier, of committing a crime against humanity under the 1964 law.

After the tortured road traveled by the Barbie and Touvier cases, many feared that the Papon case would never be heard. Although the documentary evidence against him was damning, as a white-collar defendant Papon's case seemed more difficult than Touvier's both from a legal (given the earlier case law) and a political perspective. For one thing, after the war (unlike Touvier) Papon's public image was completely rehabilitated. Indeed, while Touvier went into hiding, Papon's career flourished. Called by de Gaulle to public service based on his resistance credentials (the bona fides of which were hotly contested during his trial), he rose through the civil service ranks to become prefect of police for the city of Paris in 1958, a member of parliament in 1968, and budget minister in the government of Raymond Barre in 1978. For another, Papon does not, unlike Touvier, appear to have been explicitly anti-Semitic; rather, the anti-Semitism of Papon, if any, lies in his apparent indifference to the fate of those whose deportation orders he signed.

Nevertheless, in a 170-page-long decision (*arrêt de renvoi*)[78] that was confirmed by the Court of Cassation on 23 January 1997[79] the Indicting Chamber of the Bordeaux Court of Appeals indicted Papon for complicity in crimes against humanity. Moreover, the court's opinion is the first decision that openly admits Vichy's collaborationist role as an "indispensable cog" in the machinery of destruction employed by the Nazis. The opinion is a tour de force, condemning not just Papon, but the entire bureaucratic apparatus used in the "administrative massacre"[80] of the Jews of France, and going well beyond the conservative stance of the public prosecutor's réquisitoire définitif filed in 1995.[81]

The opinion is also interesting in its response to Papon's defenses. Papon's primary contention was that he was just doing his job and that he did not know what would happen to the deportees. Thus he claimed that he lacked the requisite intent for a crime against humanity. The court forcefully rejected this argument. According to the court's opinion, "everyone knew" what was happening (and particularly someone as well-educated and well-placed as Papon) given the news reports at the time and the personal accounts of Jews escaped from the East who had sought refuge in France. The indicting chamber explored Papon's pre-Vichy career in detail, noting that he spoke German and had, according to witnesses' testimony, engaged in political debates about the National Socialist program in the late 1930s. The court also noted that the record contained written evidence of memoranda from German officers. Indeed, one such document requested the prefect to make a report on the "elimination of the Jews."[82] As if this were not enough, the court underlined the fact that the Germans would not free children and the aged, and that those deported had their property confiscated. This, it said, was clear evidence that no one ever intended the deportees to return. The court concluded: "Thus Maurice Papon . . . had, even prior to taking office, a clear, reasoned, detailed, and continuous knowledge of the Nazis' plans to murder these people, constituting premeditation, even if he may have been ignorant of the exact conditions of their last sufferings and the technical means whereby they were killed."[83]

The Indicting Chamber also rejected any defense of duress, finding that the pressures brought to bear upon civil servants were not of an intensity that would have negated Papon's free will. The defense's reliance on claims of superior orders and subordinate responsibility were equally unfruitful. As the court notes, the orders given were manifestly illegal.[84] Indeed, the court suggested more than once that the appropriate response of Papon to Nazi (or Vichy) pressure should have been to resign.

The Court of Cassation confirmed the *arrêt de renvoi*, and rejected Papon's appeal. Most of the decision is unremarkable, with one exception. Papon argued, among other things, that his acts could not constitute "complicity" in the legal sense, because there was no proof that he adhered to the "hegemonic political ideology" of the Nazis. Indeed, he pointed to his membership in the Resistance as evidence that he opposed Germany's Final Solution and the occupation of France. Citing article 121-7 of the New French Criminal Code (on complicity),[85] but ultimately relying on article 6(c) itself, the High Court held that article 6 did not require the accomplice (*complice*) of a crime against humanity to himself adhere to the hegemonic political ideology of the principals, nor to belong to one of the organizations declared criminal at Nuremberg. Rather, it sufficed that he knowingly facilitated the preparation or consummation of the crime. One could argue that this was not a particularly remarkable holding under French municipal law,[86] and simply clarified the court's position in the *Barbie III* opinion.[87] Certainly the holding is fortunate from a prosecutorial perspective. For had the court held that the state was required to prove that each perpetrator subjectively adhered to the policy under which the crimes against humanity were being committed, it could make prosecution of the kind of heinous crimes with which Papon was charged difficult indeed.

The Trial and Verdict

The trial of Maurice Papon defeated all expectations. After the *arrêt de renvoi*, the trial's outcome was a foregone conclusion: life imprisonment. That was the sentence Paul Touvier received for ordering the murder of seven men at Rillieux; surely the deportation and ultimate death of more than one thousand souls warranted the same. But from the outset the trial surprised. From the opening day of 8 October 1997, Papon ably defended himself, and his lawyer, Jean Marc Varaut, proved more than capable of the same.[88] In contrast, the lawyers for the civil parties often seemed in disarray. Papon requested and received his liberty for the duration of the trial.[89] His illness caused the trial to be recessed several times.[90] Maître Arno Klarsfeld again surprised by requesting the president of the court to recuse himself on the grounds that he was related by marriage to some of the deportees in question. (The president refused.)[91] Repeatedly, documentary and witness testimony established Papon's knowledge of the fate that awaited the deportees, and his complicity in their deportation and death.[92] In his defense, Papon called historians, members of the Resistance, and highly prestigious individuals such as Maurice Druon, permanent secretary of the Académie française, who suggested that the trial benefited only the Germans.[93]

As the trial wore on, so perhaps did the judges, jury, and public prosecutor. Finally, although originally scheduled to end on 23 December 1997, but after more than six months had elapsed, the trial concluded with a demand for twenty years' imprisonment from the prosecutor.[94] Some even feared an acquittal.[95] Seven hundred and sixty-four questions were put to the jury. With respect to each of the victims ultimately named in the *arrêt de renvoi*, each member of the court and the jurors had to respond to several questions. First, were they the victims of an illegal arrest, an arbitrary detention, or a murder? Next, did those actions constitute an "inhumane act or persecution committed in systematic fashion in the context of a *plan concerté* carried out on behalf of a State practicing a hegemonic political ideology, against individuals on account of their membership in a racial or religious group"? Finally, was "the accused, Maurice Papon, guilty of having, at Bordeaux [on the relevant date], knowingly (*sciemment*) facilitated the preparation or consummation [of the acts in question]"?[96]

Ultimately, after nineteen hours of deliberation, on 2 April 1998 the jury rendered its verdict: ten years' imprisonment.[97] Conviction on the charges of complicity with respect to the arrests and detentions of some of the victims; acquittal on all the charges of murder. Why? Although the court's reasoning is unclear, and of course the jurors give no reasons at all (although they did respond to each of the 764 questions posed), essentially it appears that the court fell back to the prosecutor's original bill filed in 1995 rejecting the conclusions of the *arrêt de renvoi*: according to the court, although the accused could be said to have known of the cruel fate (even death) that awaited the deportees, his knowledge did not rise to the level of premeditation. With respect to the arrests and detentions, however, these could be qualified as crimes against humanity because they were being carried out as an integral part of a Nazi plan, of which he had knowledge.[98]

The decisions in the Papon case have received mixed reviews. On the one hand, the indicting chamber's opinion is extremely encouraging. Not only rejecting the revisionist version of Vichy's history proffered by the Paris Court of Appeals in the Touvier case, but squarely holding a "white-collar" administrative collaborator responsible for his acts, the decision is one of the most significant crimes against humanity cases ever to issue from any court. It sends a clear message that those who facilitate the commission of crimes against humanity are as culpable as those who conceive them, incite others to their commission, and execute the orders to carry them out. In this way, the decision closes a gap in the law to date, which tended to focus only on leadership (Nuremberg) or direct participation in atrocities (Touvier).

On the other hand, Papon's trial shows how difficult white-collar cases are to prove. The Court of Assizes did not technically depart from the legal standards announced by the Indicting Chamber. Yet, when pushed, the court was reluctant to convict Papon of murder without demonstrating the kind of specific intent that the Indicting Chamber seemed inclined to infer from the evidence. While the apparent incongruity in result is disappointing (Touvier dies in prison), it is nevertheless understandable that a court could not find him guilty on the murder charges under the circumstances, fifty years after the facts giving rise to the indictment had occurred. Also, Touvier essentially confessed to the crime; Papon bitterly contested it. Thus, if the decision of the Indicting Chamber stands undisputed as a matter of law, the trial itself sends a cautionary note to would-be prosecutors.

In a final footnote to the case, Papon, denounced the verdict in a forty-minute speech to the court issued at the end of the verdict.[99] His lawyer, of course, appealed. In a final bizarre twist to this unusual case, the day before Papon's appeal was to be heard, the newspapers reported he had disappeared rather than turn himself in as the law requires. It seems that the legalistic and formalistic Maurice Papon had, for once, chosen to disobey orders. He was ultimately captured in Gstaad, Switzerland, and taken into French custody to serve out his ten-year sentence.[100]

IV. THE IMPORT AND SIGNIFICANCE OF THE FRENCH CASE LAW

It is often said that "hard cases make bad law." To some extent, the French crimes against humanity decisions are no exception. Crimes against humanity as defined at Nuremberg was a category of offense originally conceived to criminalize the massive human rights abuses perpetrated by the Nazis that did not fit into the existing category of war crimes. They were particularly aimed at the commission of atrocities that were authorized, indeed required, under German law at the time. Yet even at Nuremberg and after there was much criticism of the prosecution as *ex post facto*; of being a retroactive application of the law in violation of the defendants' human rights. For if there were international treaties of nonaggression and international treaties defining the laws of war, nowhere was there an international treaty defining the crime against humanity. Yet the acts of the Nazis were so atrocious that for law to admit it was helpless to address the case would have been a mockery of the law itself. And of course customary international law had always been considered part of the law of nations, and many argued that the prohibition against crimes against humanity could be found therein. As Justice Jackson noted in his opening statement, "The refuge of the defendants can be only their hope that International Law will lag so far behind the moral sense of mankind that conduct which is crime in the moral sense must be regarded as innocent in law."[101]

International law was not found wanting at Nuremberg, and the tribunal convicted several of the Nazi defendants of crimes against humanity. But if it was arguably proper for an international tribunal, representative ultimately of twenty-three nations, to apply international law to condemn as criminal actions the Nazi leaders believed to be lawful in their own country, the application of this international law to new defendants, decades after the war had ended, by France as a matter of French *municipal* law strained the legal construction of the crime against humanity nearly to the breaking point. Yet ultimately the French courts, like the Nuremberg Tribunal before them, reached the conclusion that to declare the law incapable of application was unacceptable. Nevertheless, uncomfortable with the clearly retroactive nature of the law's application, and schizophrenic in their feelings about the Vichy regime, the French courts restricted article 6(c) considerably: they read it narrowly, very technically, and arguably improperly. This was particularly true with respect to their conclusion that much of the language the drafters of the London accord and IMT charter had included in the text as limitations on the jurisdictional reach of the IMT, were substantive limitations of the crime itself. Thus they limited the scope of the crime in French law to those working "in the interest of the Axis nations," as part of the policy of a "hegemonic [read totalitarian] State" that has a state policy of committing human rights abuses on discriminatory grounds. This caused the lower courts to repeatedly dismiss the indictments against Touvier and Papon, on the grounds that those working for the Vichy regime could not be charged with a crime against humanity under the 1964 law. The Court of Cassation ultimately reversed, but on the grounds that the two defendants were in fact carrying out a Nazi plan. This finesse permitted the court to avoid the unpalatable result of holding that the 1964 law applied only to Germans, while at the same time preserving the fiction that Vichy itself was not really implicated by the prosecutions.

Yet if the political cast of the cases caused an unusual reconfiguration of the law, there were many positive effects as well. First, the prosecutions, most would argue, were ultimately quite beneficial for French society as official public fora within which the Vichy period could be reexamined as a matter of law. Second, the trials were of great importance to the victims. As Henri Glaeser stated to the jury in Touvier's trial:

> Remember the last photograph [of my father], taken at Rillieux, his mouth wide open. . . . For years and years, I had the impression that someone wanted to pour concrete in there, to stop him from speaking, to stop me as well. Now I am happy to find myself in front of a court that is democratic, engaged in an adversarial debate where everyone can speak, anything can be said, even by the accused. My father was not judged by anyone. He was arrested, thrown five hours later against a wall, and assassinated.[102]

Third, the cases represent important contributions toward the task of building a legal culture where government leaders are held accountable for their actions and are unable to commit human rights abuses on a massive scale cloaked behind the power and legality of the state. While one can argue that the French cases do not go far enough, France is one of only ten countries in the world reported to have any legislation at all criminalizing the crime against humanity. Moreover, in 1992 the French legislature adopted a new crimes against humanity law, incorporating substantial aspects of the jurisprudence cited above, but rejecting the "hegemonic State" requirement. This would foreclose any future arguments concerning retroactivity, at least as regards crimes committed after 1992, although obviously the law could easily be repealed if a totalitarian government were subsequently to come to power in France. Building legal cultures at the domestic level that reject the right of state leaders to abuse their citizens with impunity is a critical step toward building a world order based on the dignity and freedom of human beings everywhere.

This leads me to my final point. If the French jurisprudence is only as strong as the French state, it should be remembered that the crime against humanity was originally the creation of the international community. Its ultimate force lies in its future application by the international community, and, one day, it is hoped, by a permanent international criminal court. For when a state becomes criminal, the international community must assume the protections of that state's citizenry. The French cases, although doctrinally problematic, have proven instructive to the international community as it has, over the past six years, actively undertaken to define and implement crimes against humanity as positive international law, first in the statute of the two international ad hoc tribunals for the former Yugoslavia and Rwanda, later in the statute of the permanent International Criminal Court adopted in 1998 by a Diplomatic Conference in Rome. The cases have been cited and discussed by the two ad hoc tribunals in elaborating the elements of a crime against humanity in international law, and were useful to the delegates at the Diplomatic Conference,[103] even if there was much disagreement about the correctness of particular holdings. For this contribution to the international rule of law, the French can justly be proud. Thus, if the verdict in Papon's case was a mixed one, the three cases taken together nevertheless suggest that the victims of these individuals did not suffer in vain. Instead, their torment spurred the establishment of a legal legacy that might, if carefully nurtured, one day prevent others from experiencing the same pain—a most precious gift indeed.

NOTES

1. The Touvier and Barbie prosecutions are discussed in detail in Leila Sadat Wexler, "The Interpretation of the Nuremberg Principles by the French Court of Cassation: From Touvier to Barbie and Back Again," *Columbia Journal of Transnational Law* 32 (1994): 289 [hereinafter Sadat Wexler, "Nuremberg Principles"]. Touvier's trial is the focus of another work, Leila Sadat Wexler, "Reflections on the Trial of Vichy Collaborator Paul Touvier for Crimes against Humanity in France," *Journal of Law & Social Inquiry* 20 (1995): 191 [hereinafter Sadat Wexler, "Reflections"]. The Papon case (prior to conviction) is discussed in Leila Sadat Wexler, "Prosecutions for Crimes against Humanity in French Municipal Law: International Implications." In *Proceedings of the 91st Annual Meeting of the American Society of International*

Law (1997). For an excellent overview of French law pertaining to war crimes and crimes against humanity, see generally Jacques Francillon, "Crimes de guerre, Crimes contre l'humanité," *Juris-Classeur, Droit International, Fascicule* 410 (1993).

2. Former President Mitterrand actually admitted that he had asked the French government to delay pursuit of several other suspected World War II collaborators, in particular René Bousquet and Maurice Papon, both of whom were much higher in the Vichy hierarchy than Touvier. See Sadat Wexler, "Reflections," *supra* note 1, at 198–99. Bousquet was assassinated in 1993, before he could be indicted, and a preliminary indictment was issued in December 1995, thirteen years after the investigations began, into the wartime activities of Maurice Papon. Papon was finally indicted in September of 1996, and his indictment confirmed on 23 January 1997. Judgment of 18 September 1996, Chambre d'Accusation de la Cour d'Appel de Bordeaux (unpublished) [hereinafter *Papon I*], affirmed Judgment of 23 January 1997, Cass. crim., 1997 Juris-Classeur Périodique [J.C.P.] II G, No. 22812 (Note Robert) [hereinafter *Papon II*].

3. The Agreement for the Prosecution and Punishment of Major War Criminals of the European Axis, 8 August 1945, Charter of the International Military Tribunal, 82 U.N.T.S. 279, 59 Stat. 1544, E.A.S. No. 472, reprinted in *American Journal of International Law* 39 (1945)(Supp.): 257 [hereinafter London Agreement]. *See also* M. Cherif Bassiouni, "'Crimes against Humanity:' The Need for a Specialized Convention," *Columbia Journal of Transnational Law* 31 (1994): 457; Egon Schwelb, "Crimes against Humanity," *British Yearbook of International Law* (1946): 178–80. For a general history of the historical legal foundations of article 6(c), see M. Cherif Bassiouni, *Crimes against Humanity in International Law* (Dordrecht: Martinus Nijhoff, 1992): 147–76.

4. Although the French only had one of the 22 defendants eventually brought to trial at Nuremberg in their possession, they took an active role in the prosecution. Court of Cassation Judge Robert Falco was their representative to the international conference on drafting, and Donnedieu de Vabres was the French member of the Tribunal (Judge Falco was the alternate). Telford Taylor, *The Anatomy of the Nuremberg Trials* (New York: Knopf, 1992): 59. See generally Donnedieu de Vabres, *Le Procès de Nuremberg, Cours de Doctorat* (Montchrestien 1946).

5. For a detailed study of these laws see Sadat Wexler, "Nuremberg Principles," *supra* note 1, at 316–18 and notes cited.

6. Professor Sweets estimates the purge at probably 10,000 Frenchmen, executed at the hands of other Frenchmen without a proper trial, although others have put the number as high as 40,000. See John F. Sweets, *The Politics of Resistance in France, 1940–1944*, (De Kalb: Northern Illinois University Press, 1976): 213, 216–17. See also Jean-Pierre Maunoir, *La Répression des crimes de guerre devant les tribunaux français et*

alliés (1956): 39 (Thèse No. 517, Université de Genève, Faculté de Droit); Herbert R. Lottman, *The Purge* (New York: William Morrow & Co., 1986): 22.

7. Eugène Aroneanu, *Le Crime contre l'humanité* (Paris: Dalloz, 1961): 225.

8. See Sadat Wexler, "Nuremberg Principles," *supra* note 1, at 317–18.

9. See G. Levasseur, "Les crimes contre l'humanité et le problème de leur prescription," *Journal du Droit International* 93 (1966): 259, 263–64. In spite of the supremacy of international law over municipal law and the essentially monist nature of the French legal system, "crimes against humanity" were arguably absent from French law prior to the 1964 law's adoption. See Claude Lombois, "Un Crime international en droit positif français," in *Droit Pénal Contemporain Mélanges en l'Honneur d'André Vitu* (1989): 367, 373 [hereinafter Lombois, *Un Crime international*].

10. Probably because no one thought of it. Levasseur, *supra* note 9, at 265 and n. 22. Indeed, none of the laws adopted by the Allies mentioned a statute of limitations, except for Article II, paragraph 5, of Control Council Law No. 10, which provided that persons accused of one of the crimes therein could not benefit from "any statute of limitation in respect of the period from 30 January 1933 to 1 July 1945." Allied Control Council Law No. 10 reprinted in Bassiouni, *Crimes against Humanity*, *supra* note 3, at 592. Jacques-Bernard Herzog, "Étude des lois concernant la prescription des crimes contre l'humanité," *Revue de Science Criminelle et de Droit Pénal Comparé [Rev. Sci. Crim. & Dr. Pén.]* (1965): 337, 338.

11. Sadat Wexler, "Nuremberg Principles," *supra* note 1, at 318–19.

12. *Journal Officiel de la République Française [J.O.]* 29 December 1964. See Sadat Wexler, "Nuremberg Principles," *supra* note 1, at 320–21.

13. Extinctive criminal prescription bars the prosecution of a defendant by the State (*l'action publique*) or the imposition of the punishment (*la peine*), if either has not been brought or carried out prior to a certain, statutorily established, period of time. In the case of prescription of the punishment, although the criminal sentence may not be carried out, the record of the conviction and the associated civil penalties remain. Although similar to a common law "statute of limitations," this essay will use the French term "prescription" to mean the French doctrine of *prescription*. See Martin Weston, *An English Reader's Guide to the French Legal System* (1991): 30.

14. See, e.g., Levasseur, *supra* note 9, at 280. In particular, one legislator, Mme. Vaillant-Couturier, wished to add a proviso that the crimes would be punishable "whatever the date and place of their commission." J.O., Débats Parlementaires, Sénat, Session of 17 December 1964, at 2428–31; J.O., Débats Parlementaires, Assemblée Nationale, Session of 16 December 1964, at 6145 [hereinafter J.O.A.N.]. Her amendment was rejected as ambiguous and redundant, J.O.A.N., at 6146 (statement of Jean Foyer, minister of justice, to the effect that this was already the clear intent of the law). Mme. Vaillant-Couturier was a survivor of Auschwitz and Ravensbruck. She

was also a witness at Nuremberg. Michel Massé, "Du Procès de Nuremberg à celui de P. Touvier en passant par l'affaire Barbie," *Rev. Sci. Crim.* (1984): 793–94.

15. The Milice was established by Law No. 63, of 30 Jan. 1943 as a special military force for combatting the Resistance and other enemies of the Vichy government. *See* Jean-Pierre Azéma, "Les Hommes en noir de la Milice," *Le Monde*, 17 March 1994, Special Supp., p. IV.

16. To say that Touvier was a "minor" figure does not, however, imply that he was powerless. Although he was not responsible for formulating government policy, by the time of the massacre at Rillieux he had risen through the command structure of the Milice to become regional head of the second division at Lyon, in charge of intelligence and operations.

17. These are similar to county courts with both criminal and original civil jurisdiction. Weston, *supra* note 13, at 75–76.

18. The attack occurred on 10 December 1943. Mrs. Vogel, who was 13½ at the time, stated in a sworn affidavit, dated 1 March 1973, that she saw Touvier's photo in the 9 February 1973 issue of the newspaper *La Tribune Juive* and immediately recognized him as an organizer of the Synagogue bombing that she had survived. Judgment of 30 June 1976, Cass. crim., 1977 Dalloz-Sirey, *Jurisprudence* 1, 1976 *Gazette du Palais [Gaz. Pal.]* Nos. 322, 323, at 699, 1976 J.C.P. II G, No. 18,435 [hereinafter *Touvier II*] [D.S. Jur.] (unless otherwise specified, all cites to the *Touvier II* decision are to the version published in the J.C.P.).

19. The history of the massacre at Rillieux is set forth in Sadat Wexler, "Nuremberg Principles," *supra* note 1, at 292–93. See also Laurent Greilsamer and Daniel Schneidermann, *Un Certain Monsieur Paul* (Paris: Fayard, 1989): 7–21 and the various court decisions issued in the *Touvier* case. See, e.g., Judgment of 13 April 1992, Cour d'appel de Paris, Première chambre d'accusation, at 133–162, reprinted in part in *Gaz. Pal.* (1992): 387, 387–417 [hereinafter *Touvier III*]. Subsequent citations are to the entire unpublished decision.

20. *Touvier II*, *supra* note 18 (Report of Counselor Mongin).

21. *Id.* Robert Nant was arrested on 27 May 1944. The deportees, Munoz-Rojo, Lopez Alder, and Charvier were rounded up in a counter-resistance operation that took place on 24 April 1944, at Montmélian, in the Savoie region of France.

22. Sadat Wexler, "Nuremberg Principles," *supra* note 1.

23. Judgment of 27 October 1975, Chambre d'accusation de la cour d'appel de Paris, 1976 D.S. Jur. 260 (Note Coste-Floret), *Gaz. Pal.* Nos. 154–55, (1976): 382 [hereinafter *Touvier IA*] (all subsequent citations are to the D.S. Jur. version unless otherwise noted).

24. For a discussion of these issues, see Sadat Wexler, "Nuremberg Principles," *supra* note 1, at 328–29.

25. *Touvier II, supra* note 18. For commentary on this opinion, *see* Sadat Wexler, "Nuremberg Principles," *supra* note 1, at 330–31.

26. The responses of the minister of July 15 (Touvier) and July 19 (Leguay), 1979 were very long in coming. When they finally appeared, they were unpublished and sent only to the court and the parties—making it difficult for practitioners and researchers to know the law. Judgment of 26 January 1984, Cass. crim., 1984 J.C.P. II G, No. 20,197 (Note Ruzié), J.D.I. 308 (1984) [hereinafter *Barbie II*] (unless otherwise specified, all cites to the *Barbie II* decision are to the version published in the J.C.P.).

27. *Barbie II, supra* note 25, ¶ 23 (Report of Counselor Le Gunehec).

28. *Id.* ¶ 27 (Report of Counselor Le Gunehec). In fact, this issue was arguably already decided by implication in the Judgment of 6 February 1975. Note *M.R. L'imprescriptibilité des crimes contre l'humanité*, 1976 Gaz. Pal. II G, at 699.

29. Such as that of Jean Leguay. Leguay was a delegate of the general secretary of the National Police in the Occupied Zone. He died before the investigation into his wartime activities was completed. See Sadat Wexler, "Reflections," *supra* note 1, at 219, n.139.

30. Brendan Murphy, *The Butcher of Lyon* (New York: Empire Press, 1983): 134 .

31. Judgment of 6 October 1983, Cass. crim., 1984 D.S. Jur. 113, Gaz. Pal. Nos. 352–54, at 710 (18–20 December 1983), 1983 J.C.P. II G, No. 20,107, J.D.I. 779 (1983) [hereinafter *Barbie I*].

32. Under the terms of the original armistice signed with the French on 22 June 1940, the Germans occupied only the northern part of France, and the Vichy government controlled the remaining southern, or "free," part of France. Hermann Mau and Helmut Krausnick, *German History 1933-1945*, trans. Andrew and Eva Wilson. (New York: F. Ungar Publishing Co., 1963): 110–11; Murphy, *supra* note 42, at 32–33. When the Allies landed in North Africa on 8 November 1942, Hitler retaliated by sending German troops across the demarcation line into southern "free" France. Lyon was retaken on 11 November 1942.

33. For a description of the charges against Barbie, see Sadat Wexler, *Nuremberg Principles, supra* note 1, at 333, n.200.

34. The four major decisions of the Criminal Chamber of the Court of Cassation are the Judgment of 6 October 1983 [*Barbie I, supra* note 1, Judgment of 26 January 1984 [*Barbie II, supra* note 26], Judgment of 20 December 1985, Cass. crim., 1986 J.C.P. II G, No. 20,655, 1986 J.D.I. [hereinafter *Barbie III*], and Judgment of 3 June 1988, Cass. crim. 1988 J.C.P. II G, No. 21,149 (Report of Counselor Angevin) [hereinafter *Barbie IV*]. The first decision was rendered on 6 October 1983. In it, the Criminal Chamber approved the ruling of the lower courts that Barbie's arrest by the French at Cayenne–Rochambeau was not an unlawfully "disguised" extradition,

but simply the execution of an arrest warrant issued by a French judge and carried out on French territory. The Court stated that it was of little consequence that the defendant was not on French territory of his own volition. The decision is interesting in that the civil parties and Advocate-General Dontenwille had argued, *inter alia,* that rules of extradition applicable to ordinary crimes could not apply to crimes against humanity as these were international crimes, *Barbie I, supra* note 1 Gaz. Pal. at 719–21. Indeed, the Indicting Chamber of the Court of Appeals of Lyon had accepted this reasoning, implying that the 1927 French extradition law was not applicable, not because there was no treaty and no extradition proceeding open, but because this law would not operate on the "international" crime against humanity. Judgment of 8 July 1983, Chambre d'accusation de la cour d'appel de Lyon, 1983 J.D.I. 782–83. The Criminal Chamber was more cautious. *Barbie I, supra* note 30, D.S. Jur. at 121. For an excellent commentary on the 1983 decision of the Court of Cassation, see Georges Desous, "Réflexions sur le Régime Juridique des Crimes Contre l'Humanité," *Rev. Sci. Crim.* (1984): 657. There were two other minor decisions, the Judgment of 25 November 1986, and the Judgment of 9 March 1988, that will not be discussed here.

35. The problem of retroactivity was still being debated by commentators at this time. See, e.g., R. de Geouffre de la Pradelle, "L'Affaire Barbie et la compétence des juridictions nationales," *Gaz. Pal. Doctrine* (1983, 1er): 131 (essay); Joë Nordmann, "L'imprescriptibilité des crimes contre l'humanité," *Gaz. Pal. Doctrine* (23 April 1983): 163 (responding to de la Pradelle); and David Ruzié, "L'Imprescriptibilité en France des crimes contre l'humanité: un faux problème à propos de l'affaire klaus barbie," *Gaz. Pal. Doctrine*(4 June 1983): 229.

36. As Professor Ruzié noted in his commentary on the decision, once given, the opinion of the minister of foreign affairs, even though unpublished, is valid for future cases, at least where the opinion is general and not tied to particular facts. Id. (Note Ruzié).

37. *Barbie II, supra* note 26.

38. Id.

39. There were 114 civil parties (including associations) to the proceedings.

40. (Emphasis added.) *Barbie III, supra* note 34. The court's choice of words was maladroit, to say the least. See Lombois, "Un crime international," *supra* note 9, at 376.

41. *Barbie III , supra* note 34, ¶ 16 (Report of Counselor Le Gunehec) (emphasis added)

42. Id. Mireille Delmas-Marty points out that this approach is consistent with the view taken by André Frossard, who suggested that the evil of the crime against humanity was killing someone just because he was born (*sous prétexte qu'il est né*). Mireille Delmas-Marty, "Le Crime contre l'humanité, les droits de l'homme, et l'irréductible

humain," *Rev. Sci. Crim.* (1994): 477, 481. In the author's view, this conception is simply too narrow.

43. "They were useful to the conduct of the war." *Id.* ¶ 56 (Report of Counselor Le Gunehec).

44. As Counselor Le Gunehec pointed out, the Resistance was arguably not an army within the meaning of the 1907 Hague Convention. *Barbie III, supra* note 34, ¶ 53 (Report of Counselor Le Gunehec). Moreover, article 6(b) defines war crimes in terms of activities "not justified by military necessity." Finally, he pointed out, citing a passage from Hitler's *Mein Kampf,* that the Nazi ideology targeted not only the Jews but all those who resisted the Nazis—particularly in France. *Id.* ¶ 64.

45. *Barbie III, supra* note 34, ¶ 18 (Report of Counselor Le Gunehec). The lower courts also found that two of the charges were barred by earlier judgments under the French doctrine of former adjudication (*l'autorité de la chose jugée*). The parties responded that, to the extent these constituted crimes against humanity (as well as war crimes), the punishment (as well as the *action publique*) never prescribed. Thus, once captured, Barbie stood reaccused with respect to these crimes, and the original investigation (*information*) would still be valid. The Court of Cassation did not specifically reach this issue (although it implied agreement by its holding), but reversed the lower courts on other grounds, id., and ordered Barbie sent to the Court of Assizes of the Department of the Rhône to be judged for these offenses as well.

46. As French Court of Cassation decisions are noted for their brevity and formulaic style, insight into the Court's reasoning is provided by a study of the report presented to the Court by the *conseiller* (the judge assigned to study the case, referred to in this essay as "counselor").

47. *Barbie III, supra* note 34, ¶ 54 (Report of Counselor Le Gunehec).

48. *Id.* ¶ 60 (Report of Counselor Le Gunehec) (emphasis added).

49. *Id.* ¶ 61 (Report of Counselor Le Gunehec) (although he admits that some commentators do not require this). By requiring this double intent, Counselor Le Gunehec rejected a more expansive reading of article 6(c) that would regard persecutions on political, racial, or religious grounds as a different basis of incrimination from "murder, extermination . . . and other inhumane acts committed against any civilian population, before or during the war . . ." Contra id., Conclusions of Advoate-General Dontenwille. Advocate-General Dontenwille took the view that article 6(c) gives rise to two separate categories of crimes against humanity: those acts that are inhumane in and of themselves and those consisting of persecutions evidently directed at a particular group. See also Bassiouni, *supra* note 3, at 38.

50. "*[D]e faire une victime collective à travers la victime individuelle.*" ("To victimize a group by victimizing an individual.") Id. at 148 (Note Edelman) (quoting Jean Graven, "Les Crimes contre l'humanité," *Cours La Haye* 547 [1950]).

51. The same issues surfaced in the International Criminal Tribunal for the Former Yugoslavia in the *Tadic* case. Tadic was tried for crimes against humanity,
among other things, and Trial Chamber II, citing the *Barbie* decision, adopted a
discriminatory intent requirement in its opinion. This was reversed by the Appeals
Chamber. Interestingly, during the negotiations for the international criminal
court statute in Rome in 1998, the French delegation urged adoption by the
Diplomatic Conference of the French definition. This position was rejected by the
delegates, who did not include this discriminatory intent requirement in the
Statute of the Permanent International Criminal Court. See also Leila Sadat
Wexler and S. Richard Carden, *The New International Criminal Court: An Uneasy Revo-
lution* (forthcoming) (88 *Geo. L.J.* [2000]).

52. It is the first decision to require this second intent, although there were hints
in the scholarly writings to support it. Levasseur, *supra* note 9, at 271.

53. *Barbie III, supra* note 34, J.D.I. at 153 (Note Edelman). One concern was undoubtedly the Algerian war.

54. The procedure is summarized in the *Barbie IV* decision. *Barbie IV, supra* note
34. On 25 November 1986, the Court, reversing the Judgment of 25 April 1986 of
the Indicting Chamber of Lyon, held that Barbie would be tried for another series
of crimes committed against the son and husband of Mme. Lesevre, one of the
civil parties. Judgment of 25 November 1986, Cass. crim., 1986 Bull. Crim. No. 353.

55. Barbie's attorneys raised 14 different grounds of appeal against the conviction. All were rejected. Most importantly, in this last opinion in the *Barbie* case, the
Court ended the debate over whether the principle of imprescriptibility applied
only to the public action or to the punishment, holding squarely that when the defendant has not suffered any punishment, the principle of imprescriptibility resulting from the IMT Charter governs all aspects of the prosecution and punishment
of crimes against humanity. Thus, the prescription (under ordinary French rules)
of the punishment imposed by Barbie's earlier convictions was no bar to the current
proceedings. Finally, the Court also held (in my view incorrectly) that participation
in a "common plan" (*plan concerté*) was an integral element of a crime against humanity, and not just an aggravating circumstance or separate offense. *Barbie IV, supra*
note 34.

56. "'Butcher' Barbie Dies in Lyons Jail," *Times*, 26 September 1991.

57. Meanwhile, other parties filed complaints with Magistrate Riss at Lyon,
the same *juge d'instruction* that had investigated the *Barbie* case. *Touvier III, supra*
note 19, at 20; see also "Nouvelle plainte à Lyon contre l'ancien milicien Paul
Touvier," *Le Monde*, 21 March 1983. A substantial jurisdictional war ensued over
whether the judges of Lyon or those of Paris would hear the case. The Court of
Cassation finally put a (temporary) end to the squabbling of the two jurisdictions

by holding that the inquiry would be conducted in Paris. Judgment of 17 September 1983, Cass. crim.

58. The charges are discussed in detail in Sadat Wexler, "Nuremberg Principles," *supra* note 1, at 347–48 and notes cited.

59. French court decisions are generally noted for their cryptic brevity, see *supra* note 45, making the 215-page decision of the Paris Court of Appeals particularly remarkable.

60. There is no accepted definition of what a "hegemonic" state is, or what the French courts intended by the use of this term. For an analysis of the decisions in the *Barbie* and *Touvier* cases discussing this criterion, *see* Sadat Wexler, "Nuremberg Principles," *supra* note 1, at 359–61.

61. *Touvier III, supra* note 19, at 206. For example, the court states that none of the speeches of Maréchal Pétain contained anything that was anti-Semitic.

62. *Touvier III, supra* note 19, at 209.

63. Seventy-three percent of French men and women reported that they were "shocked" by the decision. "73% des Français sont "choqués" par le non-lieu," *Le Monde*, 17 April 1992. A document entitled "nous accusons" (after Zola's *J'accuse*) was signed and published by 188 famous personalities accusing the three appeals judges of a miscarriage of justice. "Après le non-lieu accordé à Touvier, Nous Accusons," *L'Événement du Jeudi*, 7–13 May 1992, at 22. Conan and Lindenberg speak of the general "stupefication" of the public in reading the decision. Éric Conan and Daniel Lindenberg, "Que Faire de Vichy?" *Espirit*, May 1992, at 6. See also Theo Klein, *Oublier Vichy?: À Propos de l'arrèt Touvier* (Paris: Criterion, 1992). The French National Assembly denounced the verdict. Pascale Robert-Diard, "Le Parti de l'indignation," *Le Monde*, 16 April 1992, at 8. See also Michel Massé, "L'affaire Touvier: L'échappée belle," *Rev. Sci. Crim.* (1993): 372.

64. *See* Michael Marrus and Robert Paxton, *Vichy France and the Jews* (New York: Basic Books, 1981): 3–5, 12 (Vichy passed laws on the Jews ("*le statut des juifs*") prior to any German dictate on the subject, and in fact "Vichy mounted a competitive or rival antisemitism rather than a tandem one:" Vichy wanted to keep Jews out and the Germans wanted to dump them in the unoccupied zone). See also generally Serge Klarsfeld, *Vichy-Auschwitz* (Paris: Fayard, 1983). Richard Weisberg, "Legal Rhetoric under Stress: The Example of Vichy," *Cardozo Law Review* 12 (1991): 1375–77.

65. Judgment of Nov. 27, 1992, Cass. crim., 1993 J.C.P. II G, No. 21,977 [hereinafter *Touvier IV*]. Subsequent citations are to the entire unpublished decision as filed with the clerk of the court, which is on file with the author.

66. The charges relating to the attack on the Synagogue at Quai Tilsitt, the assassination of Mr. and Mrs. Basch, the arrest, torture, and deportation of Jean de

Filippis and the arrest and deportation of Eliette Meyer and Claude Bloch, and the murder of Lucien Meyer were dismissed.

67. The appellants based their attacks on articles 211, 212, and 593 of the Code of Criminal Procedure, arguing that in evaluating the evidence before them, the judges of the Court of Appeals failed to state proper reasons (or any reasons at all) for reversing the *juge d'instruction* and had thus deprived their decision of a legal basis. The Court of Cassation, finding that the reasons given were neither "insufficient nor contradictory," affirmed. *Touvier IV, supra* note 65, at 11, 13–14, 15, 19–20 (citing the attack on the Synagogue, the Basches, de Fillippis and Meyer/Bloch, respectively).

68. *Touvier IV, supra* note 65, at 47. Of course, the Court of Appeals really did not say this—it, in fact, argued that it was a "French affair." *See supra* note 65, and accompanying text.

69. Judgment of 2 June 1993, Cour d'appel de Versailles, Premiere chambre d'accusation [hereinafter *Touvier V*]. For an analysis of the 2 June indictment, see Sadat Wexler, "Nuremberg Principles," *supra* note 1, at 351–53. Interestingly, the court referred to "governmental *or* state policy of exterminations and persecution" (emphasis added). Query whether this choice of words was deliberate, representing a disagreement with the Court of Cassation, or whether it was unintentional. Because the Court found that Touvier was an accomplice of the Gestapo, it did not address the question of whether the Milice and the Vichy Government could also be so considered. *Touvier V*, at 34.

70. Witnesses (*les témoins*) are called under oath to testify "without hate or fear, and to tell the truth and nothing but the truth." C. Pr. Pén. Art. 331. The defendant and the civil parties (C. Pr. Pén. Art. 331(6)) are not, technically speaking, witnesses at all, however, and do not testify under the witnesses' oath.

71. The press was of course referring to the film *Schindler's List*, which portrayed the efforts by German industrialist Oscar Schindler to save Polish Jews from Hitler's Final Solution.

72. Laurent Greilsamer, "Paul Touvier fait la grève de la mémoire," *Le Monde*, 24 March 1994, at 12 (denies knowing Klaus Barbie in spite of clear evidence to the contrary); Pierre Bois, "Paul Touvier devant les assises des Yvelines: Un chapelet de sourvenirs," *Le Figaro*, 25 March 1994, at 1; Laurent Greilsamer, "Paul Touvier sous les masques du mensonge," *Le Monde*, 25 March 1994 available in LEXIS, NEXIS Library, Monde File (claims his division never arrested anyone because they were Jewish, contradicting extensive evidence proving the opposite).

73. Next to a newspaper clipping by André Frissard, a respected French writer, for example, was the notation "horrible Jewish shopkeeper" ("*sinistre commerçant*

juif"). Laurent Greilsamer, "Les Obsessions antisemites de Paul Touvier," *Le Monde*, 1 April 1994 available in LEXIS, NEXIS Library, Monde File.

74. Laurent Greilsamer, "Provoquant un vif incident d'audience Maître Arno Klarsfeld affirme que Touvier à agi de son propre chef," *Le Monde*, 4 April 1994 available in LEXIS, NEXIS Library, Monde File. Thus he attacked Commissioner Delarue (who had originally asserted that the Gestapo was not involved in the massacre but later on the stand said they were involved), asking him point blank whether he had changed his story under pressure of blackmail for his wartime activities. Mr. Delarue, outraged, responded that he was going to sue Klarsfeld for defamation of character. Another of the civil party lawyers, Ugo Iannucci, loudly disagreed with Klarsfeld, to general applause. Id. Subsequently, Klarsfeld nuanced his position: while convinced that the Gestapo had nothing to do with Rillieux, he stated that did not imply that Touvier's crime had prescribed, because, in his opinion, the entire Milice was an accomplice to the Gestapo. Laurent Greilsamer, "Au Procès de Paul Touvier devant la cour d'assises des Yvelines: La dissidence de Maître Arno Klarsfeld," *Le Monde*, 16 April 1994, at 12. See generally Arno Klarsfeld, *Touvier, Un Crime Français* (Paris: Fayard, 1994).

75. See *supra* note 74.

76. Ultimately, the Jews of Bordeaux captured by French or German authorities would, for the most part, be sent by train from the Mérignac prison camp in the south of France, to a larger prison camp, Drancy, in the north, and finally to Auschwitz, where they would be exterminated.

77. Information regarding the Slitinsky case as well as the other cases involved in the Papon case can be found in the opinion of the Court of Appeals of Bordeaux, Indicting Chamber, Decision of 18 September 1996. *See Papon I, supra* note 2. *See also* Michel Slitinsky, *L'affaire Papon* (Paris: Alain Moreau, 1989).

78. The *arrêt de renvoi* is the functional equivalent of an indictment in a common law system, and is also known by the term *"acte d'accusation."*

79. *Papon II, supra* note 2.

80. The term is Professor Osiel's. Mark J. Osiel, "Ever Again: Legal Remembrance of Administrative Massacre," *University of Pennsylvania Law Review* 144 (1995): 463.

81. The *réquisitoire définitif* that was filed in 1995 gave Papon the benefit of the doubt as to whether he knew the ultimate fate of those he deported from Bordeaux. On this point see Éric Conan, *Le procès Papon: Un journal d'audience* (Paris: Gallimard, 1998): 11, 314.

82. *Papon I, supra* note 2, at 133.

83. *Papon I, supra* note 2, at 140.

84. The court also noted that the order given from London on 8 January 1942, which told French civil servants to remain at their posts but to impede insofar as possible the orders of the German occupants, did not exonerate Papon, for this "*ordre de mobilisation*" could not serve to justify operations resulting in deportations. The Court of Cassation confirmed this holding in its opinion of 23 January 1997.

85. Article 121–7 provides that complicity is accomplished when a person "knowingly (*sciemment*), by aiding or abetting, has facilitated the preparation or consummation [of the crime]." *N. C. Pr. Pén.* (Fr.) 121–27.

86. *Papon II, supra* note 2, note Robert.

87. At least one French scholar strongly disagrees (while nevertheless supporting the solution of the Court in the Papon case because of the particularity of article 6(c) and the ability to impute knowledge in the case of the horrific crimes involved). *Papon II, supra* note 2, at 1997 D. Jur. 147, note by Professor Jean Pradel.

88. Jean-Marc Varaut, *Plaidoirie* (Paris: Plon, 1998).

89. Pascale Nivelle, "Papon ouvre son procès en demandant la liberté," *Libération*, 9 October 1997 (visited 21 May 1998) <http://www.liberation.com/papon/proces 1009.html>; Jean Michel Dumay, "L' État de santé de Maurice Papon pesera sur la suite du procès," *Le Monde*, 11 October 1997; Éric Conan, *Le Procès Papon, Un Journal d'Audience* (Paris: Gallimard, 1998): 12–21.

90. Conan, *supra* note 89, at 317–20.

91. Jean-Michel Dumay and José-Alain Gralon, "Serge Klarsfeld demande la récusation du président Castagnède," *Le Monde*, 30 January 1998, at 7; Jean-Michel Dumay, "Le procès est déstabilisé par la mise en cause du président Castagnède," *Le Monde*, 31 January 1998, at 10; Jean-Michel Dumay, "L'audience reprend son cours, sourde aux remous extérieurs," *Le Monde*, 4 February 1998, at 10.

92. Jean-Michel Dumay, "Maurice Papon convient de l' "anéantissement" vers lequel partaient les déportés," *Le Monde*, 20 December 1997, at 11.

93. To the distress of some of the civil parties, Druon rendered his opinion of the occupation: hunger, cold, knowledge of the camps, but ignorance of the exterminations. If only we had known, he said, the Jews could have left rather than waiting like sacrificial lambs. Jean-Michel Dumay, "Les derniers témoignanges des partisans de Maurice Papon," *Le Monde*, 24 October 1997.

94. Jean-Michel Dumay, "Vingt ans de réclusion criminelle sont requis contre Maurice Papon," *Le Monde*, 21 March 1998; Pascale Nivelle, "Tout ça pour announcer vingt ans. . . ," *Libération*, 21 March 1998.

95. Daniel Schneidermann, *Lé Trange procés* (Paris: Fayard, 1998).

96. Anne Chemin and Jean-Michel Dumay, "764 questions posées à la cour et aux jurés," *Le Monde*, 2 April 1998, at 10.

97. Craig R. Whitney, "10-Year Term Ordered for War Crimes," *International Herald Tribune*, 3 April 1998, at 1.

98. Jean-Marc Varaut bitterly denounced the verdict. Varaut, *supra* note 87 at 7—18.

99. Jean-Michel Dumay, "Pourquoi moi? D'un coupable désigné, deviendrais-je un symbole nécessaire?," *Le Monde*, 3 April 1998, at 7.

100. "Switzerland Returns Former Vichy Official to Prison in France," *St. Louis Post-Dispatch*, 23 October 1999, at 3.

101. Robert H. Jackson, *The Nuremberg Case* (New York: Cooper Square, 1971): 94

102. Laurent Greilsamer, "Le Procès de Paul Touvier devant la cour d'assises des Yvelines: 'mon père. Lui, on ne l'a pas jugé,' " *Le Monde*, 10 April 1994, at 13.

103. See, e.g., Prosecutor Jean-Paul Akayesu, Judgment, Trial Chamber of the International Criminal Tribunal for Rwanda, ¶¶ 569—76, 2 September 1998, discussing the Barbie and Touvier cases; Prosecutor Duško Tadi, Opinion and Judgment, International May 1997, discussing French jurisprudence as to discriminatory intent and persecution crimes, and adopting French holdings, *reversed in part* by Prosecutor Duško Tadi, Judgment, Appeals Chamber of the International Criminal Tribunal for the former Yugoslavia, 15 July 1999.

Part II

PAPON'S TRIAL FOR CRIMES

AGAINST HUMANITY

AN INTERVIEW WITH

MAURICE PAPON

Libération, 6 March 1996

Annette Lévy-Willard

"I am the scapegoat in a political plot."
Papon reveals his defense to *Libération*:
he was only a minor official and a "powerless onlooker."

A. L.-W.: The Maurice Papon investigation began fifteen years ago. Do you think your trial will ever take place?

M.P.: I know that I have nothing for which to blame myself. Just the opposite. I did things which, if they had been known about at the time, would have put me in a [German] cell. My conscience is absolutely clear. In spite of many disillusionments and disappointments, I have confidence in the legal institutions of my country. If they judge me according to the law, a dismissal is inevitable. If the political factor enters into it, anything is possible.

A. L.-W.: You were first with the Ministry of the Interior, then at Vichy, then secretary-general of the Gironde prefecture. What did you know about the anti-Semitic policies of Vichy?

M.P.: There were the famous 1940 laws on the status of Jews. In Bordeaux, to point out an example, a brilliant young law professor called Maurice Duverger,[1] declared, "At bottom, this distinction between the Jews and others is legitimate, this public law does have validity." That's all I knew about it.

A. L.-W.: However, you personally carried out this policy.

M.P.: I was secretary-general of the prefecture with an appointed prefect above me and still higher up a regional prefect, Maurice Sabatier. It was a very minor, low-profile position, a post in which one carried out orders. The chief of administrative bureaus has no responsibility for policy, he directs the departments, the personnel, and budget allocations. Why should this low-level secretary-general be taken to task in this way? Because, after the war, he made an exceptional career for himself and for that he was never pardoned.

A. L.-W.: Or because documents, signed by Maurice Papon, were found which organized roundups and deportations? Like the one of 3 July 1942, entitled "The Arrest of Jews," organizing the arrest "of Jews of both sexes under the auspices of the French police," who were to be held and then "sent to an unknown destination."

M.P.: You must understand what kind of documents those were. They were not orders; they were reports. Is this participation? For example, there was a handwritten note, dated 24 August 1942, about a telephone communication received from the Paris delegation of the interior minister, the famous Mr. Leguay.[2] Leguay had been in contact with the director of the office of the regional prefect on the very subject of the roundup of the Jews. Unable to find him, Leguay called me. And I, let me repeat, in a passive way, made a note of his communication. I immediately sent it to the regional prefect. Why was it handwritten? Because, for me, it was a matter of seconds. Waiting an hour would have been too slow to react. I didn't bother about getting a stenographer and I sent it on to Mr. Sabatier. I was only a telephone operator in this affair.

A. L.-W.: But you were responsible for the Department of Jewish Affairs [at the prefecture in Bordeaux].

M.P.: There were two completely separate departments, the Commissariat-General of Jewish Affairs of Xavier Vallat [and later under the direction of Darquier de Pellepoix], which had both regional and local representatives charged with overseeing the fate of the Jews. And, at the prefecture, along with the departments of supplies and of fuel, there was the "Administration of Jewish Affairs." This office was purely administrative and its purpose was simply to keep tabs on what was happening, to receive Jews in difficulty and provide for their needs. When the police, or the Germans themselves, arrested the Jews, they most often penned them up in the synagogue, and the chief rabbi wasn't able to feed them. At those times we mobilized the supplies division and furnished blankets for them. Those unfortunate ones often spent several nights like that.

A. L.-W.: The prosecution's indictment holds you responsible for the departure of four convoys which took the Jews of Bordeaux to Drancy, then to Auschwitz . . .

M.P.: We didn't know about Auschwitz, but we did know about Drancy. I have the feeling that these assertions were added to the indictment at the last minute, that they were quite improvised, and that they won't hold up legally. Take the convoy of 1944. At the time, the Germans did not use the French police anymore because they had found out for certain that they were being deceived, that the people were being warned. . . . They carried out their operations themselves. The prefecture was presented with the fait accompli. We were helpless onlookers.

A. L.-W.: And the three other 1942 convoys?

M.P.: I don't know what I'm being blamed for. That claim comes from notes of reports with the address of the prefect responsible for it. Legally, that won't hold. There are two things I did do that I am proud of. I claim them even though they are the two things my adversaries hold against me. At first, I managed to replace the *Feldgendarmerie*, which was escorting the convoys, with French police. Afterwards, the Germans did it themselves.

The rabbi begged us to do this because the *Feldgendarmerie* hit these poor Jews with rifle butts to make them get in cattle cars. He said, and it made good sense, "At least with French police, my religious brothers will be sheltered from these brutalities." Later, I replaced the cattle cars with passenger cars, on one occasion.

A. L.-W.: From 1942 on, you knew, through one of your subordinates, that Drancy was only a stopping place, that the internees were deported in the direction of Germany. What did you do?

M.P.: He didn't reveal the destination, only the fact that they had been deported. Absolutely no one knew it. I discovered it when Churchill talked about it at the time of the Liberation. My margin of maneuver at the time? There was a registry, naturally of Jews, which the Germans had had since 1941. The list had been compiled by the UGIF,[3] and by the chief rabbi. Secretly, and day by day, I struck out the names in such a way that the day the Germans rounded up or arrested Jews. . . . The maneuver was discovered by the Commissariat-General of Jewish Affairs, which was headed first by Xavier Vallat, then by Darquier de Pellepoix. I was denounced by the local representative, which caused an uproar. An analysis by the experts made it clear that I had removed 139 Jews from the list.

A. L.-W.: After the war, did you inquire about what had become of those Jewish families from Bordeaux that you had turned over to the Germans?

M.P.: In 1945 I had already left Bordeaux. I believe that—alas, alas, as General de Gaulle said—after the Liberation, no one was preoccupied with the fate of these poor people.

A. L.-W.: Isn't it time to put Vichy on trial, a government that had collaborated in the deportation of French Jews?

M.P.: If you put Vichy on trial, I would find nothing wrong with that. In fact, I see only advantages, but I wouldn't want to see this trial take place on my head. The secretary-general of the Gironde prefecture did not govern all of France. Those in high places were wrong to concede the cooperation of French police to the Germans . . . as a matter of policy, I myself would never have done it. But if you compare this to what happened elsewhere, all the evidence shows that the regime of Marshal Pétain, during a certain period, unfortunately it was not until the end, saved France from the outright horrors that swooped down on countries such as Holland. You cannot avoid the fact that, in daily activities, the intervention of certain French officials, under certain circumstances, lessened the hardships. I am not a Vichy defender. No one claims that and no one questions my being a good member of the Resistance. Why was I a member? Because I had an innate feeling for my country.

A. L.-W.: President Chirac has officially recognized the French government's responsibility in the deportation of Jews. Do you feel you are being targeted?

M.P.: No, I don't need to assume responsibility for that. I understand very well that Chirac did make that statement. But he was speaking of the policy level and not of government agencies. There is no unintentional blurring of government agencies with government policy.

A. L.-W.: Why do you present yourself as a victim?

M.P.: This affair has been dormant for nearly forty years. The problem of deporting Jews was uncovered around 1975 or 1980. A political trial was called for so they created one for me. If an unknown government worker had been chosen, the crowd would not have been stirred up. But Maurice Papon had been prefect of Constantine, prefect of Corsica, a minister and deputy for thirteen years. I was in the spotlight. It is a political trial whose inspiration is not entirely French. Part of it comes from abroad. In fact, Mr. Klarsfeld is a paid worker for the American organization created by German Jews who are naturalized Americans, whose transatlantic propaganda has always been to prevent Germany from being sole defendant in this completely unacceptable trial about the eradication of the Jewish race.

A. L.-W.: What American organization?

M.P.: The ADL, the Anti-Defamation League.[4] These people have participated largely by giving money.

A. L.-W.: Why would they want to "rehabilitate" Germany?

M.P.: To reduce German responsibility by having the French share in it. I am the scapegoat, but this political plot has almost nothing to do with me. Don't you think that it hurts me to be associated with Touvier, an assassin, with Bousquet, who was responsible for policy? I am a kind of expiatory victim for the evils of our age.

ANALYSIS BY ANNETTE LÉVY-WILLARD

The "Serenity" of an Ambitious Man
Without remorse, Papon minimizes his role and does not hesitate to lie.

At eighty-five, Maurice Papon, seems to have a clear conscience. He is a French official whose career has been punctuated by dramatic events—1,600 Jews, including 240 children deported from Bordeaux while he was secretary-general of the prefecture, 200 Algerian bodies recovered from the Seine on 17 October 1961, and nine dead, crushed against the bars of the Charonne metro station during a demonstration against the Algerian war on 8 February 1962 when Papon was chief of the Paris police.

In spite of documents, signed "Maurice Papon," organizing roundups and the deportations of Jews, in spite of lists of Jews to be arrested furnished to the Germans by his departments (and not by the UGIF as he claims in the accompanying interview), in spite of the Jewish children whom the prefecture took away from sheltering families in order to send them to their deaths, this man is "serene."

The serenity of a government official, neither pro-Nazi nor pro-Vichy, a civil servant who never questions himself. Anyone else would have performed duties just as he did, and less well, he declares, as he points out his positive actions and his participation in the Resistance (beginning in 1943 when a German defeat became obvious). And he minimizes his role at the prefecture as he rewrites history. "I only wrote reports," he explained to justify the directives from the prefecture for the hunting down of Jews by the French police in Bordeaux. This is a new tactic of his defense. He originally claimed the documents were false in the opening days of the investigation.

Another lie, "No one knew what the deportations meant," was repeated for a long time by those who collaborated with the Germans. However, the meaning was clear in the Nazi literature and in the anti-Semitic policies of Pétain. In the case of Papon, the lie is even more flagrant since it was disproved in the investigator's notes by the unique testimony from Marie Reille, a Catholic deported to Auschwitz by mistake in the convoy of 23 September 1942 and later liberated. She returned to the prefecture to tell them of the horrors of the camp.

Maurice Papon will not allow himself to be accused of human rights crimes as was Paul Touvier, the Milice murderer. He also refuses to be compared to René Bousquet (shot down in 1993 by a deranged gunman), the chief of Vichy police who agreed to having the French police arrest, jail, and put on trains to Auschwitz all the foreign Jews who had taken refuge in France as well as their

French children. However, he does share with Bousquet a thirst for power, the assurance of those who had a brilliant career after the war, and the certainty that he has served France. And this without ever, ever having spoken a word or made a single gesture toward those innocent families who were murdered.

Like Bousquet, he was not disturbed about the future of these people who were herded together at Drancy and later deported toward "the East." Like Bousquet, he did not go to see, did not take part in the roundups, was not confronted with the stares [of the victims], but [instead] restricted himself to signing the papers and passing on the orders. And again like Bousquet, he did not hesitate to put on the trains, alone, children not yet five years old, whose parents were already dead.

And now, from the "neutral" mask of the conscientious government official, a strange discourse emerges in which we hear that the exclusion of Jews from French life was not so shocking when even the eminent jurist Maurice Duverger saw a legal foundation for it. Curiously, the eighty-five-year-old official who so willingly identifies himself with France now takes up once again the traditional anti-Semitic terminology, speaking of his trial as a Jewish-American plot. And of course, involving money.

NOTES

1. Maurice Duverger, 78, former law professor, had, in 1941, discussed in the *Revue de droit public et de sciences politiques* (vol. 57) the first laws passed by Vichy excluding Jews from holding public office.

2. Jean Leguay, representative in the Occupied Zone of the secretary-general of the national police, René Bousquet, from May 1942 to January 1944. Accused of crimes against humanity on 12 March 1979, he died on 2 July 1989, without having been brought to trial.

3. Union générale des Israélites de France, created 29 November 1941 by a decree encouraged by the Germans, charged with representing the Jewish community in its entirety under the Occupation. It was dissolved 12 September 1944.

4. An international association created in the United States in 1913 in reaction to anti-Semitic demonstrations that were breaking out in Europe. It is an offspring of B'nai B'rith, a Jewish organization founded in 1843 to defend human rights.

VICHY

ON TRIAL

The *New York Times*, 16 October 1997

Robert O. Paxton

FINALLY, FRANCE CONFRONTS ITS NAZI SHADOW

F ifty years is a long time to wait to bring a World War II collaborator to justice. But France has finally put Maurice Papon, secretary-general of the Gironde prefecture in Bordeaux during the Vichy regime, on trial. He is charged with crimes against humanity for organizing the arrest of nearly 1,600 Jews during World War II and arranging for their transport to a transit camp in Drancy, a Paris suburb. From there, the Nazis took them to Auschwitz.

It was remarkable to see Mr. Papon, now eighty-seven years old, take the stand yesterday in his own defense. But as someone scheduled to testify as an expert witness, I find it more remarkable that this trial is happening at all. Mr. Papon represents a part of French society—the administrative elite—that largely escaped scrutiny for its actions during World War II.

At the close of the war, France punished many Nazi collaborators: 9,000 were summarily executed during the liberation campaign, 1,500 were executed after a trial, and 40,000 were sentenced to prison.

The French, however, concentrated on the most visible collaborators, like members of Vichy's "Milice," a parapolice squad. In general, civil servants and businessmen who had cooperated with the Germans on a day-to-day basis were spared punishment, because they also claimed to have worked for the French Resistance.

In reality, the Vichy government helped the Nazis. In 1940 the Nazis wanted only to dump German Jews into unoccupied France. Yet the Vichy government went further and registered its Jews, excluded them from jobs, and forced many foreign Jews into camps. By 1942, when the Nazis began their extermination program, the French Jews were vulnerable.

After the war, the government decided to continue the myth that nearly all French citizens supported the Resistance, because it desperately needed the Vichy civil servants to help revive France's crippled government and economy. General Charles de Gaulle hesitated to hand such responsibilities over to Resistance heroes, many of whom were Communists and better with dynamite than with budgets.

Attitudes began to change after the student demonstrations of 1968. The students, who were protesting the Vietnam War and the bourgeois establishment, also began to question their parents' role in the war. In 1970, *The Sorrow and the Pity*, a documentary by Marcel Ophuls, vividly portrayed a France more collaborationist than resistant.

By then, Jewish survivors, who in 1945 had preferred not to call attention to themselves, decided to tell their stories. And new archival research proved that Vichy France was the only Western European country under Nazi occupation that enacted its own measures against Jews.

But this evidence wasn't enough to persuade French leaders to bring Vichy officials to trial. In the 1980s they quietly blocked cases against Vichy officials from proceeding. For example, President François Mitterrand delayed the prosecution of René Bousquet, the police chief most responsible for official French assistance to the Nazis. Mr. Mitterrand preferred to sidestep the issue, having himself (like so many others) served the Vichy regime before joining the Resistance.

It took a new generation of French leaders to let the trials proceed. The changing of the guard took place with the election of Jacques Chirac as president in 1995. Soon after his inauguration, Mr. Chirac, who was only twelve years old in 1944, publicly recognized the state's responsibility in abetting the deportation of Jews. A majority of French people are finally ready for justice to be done.

"TODAY, EVERYTHING CONVERGES

ON THE HAUNTING

MEMORY OF VICHY"

An Interview with Pierre Nora

Le Monde, 1 October 1997

Nicolas Weill and Robert Solé

R.S. and N.W.: As an historian of the impact and the memory of Vichy, doesn't Vichy seem to you to have a unique destiny as shown once again by the Maurice Papon trial? The more time passes, the more this memory seems to deepen, to weigh more and more heavily on the collective conscience. How do you explain this?

P.N.: Indeed a strange story, this wound that festers instead of healing. It obviously cannot be explained by only one cause, but rather by a constellation of events that have resounded for thirty years. To be more precise, Vichy—I mean the memory of it—seems to me to be at the intersection of two important phenomena, apparently independent, which have influenced each other: the creation of a special Jewish identity, and the creation of an identity belonging to one generation whose beginning was marked by the events of May 1968.

We forget too often that these are two worldwide phenomena even though each one does have French characteristics. Also, the two phenomena are contemporary, 1967–1968. It is clear that at that moment the procedures were put in place that continue to stir up painful memories.

In my opinion, it all began with the Six-Day War, when the specter, quickly dissipated but disturbing, of a second holocaust suddenly revived the reality of the first one. The wave of emotion for Israel set in motion a lengthy movement by French Jews to rediscover a religious, cultural, historic space that had been obliterated by assimilation "*à la francaise.*"

Although the movement was worldwide, it was particularly strong in France, probably because Jews have a special rapport with this country whose most important moments have also been key dates in their own destiny. Let's not forget that France was the first country to emancipate them, in 1791. It was also the country of the Dreyfus affair, with its effect on the birth of Zionism. Because of this overlapping, the scandal of the Vichy exclusion was felt even more violently.

This awakening of a community conscience has actually nothing particularly French or Jewish about it. It is a general movement of identity reaffirmation of all the minorities moving toward emancipation—women, workers, Corsicans, etcetera.

R.S. and N.W.: Don't you think that the movement you're talking about also has older roots?

P.N.: It is likely that what prepared the ground, in the case of French Jews, was the massive return, beginning in 1962, of French citizens from Algeria. The arrival of the North African Jews, who were much closer to religious practices and traditions, helped to give a true sense of "community" to a group without a communal identity, thus breaking with the habits of consistorial Judaism that demanded that one be Jewish in the synagogue and in the family, but not in the street or in public life. Besides this, on the level of memory and the imaginary, we could believe that Algerian Jews returned armed with a feeling of abandonment that they transferred onto Vichy and that, as Algerian French, they had very good reason to feel. This is unprovable but likely.

R.S. and N.W.: Hasn't the irruption into the public arena of the question of the genocide of the Jews played a role in the crystallizing of the memory of Vichy, especially after the Eichmann trial that opened in April of 1961?

P.N.: We must take into account, certainly, that the Shoah took a more and more central place, even that of an originator, in the forming of a Jewish identity. There again, it is a question of a worldwide movement beginning in the sixties. The Shoah became a pillar of a new type of secular religion. Three days before the Six-Day War, a meeting took place in New York organized by the journal *Judaism,* an important symposium with Rabbi Fackenheim,

George Steiner, and especially Elie Wiesel, who played a very important role. For the first time there was a discussion of "Jewish values after the Holocaust."

Why at that particular moment? It is understandable that it took a certain amount of time after having endured it to look for the meaning of such a monstrous event. The nearness and the enormity of the shock favors two kinds of explanations: a secular explanation, which finds the cause of the phenomenon in the human era and in history, and a theological one, which, for better or for worse, finds it in the tragic stigma of the chosen. The two versions are radically opposed to each other, but they can, in a strange way, exist together. The Shoah works in the direction of a double demand for historical enlightenment and moral strictness. It has made Judaism powerful historically in making itself sacred. It has emphasized the ethical dimension, which goes in tandem with the contemporary generalization of human rights, a post-1960s ideology that becomes more and more powerful in the seventies and eighties. This human rights ideology is very important in understanding the current fixation on Vichy.

R.S. and N.W.: Would you say, then, that Vichy seems a perfect countermodel of what you call the "ideology of human rights"? In other words, that the reinforcement of the memory of the Occupation is in proportion to the sensitizing of ethical questions?

P.N.: Certainly. Law and ethics are linked in the idea of human rights, and Vichy was its negation and the crime against humanity is its symmetrical counterpart. There again, the tendency is universal. In addition, from 1962 to 1965 a major event took place without which we would be unable to understand how a purely Jewish memory—in this case, Shoah—had such reverberations. I'm speaking of Vatican II. In lifting the opprobrium that weighed on the Jews, the council, in great part, permitted the launching of the idea of Christian responsibility in the Shoah.

So much so that the moment corresponded, in France, to the crumbling of the Gaullist version of the "unanimity" of the Resistance, a collapse that began in 1971 with the scandal that surrounded the film *The Sorrow and the Pity,* of Marcel Ophuls, followed by the revelation of Vichy's responsibility first recognized in Robert Paxton's book *Vichy France* (Seuil, 1973) and continued with the Touvier affair. Between a growing Christian guilt and the fading of the notion of the "unanimity" version of the Resistance, the way was open to questioning the direct or indirect responsibility of Vichy in the Final Solution.

The end of Marxism-Leninism has also evidently played a role in this configuration. It opened the way to an explanation of history that includes individuals and their personal responsibilities. The coincidence is striking between the intellectual defeat of Marxism and the explosion in the late seventies of the Darquier de Pellepoix affair, a former commissioner-general of Jewish affairs, followed by that of René Bousquet, secretary-general of Laval's police force, and Jean Leguay, his representative in the Occupied Zone.

There is a sort of fatality that led to this questioning of Vichy that was not possible in previous years. And if a study is not done of the path memory took in arriving at this point, it is impossible to understand why, more than fifty years after the fact, we are still there!

R.S. and N.W.: You belong to a generation—that of the fifties—which came of age after the war, but before the memory of Vichy occupied the place in the collective conscience that it does today. How would you judge this "silence" that you believe was broken at the end of the sixties? Didn't it have certain advantages?

P.N.: Actually, I belong to an intermediate generation between, let's say, the one of Aron and Berl and that of Modiano and Finkielkraut, the generation of '68. Besides the advantages or disadvantages of silence, another explanation is necessary. This period, in which there was not so much talk of Shoah—the use of this word came later, it dates from the 1985 Claude Lanzmann film—or of Vichy, was a time of a memory that was either combative or shattering. I remember that in 1945, when I was thirteen, my father showed me the photos of the camps that he had gotten from a Communist journalist who had just died at the Rothschild Hospital. I was devastated by them. But that was a rather normal way of fulfilling the classic Franco-Judaic contract. French Jews themselves considered their suffering or persecution as a contribution to a patriotic and national sacrifice. And much time and many things were necessary, beginning with the creation and consolidation of the state of Israel, for a man like me to find myself, on the morning of 6 May 1967, at the Israeli embassy and on 12 May in Tel Aviv.

R.S. and N.W.: Do you think that this memory can sometimes bring about a distortion of the historical reality established by the historians?

P.N.: Yes. This coming together of phenomena is, for example, the source of the feeling prevalent today in public opinion that there was no Purge. But the Purge certainly did take place. It was very violent, but at the very moment when the historians were continually revising the figures upward, the collective conscience was erasing them more and more. Why this strange reaction? Because a purge of specifically anti-Semitic persecution did not take place, a separate grief was not recognized at the time of the Liberation nor even felt as such by the Jews themselves. Everyone had good reasons to participate in this general erasure, from Communists to Gaullists. And even more so, the judges of the Purge, with their own dose of ordinary anti-Semitism that Vatican II had not yet ruled against.

This is a recent perception, with all that that implies, about the rereading of Western history. Take for example, in 1949, the trial of René Bousquet, responsible for the Vel d'hiv roundup. All the elements for a charge of a crime against humanity converge here, and yet no one thought about it. The problem certainly exists, but it exists in retrospect. It is true that France came out of the Second World War in an ambiguous situation, half victor, half victim. The management of this ambiguity has never been easy.

The treatment of this memory by those in power could even be called disastrous, and this has not been unimportant in the reactions of the public. Let's go back again to 1967. The statements of de Gaulle about "a people sure of itself and master of its destiny" [about the Israelis], opened the way. We watched Raymond Aron's first and only pronouncement on the Jewish question (the year of publication of his *de Gaulle, Israel and the Jews*), and also the publication of Patrick Modiano's *La Place de l'Étoile*, a typical novel of the generation of '68 and which was also Jewish. After de Gaulle and his version of a country united around the Resistance, historically in error but politically constructive and accurate, came Pompidou and Touvier, then Giscard d'Estaing, who understood nothing about the problem and saw Israel from a Jordanian viewpoint, displaying a provocative indifference to the attack on the rue Copernic synagogue in 1980. Those in power had not become conscious of the singularity of the tragedy and the memory it carried with it. The arrival of François Mitterrand appeared to calm the waters until his friendship with Bousquet was revealed, which once again compromised everything. And the last years of Mitterrand's presidency themselves poisoned the atmosphere to the extent that the "purge" [accomplished by Jacques Chirac's] 16 July 1995 speech was a real relief. The Papon trial seems a logical conclusion to this declaration which finally recognized the mistakes committed by the state in the persecution of the Jews. Jacques Chirac's declaration did perhaps choose what it wanted from historical truth, but it had the merit of letting in a little fresh air.

R.S. and N.W.: Do you think that a trial like Papon's is a good way to clarify the memory of the Shoah, especially for future generations?

P.N.: There is no way of knowing. It's hard not to ask oneself what pedagogical results we can expect from a trial already lost by the defendant, and without taking into account the catastrophic results that, inversely, would be those of a "bungling," as was the case in the late eighties with the Demjanjuk trial, when Demjanjuk was suspected of being one of the murderers of the Treblinka extermination camp. These are long-term effects. The Eichmann trial did not produce in Israel the results its organizers expected. In addition, today a new generation wants to revise the judgment of the preceding one. In France, too, we need a little critical distance as well.

R.S. and N.W.: Is the Papon trial different from recent trials for crimes against humanity?

P.N.: The Papon trial is unique. Certainly it is an action taken against a man for what he did. But since Papon was a rather unimportant link in the French administration, the responsibility of the Vichy government in the Holocaust is also being judged. A criminal as such is not the only thing that is being tried here, as was the case with Barbie or Touvier. Papon is a double substitute for Bousquet and Jean Leguay, who are both dead.

Moreover, insofar as it is a question of Vichy's anti-Jewish policy, there is a tendency to mix in an identical perspective two radically different aspects. Papon is being judged for participation in the Final Solution, a by-product of the state's policy of collaboration. As horrible as the consequences of this policy were, it was put into action by individuals like Bousquet, like Laval, even like Papon himself, who were not especially anti-Semitic, in any case no more so than the average Frenchman of the times.

The other dimension, the "motu proprio" policy of Vichy, which instituted the anti-Jewish Statutes in 1940 and 1941, derives from something completely different from the collaboration. Here we are engaged in a settling of scores between the French themselves, whose source must be looked for in an antidemocratic movement that goes back to the thirties, to the Dreyfus affair, to the entire nineteenth century, and, finally, to a counterrevolutionary France. Maurras, following the outcome of his trial in 1945, did not say, "It is the revenge of Auschwitz" but, "It is the revenge of Dreyfus." Whether or not Vichy's policy of exclusion prepared the policy of extermination is open to discussion. Nevertheless, it remains that only the result of a retrospective alignment accounts for the confusion of the two kinds of policies. It must also be pointed out that, in fact, only the fate of Jews brings the charge of a crime against humanity. That led inevitably to an overestimation of the anti-Jewish policy of Vichy. Now, if the anti-Semitic policy is one dimension of the Vichy regime, it isn't the only one, and, no doubt, not the principal one.

In the Papon trial, behind the issue of collaboration in the extermination, the policy of exclusion is also being targeted. The anti-Jewish Statutes strike more at the older generation. The new generation is more sensitive to the policy of extermination.

R.S. and N.W.: Do you mean that Maurice Papon is not the most representative of those accused?

P.N.: As an individual, the countenance of Maurice Papon is displeasing in every way, his political personality includes what was worst in all the governments, it contains everything that encourages antisocialism, anti-Vichyism, anti-Gaullism, and anti-Mitterrandism. His personal haughtiness excludes any kind of compassion—a compassion that he himself never permitted himself to feel, to say the least. It goes along with the cruelty he later showed as chief of police when he allowed Algerians to be thrown into the Seine during the demonstration of October 1961. Later on, Papon was also the budget minister, "Mr. Taxes!" Also in his career maneuvering he represented everything the young generations are likely to despise, a sort of technocratic nomenklatura. But finally, this will be the last trial of this kind because there are no more adversaries. Will it really turn the page on the "Vichy syndrome," as it is called by its best analyst, Henry Rousso? We can certainly ask ourselves this question.

R.S. and N.W.: Will your explanation of the memory of Vichy last even though the last witnesses of that period grow old and die?

P.N.: It is difficult to say at present if, one day, Vichy will be like the quarrel of the Armagnacs and the Bourguignons, which ended by losing its acuteness, or if, instead, the scars left by Vichy will remain deep. In any case, right now the obsession with the Papon trial has come to a kind of pause. Everything today is converging on the obsessive memory of Vichy. Novelists like Marc Lambron or Lydie Salvayre,[1] who must be in their forties, are haunted by it to the point of hallucination. This is truly the "Bousquet Generation." The problem is that moral judgments imply a total manicheanism in the way we look at the period.

R.S. and N.W.: How should a historian act since his role is to explain and understand?

P.N.: There is a general confusion today between judges and historians as to their proper roles. The historians have too much of a tendency to act as judges, even supreme judges. Certainly, calling historians into the courtroom is absolutely legitimate. Furthermore, I understand perfectly that the complexity of contemporary history calls for clarifications for the general public. But there is a limit to the historian's expertise. As professionals, we should, I think, ask ourselves about our ethics.

It seems to me that this abusive expertise began in the columns of *Le Monde*, in 1979, on the subject of negationism, and against which a certain number of my most respected colleagues, nonspecialists of the period, circulated a petition aimed at banning, on principle, the questioning of certain accepted truths. Even though I shared their point of view on negationism, I did not at the time associate myself with this effort.

There is certainly a historian-judge, I think. But in wanting too much to become, as Chateaubriand put it, the instrument of "the revenge of the people," there is a risk of becoming the prosecutor. This must be avoided because it increases the risk that we historians might appear to be the "paparazzi of the past."

NOTE

1. Nora refers here to Marc Lambron's *1941* and Lydie Salvayre's *Le Campagnie des spectres*.

"THOSE WHO ORGANIZED

THE TRAINS KNEW

THERE WOULD BE DEATHS"

An Interview with Robert O. Paxton

Libération, 3 October 1997

Annette Lévy-Willard and Béatrice Vallaeys

A. L.-W.: Are you surprised that the [French Catholic] church is now asking for forgiveness for its silence during the war?

R.P.: This is a time of asking for pardons. President Reagan asked for forgiveness from the Japanese-Americans who had been imprisoned during the war. Native Hawaians were asked for forgiveness, the king of Spain asked for a pardon from the Arabs for the 1492 crusade. The time of pardons has arrived and it is a good thing for the general population.

A. L.-W.: In the 1970s, when you wrote *Vichy France: Old Guard and New Order,* did you think we would one day arrive at this? A president of the republic [Jacques Chirac] who publicly admits the state's responsibility in the deportation of the Jews of France? With a Papon trial taking place next week?

R.P.: Certainly not. In 1970 the French were not much interested in Vichy. At the time, my book had been refused by an editor—before being accepted by Le Seuil—who explained to me, "It's a good book for the Americans but it won't interest the French." Looking back, we now know that 1970–72 marked a turning point in the acknowledgment by the French of what had happened with the Marcel Ophuls film *The Sorrow and the Pity* and the young generation of 1968 demanding explanations from their parents. A new generation may arrive to call this questioning only excessive moral puritanism and an obsession, but right now there is intense interest in it. We must also understand that the Jews who survived are preoccupied with the idea that they will die without the whole story being told. Perhaps the Papon trial will bring a close to this chapter of France's history.

A. L.-W.: Is the myth that Vichy was a protective "shield" against the Germans permanently buried?

R.P.: This myth is a little shaken but it still persists. Not among historians, but the idea remains widespread that Pétain and de Gaulle were both necessary to protect the French from the worst, and that they succeeded in this. The idea that Vichy's only purpose was to ward off German blows had been carefully cultivated by Pétain and was devised at a precise moment, in August 1944, and again during his trial, when Pétain said, "I was a shield and de Gaulle was the sword." Obviously this idea corresponds to the wishes of a majority of the French during the Occupation. They hoped it was true and that there was collusion between the two men.

Now, the real goal of Vichy was not to ward off German attacks. At times the Vichy officials did say no to certain German demands. For example, they refused to let the Germans use the French military bases in North Africa in July 1940. Later, in the summer of 1942, when it was more difficult to say no, Vichy opposed forcing the Jews in the Unoccupied Zone to wear the yellow star and Laval refused to order the denaturalization of the Jews. But these few refusals mask the true objectives of Vichy, whose main goal was to change French traditions and install a more traditional and conservative anti–Popular Front kind of government. Vichy also hoped that France would have an important place in a Europe dominated by the Germans, as the principal colonial and maritime power, a more promising future than that offered by an Allied victory. These two objectives are at the heart of the Vichy regime, and they reinforced each other in such a way as to implicate France in an active participation in the difficult tasks of the Occupation, such as the struggle against the Resistance, the seizure of Jewish property, the arrest of Jews, and the function of French police acting at the side of the Germans. To achieve these two goals, the sovereignty of the state had to be maintained.

A. L.-W.: Another myth that never dies: the French government would never on its own initiative have instated the anti-Jewish Statutes that deprived them of their rights as citizens and excluded them from public life.

R.P.: Most French citizens still believe today that the Germans demanded it, but a study of German documents proves the opposite and even that the Germans themselves did not want it. Their policy at that time was to expel the German Jews to other countries. Moreover, during the entire autumn of 1940 they sent trainloads of German Jews into France in an attempt to make unoccupied France a "dumping ground for Jews."

It is true that, on 28 September 1940, the Germans had prepared a decree in preparation for measures to exclude the Jews in the Occupied Zone. The documents clearly show that the Germans were in a hurry to have this decree passed because they had gotten wind of the fact that Vichy was preparing its own anti-Jewish statutes and they were determined to be the first. But the law adopted by Vichy went further and this decision came from within the government and was not imposed on it by the Germans.

A. L.-W.: So the Vichy government had its own ideology?

R.P.: It was a continuation of the anti-Semitism of the thirties. At the end of the First World War, anti-Semitism was declining, but it reappeared with the waves of refugee immigrants and with the unemployment and the unsettled atmosphere surrounding the Popular Front. The climate of the thirties is difficult to recreate, but it was at that time that the talk began about a Jewish problem, and the defeat exacerbated these feelings. Many were looking for a scapegoat and claimed that the Jews had dragged France into war against Germany and that the decadence of France in the final years of the thirties came from the presence of foreigners and Jews in the culture, in the literature, the cinema, and all these "cosmopolitan" influences had weakened French will. The idea of a "rebirth" implied a "purification."

A. L.-W.: Members of the government who had sworn allegiance to Pétain could not ignore his program. Did they agree with these policies or were they signing the papers as a matter of procedure?

R.P.: I think the atmosphere of the thirties had prepared them for it. With the rupture of defeat came the disappearance of the politics of the left, and the nationalists were installed. Very few officials left the government. Jews, Masons, and Communists were excluded from public functions, the others remained and accepted the application of the anti- Jewish Statutes. It was very rare to see a government official resign from his job. I have one example, General Robert de Saint-Vincent, regional commander at Grenoble, who in August 1942 refused to mobilize his troops to accompany the deportation of Jews. He was removed and forced to retire. This courageous act was punished, but not very seriously. He was neither hanged nor executed for disobeying orders. But that was rare. In the government one is taught positive law and not natural law. The law is the law.

In 1973 I wrote a little schematically, "Vichy was everyone in 1940, and no one in 1944. De Gaulle was almost no one in 1940, and everyone in 1944." French historians who have since had access to prefecture reports and other documents have modified this analysis. But I continue to believe that Vichy was favored by a vast majority in 1940. There were few enthusiastic collaborators and few armed and active resistants, but a large majority who tried to get along and worried about questions of survival.

A. L.-W.: Why were almost all the government officials kept on by de Gaulle?

R.P.: First of all, the Purge struck at men of words (journalists, commentators, intellectuals, artists) much harder because the courts had published documents at their disposal. For the others, there was little time to search the archives for material.

At the time of the Liberation, France was living through a very grave crisis. Living conditions were even more difficult than during the war and the first winter was a cold one. In the middle of such a crisis, all the institutions of Vichy were kept in place, often under other names, for technical reasons. There was a personnel problem because the important Resistance fighters who emerged from the maquis with pistols still in their hands were not able to replace the civil servants and the system had to continue.

A. L.-W.: Can we say that Papon's career was one of an "important civil servant" in the same way that Mitterrand's was one of a "French youth"?[1]

R.P.: Mitterrand's course of action was typical of the majority of French civil servants. At first they agreed to become civil servants in the Vichy government, and then, in 1942, they began to have doubts. Some joined the Resistance, and many others at least had Gaullist sympathies by 1944. As a participant in the Maurice Papon trial, I can't say more than that, but I can quote myself. In *Vichy France and the Jews*, Michael Marrus and I tried to find out up until what moment the French police participated in arresting Jews. The last case we were able to find was Bordeaux, in March 1944. Police went further in Bordeaux than elsewhere.

A. L.-W.: Can these important government officials claim they knew nothing of the fate of all kinds of men, women, children, and old people who were turned over to the Germans?

R.P.: At first those who organized the trains knew that there would be deaths on them. Later, when they deported old people and children, they obviously knew that they were not being sent to work camps. Their exact fate was not known, but the fact that they would be mistreated could not be ignored and they knew this treatment would be inhuman.

NOTE

1. Lévy-Willard is referring here to Pierre Péan's book dealing with François Mitterrand's right-wing youth and Vichy past, Une Jeunesse Française: François Mitterrand 1934–1947. The book created a national scandal when it was published in 1994.

MAURICE PAPON

WAS NOT ALONE

Le Monde, 24 September 1997

Zeev Sternhell

The Papon trial will make no sense unless it is used to reflect on a major chapter in the history of France. The interest in the debates soon to begin lies as much in their historical dimension, in the firm intention to examine the reasons for waiting a half century, as in the determination to investigate the origins and the nature of the Vichy dictatorship.

It is not a question of determining the facts, which have all been known for a very long time, but of trying to understand the intellectual context that made them possible, if not altogether natural. If no attempt is made to account for the fervor with which the National Revolution, in which the characteristic signs of fascism were evident, was welcomed by vast sectors of public opinion, the moral and pedagogical objective of this trial will be lost. If we prudently abstain from asking about the responsibility of the elites who served the new regime and concentrate only on the moral qualities of the accused, the efforts made to bring the former minister to justice will have been in vain. For Papon, a truly emblematic figure, is anything but a docile bureaucrat, without principles, a servant of the state whatever the state happens to be, capable of better and worse, just as the anti-Jewish policy of Vichy was not a simple improvisation and the regime did not come out of a void, nor did it simply create itself the day following the defeat. The opposite corresponds to reality. The defeat only created the conditions that allowed a policy that had been developing since the turn of the century to give birth to a government.

This alternative solution to liberal democracy, which had deep roots, waited for its time to come, just as elsewhere in Europe a lost war furnished the opportunity to translate ideas into action. All the Papons, and they were not the only ones, knew exactly what they were doing. They came forward to serve a "new order" that large sectors of the public had never ceased to call for throughout the period between the two world wars. This is where the basic problem lies. Thanks to this mobilization of minds, the "National Revolution" was set in motion with extraordinary ease. In less than six months, the face of the country would change as it never had since 1789.

Certainly the defeat had created a shock without equal. The French were almost unanimous in deploring the country's misfortunes, and they were deeply divided in the analysis of the reasons for them. Among the elites—it was always the elites who governed—there were many who, for many years, had seen in liberal democracy the basic source of French decadence. The "National Revolution" expressed a beginning that had to be given a chance. For these men, this revolution was a system that might have unpleasant aspects to it, but that had to be accepted to avoid the risk of seeing the country slide into the worst kind of anarchy. Therein lies the answer to a question that is fascinating in itself: how to explain the fact that the fate of the Jews could arouse so few reactions, even in the most enlightened part of public opinion?

The destiny of the Jews, more than that of any other group of men and women in Europe was, from the early days of emancipation, tied to that of values rooted in the French Revolution. The Jew, member of a group of free citizens who had equal rights, was the living symbol of this revolution that, at the end of the eighteenth century, had turned the world upside down.

That is why all those who in the summer of 1940 rushed to undo the work of the men of 1789 and save France from the liberal and democratic decay could not be too disapproving of the anti-Jewish laws. At any rate, the largest number thought that democracy, human rights, and other "great principles" already belonged to the past.

At the same time, all those who saw a Nazi victory as the end of an era could profess an ardent patriotism, despise the conqueror, and be free of all anti-Semitism. But wouldn't being patriotic and hating the Germans demand a ceaseless effort to foster the "National Revolution"? Wasn't it obvious that the Jewish laws reflected the most profound and basically essential concerns of this same "National Revolution"? Under these conditions was it reasonable to sacrifice, for the sake of the Jews, the only chance left for the country? It was in this atmosphere that the machine of exclusion and later extermination was set in motion, ending with Touvier, Bousquet, and Papon.

This is why, in putting into place this brutal and destructive regime, in many ways much more severe than that of Mussolini, the responsibility of intellectuals, writers, editors, newspaper and magazine publishers seems greater by far than that of the officials of the administration. The intellectuals who worked within the framework of the system, including those who would move into the Resistance in 1943, a long time after El Alamein and Stalingrad, gave legitimacy and respectability to the regime. They served as guarantors and thus allowed the civil servants to fulfill their duties without problems.

Many Resistance members had started out as more or less ardent and convinced supporters of the National Revolution. Maurice Papon chose to be both at once, not one after the other, but at the same time. In this way he too would have served his country in two ways: he would have contributed to the purification work of Vichy, and, on the other hand, he would have fought the enemy. From important intellectuals he had learned throughout the two long years that followed the fall of the Republic that in remaining at his post he was contributing to the rehabilitation of the country that had been hollowed out by liberal democracy. And others, did they not at the same time set about creating schools and directors to govern a new France closer in spirit to the "National Revolution" than to liberal democracy, and did they not do all this for a regime that first banned Jews from the national community and then turned them over to the Nazis?

The big roundups in Paris took place in July 1942. Why should the secretary-general of the Bordeaux prefecture, named to that post in May of the same year, have revolted against his own superior when so many other future Resistance fighters and important names in postwar French governments lent support to the regime? From our vantage point at the end of the century, who, after all, bears a greater responsibility?

THE PAPON INVESTIGATION

BRINGS TO LIGHT THE TRUE ROLE

OF FRANCE IN NAZI EUROPE

An Interview with Philippe Burrin

Le Monde, 24 September 1997

Thomas Firenczi

T. F.: Unless there is an opposing opinion from the Court of Appeals, Maurice Papon will be brought before the courts for crimes against humanity. Do you think this event has changed the way we see "France on German Time," to return to the title of your last book?[1]

P. B.: After the death of Bousquet, the investigation once again brings to the forefront the complicity of Vichy in the Nazi policy of extermination. This complicity is no longer obscured by valuable services rendered by the Resistance. Of greater interest is that Papon's judges are attributing a justifiable significance to the fact that an important government official like Papon could have known the importance of his actions at the time—in other words, he could have known the fate of the Jews whom he ordered deported. It is the attitude of those who served Vichy, and indirectly the attitude of the civil service, that is thrust into the limelight. As a result, more than ever before, France's exact role in Nazi Europe is being established.

If there is a Papon affair it is because of the wide latitude the Germans allowed the Vichy regime and that gave it a margin of negotiation. We know how it was used in the case of the Jews. In 1942, faced with German demands, Vichy handed over foreign Jews, hoping once and for all to encourage collaboration. Then, in 1943–44, it slowed down the handing over of French Jews without ever declaring a refusal in principle, so as not to block this same policy of collaboration that was falling apart nonetheless. But Vichy's frailty also provided a wide latitude of action for employees of a government whose legitimacy, they knew, was at least questionable. Not even considering the possibility of resignation, which was rare, for these employees there did exist the possibility of certain kinds of behavior that would show reluctance.

During the period of German occupation, France was, for me, a myriad of compromises between the restrictions endured under an occupation and the attempt to look after its own interests as much as possible, whether they were ideological or material, corporate or personal, and this was an attitude that Vichy's actions could only encourage. The government officials, especially the important ones, were particularly exposed to the temptation to make such compromises. They were on a terrain shared by Vichy and the occupying forces. They were forced to compromise between patriotism, service to the nation, personal interest, German pressure, and policies more or less approved by Vichy. In the case of Papon, and even more so in the case of Bousquet, at least until 1943, it was clear that worries about their careers were mingled with a belief in national glory, political ambition, and loyalty to Vichy.

T. F.: Revelations about the gold Nazis kept in Swiss banks have created an outcry, so much so that the government is proposing, for this investigation, to set aside the policy of secrecy. Isn't it time to investigate the attitude of the Swiss during and after the war?

P. B.: The story of German gold is well known, at least in Switzerland where it has already been much written about. Echoes in the national press nowadays will have the advantage of pushing the Swiss authorities to act, which in turn will allow the historians to go further in their research. If we set aside the caricature made of this—the little Swiss sitting on a pile of gold gained from shady transactions with the Nazis—this affair deserves consideration because it goes back to a larger policy of economic and financial accommodation carried out by the Swiss in order to placate their powerful neighbor and, along with a military deterrent that was small but effective, to divert it from actual invasion. In addition, it cannot be separated from the closing of frontiers to those persecuted in Nazi Europe, and the refusal to make an official protest against the extermination of the Jews.

This selfish and cowardly policy takes us back to the freedom of action I was talking about, even though the situation is far from identical with that of France. Precisely because Switzerland had more assets to offer in dealing with the Nazis, it could have shown itself more faithful to its humanitarian calling than it really was and indicated more clearly than it did where it stood in the worldwide conflict.

T. F.: How do you explain the continuing interest of the public in the Second World War?

P. B.: I see this interest as a broadening of our civic role and, at the same time, a challenge that is clearly intellectual. The formative role of national identity is becoming outmoded, if it isn't already exhausted, and this change in attitude is shown by the interest in the Second World War. To put it briefly, we are experiencing a shift toward humanitarianism and a European conscience. This change presents the historian with a reduction in his civic function. The intellectual challenge is directly linked to the fact that this trend exerts, through the demands of the media and the expectations of the public, a pressure that can impede reflection. The demands of civic conscience are not enough to make for good history.

NOTE

1. The book in question appeared in English translation as *France under the Germans: Collaboration and Compromise* (New York: The New Press, 1996).

PAPON:

TOO LATE

Le Monde, 14 October 1997

Alain Finkielkraut

P rior to the twentieth century, Europeans, in considering evil, could rely on solid pairs of opposites: legislative reason against primitive lawlessness and murderous impulses, civilization against barbarism, law against crime. We no longer have this comfortable choice. In fact, in the twentieth century and in the heart of Europe, barbarism took the form of civilization, the rational became separated from all ethics, and the most abominable crimes were bureaucratic and not sadistic, they were legal crimes, atrocities of the system, and not great saturnalian transgressions.

This confusion is disorienting, and this is why the memory of it haunts us, or should haunt us. It would be irresponsible to turn the page and act *as though nothing had ever happened*. But does the decision to judge Maurice Papon in extremis allow us to escape such irresponsibility? I doubt it for three principal reasons.

First of all, Maurice Papon is a survivor. Over fifty years after the crimes he is accused of took place, nearly all of those around him at the time, those superiors and those under him, friends and adversaries, are dead. The youthful jury knows only what the media and the historians have told it about that criminal period. As Paul Thibaud wrote, there is no personal experience of this reality and, for example, of what one knew or didn't know of the fate of the deported Jews at the time. The risk of anachronism is therefore great, and I do not see what legal truth can result from a debate in which the accused is, in a way, his only contemporary. In addition, it is painful to watch the race taking place between life imprisonment for Papon and his natural death.

There is a second problem, and that is the collective massacres and crimes against humanity, other than the extermination of the Jews, that have been carried out in the second half of the twentieth century. These are certainly not as extensive. Only the Nazis have made the inconceivable decision to make an entire people disappear from the earth. But these actions are no less frightening, and they have not been brought to justice. The crimes of communism have not been judged, and neither have the crimes of colonialism. As for crimes committed in Croatia and Bosnia, they did lead to the creation of an international criminal tribunal, but it has only laid hands on some Croatian small fry while the eulogist of ethnic cleansing comes in first in Serbian presidential elections and the instigator of the carnage governs what is left of Yugoslavia with the consent of the civilized world.

In short, everyone cried "Never again!" when they emerged from World War II, but this promise was betrayed, and such treason conceals itself behind endless trials aimed at nazism. These trials offer, in addition, the opportunity for wrongheaded and senile sermonizing on the theme "The society that forgets its past is condemned to repeat it." And the institutions are not the only ones involved. Among the forty million devout anti-Nazis currently in France, who have their finger on the trigger, how many could name a single European town totally destroyed by violence in 1991? "To be ahead, to be behind, what lack of precision! To be on time is the only exactness," said Péguy in a profound statement.

Contrary to what one may hear, the Pétainist past of France has not been taboo for a long time. If it is true that in 1970 one could still have a conference in Paris on Vichy without the word "Jew"[1] being mentioned, the situation since then is radically different. French studies on the government's collaboration and Vichy's part in the Final Solution are many and for the most part excellent. What appears more and more often is the reverse of the taboo, the willingness of a small sector of public opinion to be contemporaries of this period. To relive Vichy, but armed with weapons. This was the curious wish of those who signed the "petition of the 121, with names difficult to pronounce," that appeared at the time of the demonstration against Debré's laws.[2] The same overwrought anxiety excites those who see Le Pen everywhere, even in the government, and who fight the limiting of the waves of immigration as if it were Vichy's statutes concerning the Jews.

The Papon trial is reinforcing this delusion. For many of those born since the war, this judicial spectacle offers an opportunity to deny that the past is the past and to relive this time of heroism and terror. Thanks to imprescriptibility, they can hoist the present to the heights of their aspirations.

So this trial is useless? Perhaps not. Maurice Papon, capable of the worst because of an indifference to anything other than career or government service, is one of the purest and most disturbing products of the age of bureaucracy. If, apart from all delusions of grandeur, and after all the hearings, we agree to think about the potential for barbarism of a reasoning that is completely professional and concerned with efficiency for efficiency's sake, and if it becomes a little less easy for us, whatever we are—civil servants, but also photographers, technicians, researchers, executives, or businessmen—to run from moral responsibility for our acts in the careful carrying out of our tasks, the trial of this arrogant and unrepentant administrator will have had a real power to disturb us. But let's not dream.

NOTE

1. Finkielkraut is referring here to the conference entitled "Le Gouvernement de Vichy 1940–1942" that took place at the Fondation Nationale des Sciences Politiques. Vichy anti-Semitism is referred to in the proceedings of the conference, but only on a few, isolated occasions [Ed.].

LETTER TO THE PRESIDENT

OF THE BORDEAUX

ASSIZES COURT

Henry Rousso

6 October 1997

Jean-Louis Castagnède, President
Assizes Court
The Palace of Justice
Bordeaux

Dear Mr. President,

I have been summoned to appear as a witness at the request of Mr. Maurice Papon, currently indicted for complicity in crimes against humanity. I first became aware of this summons through the press, without the accused or his counsel having notified me beforehand. I must therefore raise the question as to what aim and purpose my name and my status as an historian are being put in public.

With all the respect due to the court, Mr. President, I would prefer not to testify for the following reasons.

First, I would like to invoke an ethical reason that is also a matter of principle. In the context of another trial for crimes against humanity, that of Paul Touvier, I wrote that I believe that the presence of historians in an Assizes

Court trial raises a number of problems. In keeping with this stated position, during the Touvier trial I declined a request made by certain civil litigants to testify before the court in Versailles. It therefore strikes me as impossible today to accept Maurice Papon's request, given that in the past I refused a similar request by civil litigants in an earlier trial.

In my soul and conscience, I believe that an historian cannot serve as a "witness," and that his expertise is poorly suited to the rules and objectives of a judicial proceedings. It is one thing to attempt to understand history in the context of one's research or teaching, with the intellectual freedom these activities presuppose, and quite another to pursue the same aim, under oath, when the fate of a particular individual is being determined. I would like to add that this a strictly personal position. It in no way entails a a particular attitude toward the participation of other historians in the trial of Papon, whether they be called by the prosecution, the civil litigants, or the defense.

Finally, having been summoned against my will, with a publicity which I deplore, and without having any direct connection to the incriminating deeds with which the accused is charged, I greatly fear that my "testimony" will merely serve as a pretext to exploit historical research and interpretations that were elaborated and formulated in a context entirely alien to the Assizes Court. The discourse and argumentation of the trial, moreover, are certainly not of the same nature as those of the university.

I would be grateful if the court would take these grounds for declining to testify under advisement.

Very respectfully yours,

Henry Rousso, Director of Research,
Director of the Institute for Contemporary History

NAZISM, VICHY, AND THE

PAPON TRIAL AS SEEN

BY A GERMAN HISTORIAN

An Interview with Eberhard Jäckel

Le Monde, 7 November 1997

Lucas Delattre

L.D.: How is the Papon trial viewed on the other shore of the Rhine? Can it have an influence on how the Germans see their own past?

E.J.: The German media is following the trial very attentively. But, happily, I see no sign of smugness or relief of the kind "So now it's the turn of the French!" I hope France will be able to avoid the shortcomings that we are familiar with here in Germany in these kinds of cases, taking a moralizing approach to them. When we try to find an ideal guilty party, the sense of history is quickly lost. The deeds blamed on Maurice Papon cannot be approached without making reference to the fact that, at the bottom of it all, there was a German initiative. However, it is important to remember that the Vichy regime was not asked by the Nazis to put in place the anti-Jewish Statutes.

L.D.: Can the Papon trial be compared to legal processes of the same kind that took place in Germany after the war?

E.J.: Yes. The first important trials took place in Germany more than thirty years ago. The trial of those responsible at Auschwitz and Majdanek, which took place in Frankfurt in the early 1960s, played an especially important role. These trials were not satisfactory from a legal standpoint nor from the point of view of the victims. What we gained from them was to find out the facts themselves. This work of memory allowed us to retrieve our dignity, something impossible to do if we live on legends and myths. I think the Papon trial will accomplish the same result.

L. D.: You were the initiator, along with Lea Rosh, of the project for the Berlin monument in memory of the Holocaust victims. Chancellor Kohl, who favored this idea, vetoed an earlier project in June of 1995. The many debates that have taken place in Germany since then have brought fears that the monument will never be built.

E. J.: This monument was conceived to honor the memory of six million European Jews exterminated by the Nazis. Those debates were generally between experts, and most of them do not question the construction itself, which is generally accepted by the public. Furthermore, there has been no intervention of a revisionist kind to disgrace the discussions of the project.

The first stone is supposed to be laid in January 1999; the site for the monument has not been changed. It is between the Brandenburg Gate and Potsdam Plaza. It was important that a large monument be erected to remind us of the greatest crime in history, and that it be placed near the former Reich Chancellery. The three partners in this project — the federal government, the Land of Berlin, and a foundation uniting the initiators — must agree very soon on the architectural project to be chosen.

L. D.: Why is the project so late in getting started?

E. J.: We already have many commemorative sites, beginning with the concentration camps of Germany, but also the Lake Wannsee Villa in Berlin where the conference on the "Final Solution" was held in January 1942, and the permanent exhibition, "Topography of Terror," also in Berlin. But the extermination of the Jews did not take place in Germany, and the German camps are not in themselves adequate to commemorate the extermination by the Nazis of a third of the world's Jewish population. A separate monument was necessary, centrally located and, if possible, with the names of the victims.

L. D.: How is the German view of the Third Reich changing?

E. J.: I find no lessening of interest among the young. In fact, the opposite is true. Films and books on the Nazi era continue to arouse curiosity and raise questions, even though there is a real lack of knowledge about it in the former Democratic Republic.

L. D.: With this in mind, how do you interpret the polemic raised by a recent exhibition on the crimes of the Wehrmacht? We had the impression from this that very strong taboos still exist in the debate Germany is carrying on about its own past.

E. J.: These days this debate is very lively, but it is more complex than it appears. It is hardly possible today to defend the idea that the Wehrmacht was a "clean army." It's a very naive idea. What shocked part of German public opinion was that the exhibition's authors wanted to demonstrate that the Wehrmacht was an almost autonomous criminal entity. It was less the Wehrmacht as such that was criminal than the government that gave it orders and of which it was a part. The decision to invade Russia was not made by army generals, for example. So I'm not speaking of a retreat on the part of a historical conscience. There are no more taboos in Germany about this period.

L. D.: The debate on the responsibility of the German population in the choice of the Final Solution was reopened last year by Daniel J. Goldhagen's book *Hitler's Willing Executioners,* which was a great publishing success in Germany. Goldhagen believes that the Germans developed a specific form of anti-Semitism in the nineteenth century, "exterminationist" anti-Semitism.

E. J.: This is a bad book, considered so unanimously by specialists of the period from all over the world. If the book was a success in Germany, it was because it put the problem in simple moralistic terms. I think it is false to present the Final Solution as coming from personal motives of the Germans. Above all, it was the structure of the Nazi state that made extermination of the Jews possible, not the will of the German people. No one, before Hitler, had had the idea of exterminating all the Jews of Europe. The Final Solution can be explained by the joining of a man like Hitler to structures ready to serve him.

L. D.: And what was the role of the German population in the Final Solution?

E. J.: It was more complex than Goldhagen would have you believe. According to sources at our disposal, we see that, in 1938, *Kristallnacht* provoked an uneasiness in the population. The deportation of the Jews stirred up various reactions, not unanimous enthusiasm. As for the average executioners, most acted out of opportunism in order to obtain personal advantages, much more than in the name of an anti-Semitic ideology. Besides, the anti-Semitism of the Germans was not the main reason for Hitler's rise to power. If we study his speeches closely, we see that his anti-Semitic propaganda becomes secondary between 1930 and 1932. At the end of the last century and the beginning of the twentieth, German anti-Semitism was not fundamentally different from others, and even less virulent than in Russia, Austria, and France.

MAURICE PAPON AND

CRIMINAL PATHOLOGY

Le Monde, 18 November 1997

Michel Dubec

A man, and not a symbol, is being judged in Bordeaux. Let us put aside for a moment France, the state, even the Vichy regime, and limit ourselves to his personal responsibility, to the limits of free choice that made him decide to remain at his job and participate in the deadly actions [of the deportations] even if he did not know how it would end.

There is a kind of criminal who can be defined by the following characteristics: they are intelligent, appealing, and, most importantly, they feel no hatred for their victims. These are the serial killers. What strikes one in first approaching them is the coldness of the contact. Since the serial killer feels no preliminary hatred, he feels no guilt.

Certainly this is only a simple analogy. It would be absurd to try to reduce taking part in a genocide to the categories of criminology. But it is not impossible to believe that the criminal motive of a person as unique as a systematic killer can be buried deep in each one of us and can find an outlet in operating in ways somewhat similar to the special circumstances of genocide.

The serial killer has no personal link with his victim. He decides on one by a single characteristic—blond hair, for example, or any other characteristic he chooses. He does not hate his victim, because he has depersonalized him or her beforehand. In an unchanging ritual, he depersonalizes his victim in order to use him or her as an object. He can kill only if he shows he is indifferent. From the segregation laws [anti-Jewish Statues] of Vichy to the stripping of bodies on arriving at the camp; from the initial extraction to the final selection, each accomplice contributes to this dehumanization.

The massacres and the mass killings were possible in Eastern Europe because of the regrouping of Jews into distinct communities. Certain villages in the Ukraine were almost 60 percent Jewish, and these percentages are comparable to those of other, earlier or later genocides. The massacres were carried out in the context of a warlike action, which has also traditionally served as a pretext. In Western Europe, on the other hand, the cultural stamp of the Jews was so great that it made this impossible. It was first necessary to single out the individuals, desocialize them, then misrepresent them in order to finally dehumanize and exterminate them. Collaborators in this dehumanization could be ignorant of its final cost but not of its significance.

Since the 1930s a great many images had been pouring out of the Nazi propaganda machine. They all wore the gaudy finery of cruelty and displayed a fascination with death. Although the methods of genocide were not discovered until the end of the war, and totalitarianism was not defined until later, the basic sign of National Socialism—sadism—was apparent from the beginning.

Adolf Eichmann was not anti-Semitic and neither is Maurice Papon. But the fact that the murder was delayed, cold-blooded, and anonymous does not rule out pleasure. We should mistrust another type of depersonalization, that of seeing the organization of genocide as only obeying a command, as if the transmission of the insanity had been so persuasive that there was no way to escape it, or, more pointedly, as if the taste for work well done could blind us to the point of not recognizing it. Let us be careful not to consider totalitarianism as an inexorable machine, capable of turning men into automatons, because we cannot understand what they have done. The way one obeys depends on the type of order that is given.

The Holocaust was not an objective of the war, it was an added pleasure. So it wasn't a question of collaborating with German strategy, but of an additional slavishness. Those who responded to it did it to please the occupying power, or because the action was not distasteful to them. Subscribing to it was made easy by the fact that the order came from the enemy and it served to satisfy a deep temptation, a buried drive that is executed in spite of oneself.

Maurice Papon probably had no personal hatred for the Jews; perhaps he had no connection with them. But these people, some of whom were recent immigrants, who spoke with an accent and lacked good manners, weren't they a blot on the landscape? If an order to cut down the pine trees, to tear out the vines, to get rid of domestic animals had been given, would Maurice Papon have hastened to carry it out?

Later on his duties "obliged" him to put down many demonstrations over the years. When it concerned others who had accents and dark faces and were Algerians, the orders given by Maurice Papon brought about two hundred deaths. There is a consistency to this important official.

For those who persist in thinking that Maurice Papon's concern was to avoid the worst—the worst is just what he accomplished. How did Maurice Papon draft administrative notes in order to delay or avoid the painful operation? Did he alert his superiors or even the German authorities of the material difficulties of rounding up the Jews or of the convoys? Did he point out that there would perhaps be negative reactions from the French population and eventually a refusal to obey? How had he composed the administrative notes to slow down the effort? In short, did he show any hesitation and what did he risk if he did? A bad grade?

Bulgaria was an ally of Germany. Later it was occupied. It never explicitly refused to hand over its Jews as Finland and Denmark did, but to the very end it was so unwilling to cooperate that it managed to save them. In no country was a citizen executed just because he refused to take part in genocide.

Understanding mankind is perhaps an impossible task, but a trial is not a teaching instrument. A trial judges the act of a man in order possibly to understand him, and not the reverse. It is never possible to know the exact degree of alienation or lucidity of the author of a crime at the exact moment. To come near measuring it we must examine closely his conduct before and after the moment. Those who did not live under the Occupation should not blame those who did for their attitudes or for the fears that took hold of them.

No one can know what Maurice Papon was thinking then, not even the man himself. But what have been his thoughts since? What were his feelings when he finally learned of the destination of the convoys he had formed? Did the important witnesses to his later career one day detect in him an expression of remorse, of regret, of emotion, or of a single doubt? Are misanthropy and a haughty attitude the results of being a leader? Does the march of events carry with it a silent conformism and, as a consequence, a forgetting, and the final heritage of denial?

We must give up once and for all judging the feeling of guilt of an accused during his trial. Anyone obliged to defend himself mobilizes all of his psychic energy to win in this situation. He puts all of his faith—good and bad—into it and is unable to leave any place in his thoughts for the victim. The accusation comes from without, and this is no time for reflecting on his own guilt.

There were expressions of guilt among some of those who committed acts or who witnessed them during those times, and this feeling exists in almost all of the victims who can't recover from the disappearance of others. Why didn't this feeling of guilt exist for the servants of nazism? Because the primacy of passivity and conformity and the taste for order over any moral preoccupation allowed them to commit this crime and later to let it stand.

The historians, whether they agreed to testify at the trial or not, were all agreed that their task was not to try to take the place of legality. And the legal system did not want to substitute for history. Therefore it is necessary to return to the man himself, both before and after the crime. In this way we can evaluate whether or not a top official can see himself as less responsible.

ARE WE

ALL GUILTY?

Le Monde, 11 December 1997

François Maspero

Is France guilty? Are the French all guilty? There is something disturbing about the present enormous wave of contrition. In 1940 and 1941, at the instigation of Catholic authorities and the Vichy government, it was accepted that France had to ask God's pardon for sins she had committed and which—by a just and divine punishment—had led her to defeat. I remember all too well the endless acts of contrition we schoolchildren were obliged to make in the churches. If, at the pleasure of every government, France is obliged to regularly ask forgiveness for past misdeeds, what sins will we be asked to beg forgiveness for in the years after 2040 (a question that, if it were asked from now on, might save those living at the time from having to do it . . .)?

I certainly don't put the charade of the Vichy government's demanding the French repent for having had the bad taste to believe in the Popular Front on the same level with the legitimate—but tardy—recognition by our Republic that the Vichy regime participated in racial extermination. The Vichy government was guilty of crimes against humanity, but to say that all Frenchmen were guilty or accomplices is not only an abdication (in the form of a globalization) in the face of history, it is also nonsense.

This is true for at least two reasons. The first is that hundreds of thousands of French were persecuted for their real or supposed religion, which was called "race." To say that "We are all guilty" would imply either that the Jews, French like the others, were also guilty like the others—which is absurd—or that the Jews, if we exclude them from this "We," were not French—which is outrageous and repeats the old accepted Vichy refrain. The second is that hundreds of thousands of French, on all sides, of all religions and all classes, opposed the pro-Nazi politics and the racial laws of Vichy. They are, or they would be, stupefied today to see themselves designated as guilty or as accomplices to the application of this political program and these laws. I feel the statement that "everyone is guilty" is an insult to those who at times paid with their lives for their opposition (which wasn't simply the passive opposition of a whole people, as Valéry Giscard d'Estaing "explained" it to us, fatuously confusing dignity and passivity).

In affirming such a collective guilt, we expel from the French community all those who, by their actions, managed not to take part in the political program and the Vichy laws, but to combat them. In short, we imply that the Resistance fighters were not French—or, in any case (like the Jews) not like the others. This is exactly what the Nazis said. Claiming that we are "all guilty" and including everyone is to end up with an absurd paradox of introducing into the national community an exclusion, or at the very least a segregation just as absurd, which expels from the community all those who were victims of the barbarity and, at the same time, those who fought against it.

I know that those [among my friends and family] who, like so many others, "died for France" by resisting, did not die for this France that loudly repents, and I continue to hope there is another France that is theirs. And feeling with every fiber of my being a part of this other France, I do not feel guilty.

MAURICE PAPON

WAS TRIED LONG AGO

IN HISTORY'S COURT

An Interview with Henry Rousso

Le Monde, 7 April 1998

Laurent Greilsamer and Nicolas Weill

L. G. and N. W.: The Criminal Court of the Gironde has just condemned Maurice Papon to ten years of imprisonment. How would you analyze this verdict, and, in your opinion, will it be acceptable in the future?

H. R.: It is difficult to foresee how posterity will judge this verdict. At present, it can be understood either as the result of hesitation, following the example of other verdicts coming from citizen juries; that is—and this is my instinctive feeling as a historian—as a reflection of the ambiguities of the case. Even if it marks a turning point, this trial and its verdict will be perceived as the explanation of what the France of the Vichy years was, and of the "Vichy syndrome." The confusion it arouses will at least have the virtue of making us think about it, ask ourselves questions, debate the past without hiding behind a legal decision and without assuming that this verdict closes the historical case just because it concludes the legal one.

L. G. and N. W.: The trial was exceptionally long. How does that strike you?

H. R.: The trial told us much about the current state of the law, the media, and our society. As a whole, it told us about the present but not about history.

The trial was perceived as having four missions, which were fulfilled in varying degrees. First, it had a mission to see justice done. But the unusual character of the event left a feeling that there were two trials—the real one and the "virtual" one taking place outside the courtroom and guided by the media, commentators, and political declarations. It is the latter that inundated the public (and those who, like me, did not attend) with inevitable distortions that became a source of increasing confusion.

In spite of itself, the court also accepted the fact that a commemorative ritual should unfold before the spectators. This was evident in the accounts of certain witnesses, with the projection on a screen of the photos of victims and with the reading of their names. And this ritual often did not fit well with the judicial procedures.

The third dimension was vengeance. Allowing Maurice Papon to go free was a shock. We had accepted the idea that it was not possible to see someone accused of crimes against humanity as a free man on the witness stand. The judges decided differently and many objected to their decision. The civil litigants' lawyers declared that the trial was over, thus refusing at the outset everything a trial offers in the way of uncertainty and open-endedness.

The attitude of Serge and Arno Klarsfeld in this regard was indicative. As the instruments of memory and of vengeance, in the noble sense of that word, they wanted to seize the hand of justice and make her write history the way it should be written in their view. This would deny the very legitimacy of the trial. If we are able to have the law available to us, it is precisely because it decides with complete independence.

L. G. and N. W.: Would you go so far as to say this independence was abused?

H. R.: It was threatened. The pressure was such, the stakes were so high and the incidents so numerous that the criminal court had trouble dealing with them. The impression given was that the law could arrive at only one verdict. That was one reason for the profound feeling of discomfort the trial engendered.

From the time the case was reopened, there was uncertainty. And here I think many did not, in the beginning, measure the risks this reopening would entail. It had not been measured or taken stock of because Maurice Papon appeared from the outset to be totally and absolutely guilty. They had underestimated the fact that, if the court decided otherwise, the entire exemplary element would be compromised. This was one of the main pressures of the trial. Finally, the fourth mission undertaken by the trial was to provide a great history lesson about Vichy for the whole nation. Here my criticisms are much more severe.

L. G. and N. W.: Would you say that the Papon trial has no lessons to teach us?

H. R.: I frankly believe there are none. Certainly we've learned much about the Occupation in Bordeaux, but, as an historian, I don't have the feeling that our knowledge of the period has progressed. On the contrary, I think it has regressed. The court of history judged Vichy a long time ago. Today Vichy is the object of public scorn in a much more blatant way than it was in the fifties and sixties. All the polls show this. Posterity's judgment is overwhelming.

So what has the trial done? It reopened the case. It questioned this viewpoint through an individual case that is very complex and whose "exemplarity" is very much open to question. The historians, faced with the questions left by the Papon trial and the confusions arising from it, will have a real pedagogical task to undertake once again. It will be necessary for us to explain once more, and to take into account the negative effects of such a trial.

The very manner in which the trial took place has weakened any widely held historical understanding the general public might have had on this question because the court deliberated once again on what history had already judged.

L. G. and N. W.: From the beginning of the trial you have maintained that an historian has no place in a courtroom. Have you changed your mind about this in the last six months or modified your opinion?

H. R.: Indeed not! And the basic reason for this is simple. Historians, from the start of the game, were used as instruments. Their presence was inserted into the framework of the legal strategies of the prosecution or of the defense or of the civil litigants. Each was intent on having "his" historians in order to weaken those called by the others. They were called on to appear in the theatrical setting of a criminal court where what matters is the rhetoric, the impression made on the jury. This procedure does not allow for historical expertise. Any historical conclusion presupposes a questioning. In a trial the court handles this and it is strictly binary: is Maurice Papon guilty or innocent within the framework of the applicable legal qualifications? Most historians who testified were caught in the prosecutorial procedure in spite of themselves.

Here is an example. Was Maurice Papon aware of the "Final Solution"? Did he know or not? Who knew what? Eichmann knew. Papon . . . ? This is a matter that requires a very detailed historical analysis. The consignment to trial as well as the debates were bogged down in this argument when it was enough to say that Maurice Papon participated in a crime by putting children, women, old people in cattle cars. The prosecution and most of the civil litigants wanted at all costs to say that the accused "knew," when the question cannot be formulated in this way. What does "to know" mean? At what level? It is very easy to possess the information and not act on it. Today, an out-of-date and moralizing view of things makes it difficult to explain that, put in such a simple way, the question does not make much sense. History is not an exact science. The historian proceeds by using a series of individual analyses and adding a particular case, which allows him to form a general picture. We can never be sure that a general historical statement can apply to a particular case or vice versa unless all the facts of the case are known, and with Papon this was legally impossible. It is one of the absurdities of the situation: the historians were almost never called on during the investigation, the only time their "expertise" would have had some use; they were called on only in circumstances in which only oral debate mattered, and not an informed opinion as to the documents. And when one historian who knew the case, Michel Bergès, did testify, he was attacked because he was treading on legal prerogatives. At Bordeaux, the "good" historian was the one who knew nothing about the legal case.

L. G. and N. W.: Do you believe it would have been better if the Papon trial had not taken place?

H. R.: Once the courts had taken it up, they had to see it through to the end. So it has no meaning now to say that it would have been better not to have had the trial. At what moment did we get involved in the procedure? In 1981? When he was accused? At what stage?

The real question is that of imprescriptibility. This is a debate that has never taken place in France. The law was voted in in December 1964, in a particular context when it was feared that the time for punishing Nazi war crimes would elapse. At that time, no one thought for a moment that the law could apply to the French—that is, that it would have as a consequence the reopening of the Purge. The law was adopted unanimously, and among these lawmakers were many who, a decade before, had voted for amnesty laws.

From the moment that imprescriptibility was considered self-evident, everything else became secondary. The procedure was set in motion, and the result would be either a mistrial (and we saw with Touvier that this was not foreseeable), or conviction. A mistrial, even if it had been found legally justifiable in Papon's criminal case—and the prosecution had for a time been inclined in that direction—was not acceptable to public opinion. People would have said that this was tantamount to acquitting Vichy, as had been argued in the case of Touvier.

From the moment part of public opinion became convinced that a trial was the only way to eliminate the Vichy question and therefore to satisfy memory and history and justice all at the same time, French society was caught in a trap. As far as history went, it was necessary that the outcome of the trial be beyond doubt. Was this possible?

L. G. and N. W.: You just mentioned the Purge following the Second World War, which we now know was seriously flawed where racial persecutions were concerned. Why are you so suspicious about the capacity of the law at the end of the twentieth century to do its work?

H. R.: It isn't a question of suspicion where the law is concerned but a doubt about the possibility of an entire society being able to fill in the gaps, fifty years later, of a political purge that cannot be judged and understood except within the context of the moment and not as seen by our own time—which is to say, a different time. Whatever one thinks of the recent trials, they did constitute a kind of "second Purge," based on other penal qualifications, other procedures, other stakes. Today's trials, such as Papon's, have taken on more symbolic weight than the trials that followed the war, except perhaps for the trial of Pétain.

L. G. and N. W.: With the Papon trial, has the "duty to memory" been fulfilled, and what remains of it?

H. R.: There is a tendency to forget that the idea of "the duty to memory" was created by the survivors of the extermination camps, beginning with Primo Levi. It was a duty the survivors imposed upon themselves—to bear witness. They feared not being understood as well as not having the courage to speak, succumbing to the temptation to forget in order to reconstruct a life. That is the duty to memory, which comes from a deep Jewish tradition aimed less at turning the past over and over than in transmitting it, in order to engage the future.

This duty to memory was transformed into an injunction formulated by generations who had never known the tragedy and who were asking contemporaries and people older than they were to subscribe to it. There is something absurd about this—even more so when the duty to memory becomes a kind of ideology, a moral of substitution with its taboos and its stereotyped language. From this viewpoint, the Papon trial will at least have had the merit of opening our eyes to the limitations of the duty to memory as it is currently understood.

The duty to memory cannot stand up very long against the duty to truth. In fact, the "hyper-remembering," the "surfeit" of the past, is as disturbing as amnesia. To avoid the one as well as the other, I agree with Paul Ricoeur that for the idea "the duty to memory" we need to substitute "the task of memory."

L. G. and N. W.: What new phase will the aftermath of the Papon trial lead us into? Have we come out of what you call the period of "Obsession"?

H. R.: With the Touvier trial in 1994, and the declaration of Jacques Chirac in 1995, I thought we had almost left it behind, we had gotten what was demanded. . . . Today, I have the impression that a summit has been reached. Will the Papon trial put an end to the "Vichy syndrome"? I hope so. But there are several cases pending—one of them is for punitive damages. I don't deny the legitimacy of these reparations, but yet again, let's think about it: is this reparation for fraudulent action?

Looking at it from the way the trial was presented—that is, not only as an effective reparation owed to the victims but as a trial of memory, an historical trial—we must ask ourselves if this raising of the stakes is the only way to take on the past.

L. G. and N. W.: Why has French society been unable to have the irreparable accepted as such?

H. R.: The singularity of the genocide carried with it a memory that is also unique and a source of great tension. Can we repair the irreparable? At the same time, can we consider the event both unique and exemplary? Can we demand justice, a verdict that by definition closes a case, hoping at the same time that the crime will remain unforgettable? Can we resolve history's conflicts at a later date? We have to deny all *political* legitimacy to the Vichy regime and yet admit that it did have legitimacy on an *historical* plane. This was the reality with which the Papon trial had to deal. The legitimacy of the Resistance was made clear during the struggle, and fortunately that is what emerged from the trial. But that does not erase the fact that there were certainly two "Frances" during the war, even several, and that they were not totally distinct from each other. Think of the career of a François Mitterrand. The complexity of the past must be accepted in order to arm ourselves against the incertitude of the present and the unknown of the future.

Le Monde, 3 July 1998

Michel Zaoui and Jean-Marc Varaut

Three months after the conclusion of the Papon trial, *Le Monde* asked Michel Zaoui, a lawyer for the civil plaintiffs, and Jean-Marc Varaut, Papon's chief defense counsel, to reflect on the trial. Their comments were published on 3 July 1998.

MICHEL ZAOUI

What a strange legal archaism it is to insist that in a criminal court the written word should be relegated to the sidelines! A criminal court judges the most serious offences, inflicts the heaviest penalties, but no "official," legally certified trace exists of the judicial debates, of the accusations and injuries claimed by the victims or of the explanations furnished by the defense. The written record has no place here because of a principle that was justified in the past by the fact that a part of the jury was illiterate. Today the principle of oral debate remains essential because it provokes an outpouring of legal truths, but one is quickly aware of its limitations. Contrary to the Barbie and Touvier trials, there was not even a stenotype of the debates in the Papon trial. The project for reform of the criminal courts cannot ignore this unacceptable incongruity at the century's end.

Furthermore, the legal report has an even more essential place since it becomes the only relay between the courtroom and the citizen anxious to know what took place during the criminal procedure. But this kind of report runs up against the impossibility of a report in extenso and the unavoidably incomplete character of the legal moments recorded.

For example, at the 6 January court session there was a lengthy discussion of the Oberg-Bousquet accord of the summer of 1942 in which Vichy freely agreed to turn Jews over to the Germans. This reminder seemed to me decisive in that Maurice Papon, as a civil servant, was acting within the framework of a government policy of collaboration. The existence of such a policy prevented him from hiding behind "German constraint" or "German instigation." I noted that many reporters did not report this discussion even though it was central to understanding what the defendant was accused of. Essentially nothing from that day's proceedings was retained except for the testimony of a witness—which, it is true, was poignant and disturbing—who was an escapee from Auschwitz. His testimony was a kind of terrible truth thrown in the face of the jury to make them understand what the Jewish tragedy must have been during the Second World War. His account had to be told in order to make sense of the accusation of complicity in the crime of assassination. But, in my view, within the framework of legal justice, a review of the Oberg-Bousquet accord should have had just as important a place, but this was not the case.

SILENCE

Since the media have an essential role and a responsibility, at the beginning of the trial, in October 1997, reading the press alone left little doubt as to the guilt of Maurice Papon. The strategy and skill of the defense consisted at the time—and for the following two months—in delaying the examination of the crimes of which Maurice Papon was accused. This created a kind of disconnection between the very object of the trial and its day-to-day procedure. When the proceedings actually began to deal with the crimes, an immense fatigue had already overcome many of the journalists, who were the first ones taken by surprise by this strategy that made the trial most unusual.

Today, three months after the judgment was handed down by the Bordeaux Criminal Court, I am particularly surprised and troubled by the silence that shrouds the event. Within a week the media had fallen silent despite a clamor from the public for more information.

The first explanation certainly goes back to this feeling of weariness. Many were relieved that the legal institution functioned at all, and that was sufficient. But can we think of the Papon trial as a passing event, as a news item already out of date, pushed out of the news by later events, no longer worth talking about?

A second way of explaining the silence that followed the trial goes back to the substance of the charge. It is worrisome that the jurists, the media, and the historians are not reviewing this strange verdict that does not retain, in the condemnation for complicity in a crime against humanity, the charge against Papon of being an accomplice to murder. We are faced with a crime [against humanity] with no deaths!

In addition to this, in Bordeaux they insisted on judging the crime against humanity as if it were an ordinary common-law crime when, by definition, a crime against humanity is a collective one that implies a chain of crimes in which each link is itself criminal. We were faced with an administrative crime. In Hannah Arendt's words, a crime of agencies. Isn't it time to break the silence on this issue?

Finally, one last explanation for this post-trial silence: the six months of hearings have shaken our collective memory and have caused the collapse of many myths and brought us back to the all-too-human truth of a painful past. Here again, the written records of the trial should assume a paramount importance and meaning alongside the work of the historians. These records [if they existed] should be read and reread in order to try to understand the meaning of what took place.

JEAN-MARC VARAUT

In Bordeaux, each evening after the court sessions, the first thing Francis Vuillemin[1] and I did was to stop the car taking us back to our hotel under security police escort in front of the newsstand near the Justice building, where we would buy two copies of *Le Monde*.

On the way to Bouliac, we would go over Jean-Michel Dumay's report, line by line, exclaiming either indignantly or with satisfaction. It recreated exactly for us the emotional or dramatic or comical or repetitive atmosphere of the preceding session. Glancing through it hurriedly, I waited for my colleague to finish his reading so we could exchange opinions.

Even though the titles and subtitles (but this was not the fault of the journalist) sometimes distorted the story to the point of contradicting it, I don't remember that we thought even once that it was dishonest. This is far from the case of many of the audiovisual reports and especially the televised ones. Nor had Dumay been deliberately and harmfully selective. The moments, the incidents, the key statements were faithfully retold. And even if Jean-Michel Dumay is not a neutral reporter and he lets his own moral judgment be known, I never doubted his impartiality.

Impartiality is not indifference, it actually is in harmony with the engaged spectator's attitude and shares the legal virtue of having only one interest, that of the straightforwardness and accuracy of justice itself.

Insofar as the courtroom proceedings exposed the gaps as well as the orientation of the investigation, tore to shreds the accusation—which did not tell the whole truth—and demonstrated what the actual charges against the accused boiled down to, showing up the ideological conflicts of the civil plaintiffs, who cared more about "winning" than honoring the memory of the victims, and revealing the impossibility of having a fair trial for one man and Vichy at the same time, I began to hope—comforted by the legal reporting in *Le Monde* and the weekly reports of Éric Conan in *L'Express*—that the media condemnation pronounced on 7 October 1997, on the eve of the opening of the trial, did not have to be inevitable. Beginning on 5 January 1998, the word "acquitted" even began to be heard. It ceased being unthinkable, even though it was still unlikely.

In rereading the articles of Jean-Michel Dumay published today, I find I have the same alternating feelings of doubt and hope that I felt during these last weeks, even after the initiatives of Serge and Arno Klarsfeld had visibly shaken and destabilized the criminal court judge.

Readers who are not partisan, even if they know the provisional end of this trial—a sentence of compromise that disappointed everyone in trying not to disappoint anyone for fear of depriving the memory militants of a conspiratorial condemnation—in reading the daily accounts of the trial in Jean-Michel Dumay's *Le Procès de Maurice Papon*[2] will feel the same alternating feelings while waiting for a decision that had become uncertain and questionable.

This trial, supermnemonic about anything concerning the French administration and singularly amnesiac about anything concerning Nazi coercion, was absurd. And unjust. The long parade of survivors of the army of shadows, ridiculed and sometimes insulted by a militant courtroom, must not obscure the fact that the principal witnesses were prevented from coming because of their disabilities or, in most cases, because they are dead, and that the real authors and accomplices in the Bordeaux deportations were not in the box of the accused.

This equitable but unreal production of an expiatory sacrifice liberating us from our shame has very little to do with justice. Neither history, nor politics, nor memory, nor even justice has been satisfied by this trial, no matter how long it was, and it was the longest in the history of France. The merit of the reporting from Jean-Michel Dumay, who obviously will not agree with what I have just written, is to offer readers, as much as is possible, all of the elements necessary for them to be able to form their own conclusions.

NOTES

1. Along with Maître Rouxel, Francis Vuillemin was also counsel to Maurice Papon.

2. Dumay's articles from *Le Monde* were published as *Le Procès de Maurice Papon. Chronique de Jean-Michel Dumay* (Paris: Fayard, 1998).

Salmagundi, Winter/Spring 1999

Tzvetan Todorov

The third trial for crimes against humanity to take place in France was held in Bordeaux between October 1997 and April 1998; it will surely be the last trial involving events from World War II. Charges accusing Maurice Papon, former secretary-general for the prefecture of Bordeaux, of participating in the deportation of Jews were initially lodged back in 1981. Exceptional in length (seventeen years of investigation, six months of hearings), the trial was also unusual for the media attention it aroused. Every day, the major papers devoted several pages to its coverage, television programs multiplied, and even now dozens of books on the trial still fill bookstore windows. What, then, can we learn from the Papon trial?

As an outside observer, I have of necessity but few things to say about the judicial case itself. I lack any familiarity with the immense file the case generated, which involved some 6,300 official documents, as well as many more that were deemed inadmissible at trial. That Papon was morally culpable for not dissociating himself more clearly from the politics of the French state under Pétain, and for not showing greater compassion for its victims, is beyond question. To claim accordingly the existence of a "duty of insubordination" is, however, a leap easily made only by those who like to play the hero in the absence of any danger. In any case, morality is not justice; was there also a crime in the eyes of the law? The answer to this second question depends upon two factors: the degree of Papon's responsibilities, and his awareness of the fate of those who were deported. The court's final decision to sentence Papon to ten years in prison for complicity in the illegal arrest and arbitrary incarceration (it set aside the charge of intent to murder) reflects how difficult it was to evaluate these factors. The sentence falls just halfway between the maximum punishment that for some seemed the only possible appropriate one, given the nature of the crime, and outright acquittal. What all could see, in any case, was the public event the trial constituted, and its effect on French social life.

CRIMES AGAINST HUMANITY

As a trial for crimes against humanity, the Papon case aroused debate about this category of offense, a debate all the more topical for being the basis of the deliberations the International Criminal Court of The Hague completed in its investigation of crimes committed in the former Yugoslavia and Rwanda. The common objectives to such a category are well known. A crime against humanity requires: (1) the condemnation of those who have not actually violated any law; (2) the pursuit of the representative of a group rather than an individual; and (3) the renunciation of prescription, or a statute of limitations, which is the capacity for forgetting that the law grants unto itself. The responses to these objections are just as familiar: certain general principles of humanity may be inferred from the very existence of law itself; violation of these principles is thus always subject to condemnation; and an individual may be indicted not just for belonging to a specific group but for the decisions for which he has been personally responsible.

The problem presented by prescription, on the other hand, raises many more difficulties. Papon was convicted in 1998 for actions committed in 1942, some fifty-six years after the fact. It is hard to imagine that those responsible for the Rwandan genocide will escape judgment until the year 2050. The problem involves more than imagination, however. The first objection to the lack of a statute of limitations comes from the difficulty it creates for the work itself of the court. If a judicial case is established on the basis of documents and testimony, then what is testimony worth when it is given fifty years after the fact? When the accounts the witnesses give to themselves and to those close to them have long since replaced their initial impressions? This was widely viewed as the reason for the acquittal in the Demjanjuk case in Israel. Written documents themselves require an intuitive familiarity with their context to be correctly interpreted.

Can we suppose that the jurors in this case had any such familiarity? Some of them were young enough to be Papon's great-grandchildren; none were chosen for their quality as historians. We take all possible precautions in establishing the truth in the murder of a single individual. Should we be any less attentive when the victims are counted in the thousands or even millions?

The judicial concept of a lack of prescription can be questioned on more general grounds too. To judge an individual for crimes committed fifty years earlier is to posit that he has remained identical to himself. Such a supposition is contrary to what biology and psychology teach us, not to mention simple common sense. What's more, it also violates the principles of humanist philosophy upon which our modern secular states are based. Rousseau claimed that man was perfectible, and that therein lay his specificity. Unlike animals, he can change, and that makes him responsible for his being. This does not mean that everyone changes, but to preclude this possibility would be to deny to a part of humanity any belonging to humanity itself, which is moreover the very definition of what a crime against humanity does. This is why the death penalty is barbarous: by taking away the possibility of change from certain individuals, it excludes them from human rights before depriving them of life.

The category of imprescriptibility appears then as an exception in the world of law. All crimes are limited after some period of time, except crimes against humanity. Now, there is no such solution of continuity among different types of crime. It is sometimes said that in a crime against humanity, people are killed for what they are rather than for what they have done. But, as Paul Ricoeur has noted, since the advent of total war, the extermination of civilian populations has become commonplace. What was the personal guilt of the inhabitants of Tokyo, of Hiroshima or Nagasaki, all of them wiped out in bombardments in 1945? They were killed for being Japanese, and war crimes are subject to a statute of limitations. To mark crimes against humanity by placing them in exceptional categories encourages us to separate them from other examples of human conduct, and to give up trying to understand them. Can anyone seriously think that is the best way to avoid repeating them?

Imprescriptibility is the law's translation of the eternal, but the eternal has no place in human justice, which no more recognizes the absolute or the sacred than the eternal. Justice deals with beings who are themselves finite, imperfect, and relative. This is why it counts amnesty and prescription among its practices, and why it dares to break with eternal cycles of vengeance by preferring peace, even if peace might seem an injustice in the eyes of God.

To renounce imprescriptibility in no way implies abandoning the idea that crimes remain crimes, regardless of the laws in force in the countries where they are committed. Crimes against humanity may transcend all spatial borders, but not temporal constraints. We should salute and encourage the international justice emerging today; for all that, it need not lay claim to eternity.

JUSTICE AS PEDAGOGY

There would not be quite so much discussion of the Papon case if it only involved finding an individual guilty. The case attracted so much attention because it was thought to educate the people, and in particular, as is often said in such instances, the younger generations, who were supposed to learn from it how Vichy's anti-Jewish policies had participated in the Nazis' "Final Solution." They would also see how a simple functionary, preoccupied only with his career, could contribute to a crime against humanity. Can it be claimed that the trial achieved its pedagogical goals?

The first trap it had to avoid was that of judgment by example, the idea that through Papon, Vichy, and even Auschwitz, were on trial. For this to happen, all those in France who had taken on responsibilities similar to or higher than those of Papon would have had to be charged. Of course, nothing of the sort took place; on the contrary, from the beginning it was understood that there would be one trial for the Gestapo (Klaus Barbie), one for the militia (Paul Touvier), and one for the administration (René Bousquet, or in his place, Papon). On the eve of the verdict, those who feared an acquittal issued a warning to public opinion that "to acquit Papon would be to exonerate Vichy!" But was this not an admission that the regime and not the man was being judged?

Several other judicial principles did not emerge unscathed from the ordeal. What is one to think of the numerous alterations and adjustments to the definition of a crime against humanity made by the highest judicial bodies in France, so that it would fit first the Touvier and then the Papon case? Or of the presumption of innocence, suddenly forgotten by the plaintiffs when the president of the tribunal authorized Papon to appear before the court while remaining free from custody? "What pedagogical benefits can one expect from a trial the accused has already lost ahead of time?" wondered Pierre Nora. Can one claim that the jurors experienced no pressure in arriving at a verdict, when all the respectable media and politicians from every party had found Papon guilty before or during the trial? Unfortunately, the lesson from the trial from this point of view was that in France, law remains subject to politics.

Then may we claim that the trial provided a lesson in history? Only with difficulty. No doubt there were some of high school age who heard for the first

time on this occasion about the suffering Jews during the Occupation, though
one wonders how they could possibly have missed the films and TV programs
that on a weekly basis present this period in history. But it is well known that
the courts are not a propitious source for the flowering of historical truth, for
historical truth is not of the same nature as judicial truth, which recognizes
only two values: guilt or innocence, black or white, yes or no. The questions
history asks do not allow for such answers most of the time. In the event, during the trial, two caricatures were substituted for the balanced and nuanced vision of the Vichy regime that has emerged in the work of historians over the
last twenty-five years; they were much easier for the public at large to retain.
The first presented the Pétain regime as a "shield" against the German invader,
sparing the French people the worst. The second assimilated it to a Fascist
regime, actively participating in the extermination of the Jews. The difference
in aims between justice and history conditioned every procedure. Thus the
court refused to allow certain documents into the file (what historian could
even imagine such a move?), or again, it imposed, as required by law, oral arguments, and then forbade the use of notes. (Try to imagine an historian who
isn't allowed to take notes!)

Judicial proceedings since antiquity have much in common with theatrical
performance. Like plays, trials must strike the minds and hearts of those attending. This rule was not overlooked in the course of the Papon trial. The lawyers
for the plaintiffs demanded the presence of the media and continuous debate
(so as to ensure the classical dramatic unity of action). They asked to be allowed
to project the photos of the child victims on a large screen, and they sought dramatic surprises to increase the tension. So goes justice. But what could such a
quest for effect have in common with the work of the historian, who aspires to
truth (even if he recognizes it can only be approximate) and equity?

Several polls demonstrated that, on the whole, the French were relatively satisfied with the existence of the trial. But ought we to rejoice in this satisfaction,
and deduce from it that the populace had made considerable progress in its political education? Or rather, should we be concerned before this tide of self-sat-
isfaction; should we realize that if the French are so unanimous in condemning
this character from another time when most of them were not yet born, it's because they do not recognize themselves in him, so they can leisurely cultivate
their good conscience: the bad guys are always the other guys? As for their political education, it's doubtful much has been achieved when we read the results
of another poll taken during the trial itself, in which 48 percent of the French
declare themselves "a bit racist." Closer still to the Papon trial: while the interrogations of the witnesses were taking place, the French minister of defense

categorically refused the request of the International Criminal Court to have French officers testify about the Bosnian and Rwandan massacres. Never, he claimed, would our soldiers lend themselves to such "justice as show business." The lesson of this sad coincidence can be easily summed up: we prosecute crimes against humanity as long as they were committed fifty years earlier, and when we ourselves are not involved.

Observing this failure to educate, this inability to draw any lessons from the past, should we conclude that it's better to forget? No, of course not. Rather, we should leave the task of education to the institutions whose declared goal it is: schools, the public media, Parliament. As for justice, it should be satisfied with promulgating the law and applying it to individuals. What's more, we have to admit that the undifferentiated evocation of the past is inadequate. To enjoy the prestige of our parent-heroes or to feel the suffering of our parent-victims contributed nothing to our moral education: such actions only serve our self-interest, whereas the task of moral education requires that we be disinterested. Recalling the past only educates us when it calls us into question and shows us that we ourselves have not always been the incarnation of good or of strength.

During the trial one French media personality said, "We mistreat our immigrants; fortunately, we have put Papon on trial today to refurbish the image of France." One would do well to ask instead whether, far from compensating for present injustices, our retrospective heroism has simply exempted us from combating them even when we are responsible for them.

Part III

THE "OTHER" PAPON TRIAL

17 October 1961

ACCORDING TO THE MANDELKERN

REPORT THIRTY-TWO WERE KILLED

DURING THE NIGHT OF 17 OCTOBER 1961

Le Monde, 5 May 1998

Philippe Bernard

According to the report drawn up at the request of the government by a senior member of the Council of State, Dieudonné Mandelkern, the police crackdown [on 17 October 1961] of the FLN demonstration against the curfew imposed on French-Algerian Muslims allegedly counted several dozen victims. This number, writes Mandelkern, remains "much lower than the several hundred victims claimed." Thirty-two dead is the "new" total for the police crackdown on the Paris demonstration of 17 October 1961. The Algerians were marching that day to protest the curfew imposed on them and in favor of independence for Algeria. This total, offered as hypothetical and issued with many reservations, figures in the report prepared by Dieudonné Mandelkern, senior member of the Council of State at the request of [Interior Minister] Jean-Pierre Chevènement.

The interior minister had ordered this work done last October, at the time the controversy over this bloody night had rebounded with the deposition of Maurice Papon, chief of Paris police at the time [before the Assizes Court in Bordeaux]. At that time *Libération* had published some extracts from a registry of the Paris public prosecutor's office that mentioned a list of bodies of Algerians brought to the Paris morgue (IML) following "assassinations" in the days after the demonstration. These developments once again cast doubt on the official assessment that stated that seven had died. In his book *The Battle of Paris*, Jean-Luc Einaudi had stated that there were more than two hundred dead.

Thirty-seven years after these events took place, Mandelkern's report does not really settle this quarrel over numbers. An assessment of the victims of this "very stiff repression" cannot be given with any "assurance," states the document, which relies on "the entry registry of the morgue . . . the most complete administrative record and the most trustworthy." According to the report, of the eighty-eight bodies of North Africans recorded at the morgue from 17 October to 31 December 1961, twenty-five were possible victims of demonstrations. Therefore, concludes Mandelkern, "allowing that a total of twenty-five cases were added to the official number of seven dead (from the Institut médico-légal NDLR) and that uncertain factors, especially those pertaining to the geographical limits of the study, justify a certain increase in numbers, we are still in the tens or twenties, which is considerable but much fewer than the several hundred claimed earlier."

The true importance of the report lies in the incredible number of gaps in the files. For example, "no copy" of the report of the police chief, Maurice Papon, sent to the minister of the interior, "which was also sent to the office of the president and the prime minister . . . seems to have been preserved in the files of police headquarters, nor at headquarters of the national police." The records of the River Authority police (Brigade Fluviale), which could have contained a list of bodies thrown into the Seine, were also destroyed "several years ago." The same lack of information is typical of the files of the official services charged with overseeing or of offering assistance to the Algerian population (Service for Coordinating Algerian Affairs, the Service of Technical Assistance for French Muslims of Algeria, the Center for Identification and Verification at Vincennes).

The report underscores the relatively small number of the forces of order for a demonstration in which twenty to twenty-five thousand people participated, and the tardy information from the police headquarters on the decision of the FLN to organize this unlawful parade. "The risk of the crowd getting out of hand might explain up to a point the violence of the clashes," writes Mandelkern. The report insists on "the extreme force of the crackdown in certain places" and the deplorable conditions in the hastily erected detention centers. Finally, the document puts the night of 17 October back into its context of a near civil war marked both by the murder of policemen and by "homicides perpetrated against the French Muslims from Algeria": 289 in only one year, 1961.

OCTOBER 1961:

FOR THE TRUTH, AT LAST

Le Monde, 20 May 1998

Jean-Luc Einaudi

Seven months after Minister of Culture Catherine Trautman's announcement that she would open the archives dealing with the events of 17 October 1961, an anouncement that occurred precisely at the moment I, as author of
La Bataille de Paris, was testifying about these events at the Papon trial, I have still
not been allowed to consult a single archival document. My letters to the prime
minister, the minister of the interior, and the minister of defense have all gone
unanswered. The opening of all the archives dealing with October 1961 and
their ready access to scholars are objectives that remain to be carried out.

By contrast, a report based on the archives and dealing with these events requested by the minister of the interior the day after I testified and submitted
by the State Councilor Dieudonné Mandelkern (president of the National
Commission for Security Control (Commission nationale de contrôle des in-
terceptions de sécurité) has recently been made public, initially in the pages of
Le Figaro.

A close reading of this report calls for several comments. First, Mr. Mandelkern and his co-authors are not happy simply to make an inventory of the
archives of the Paris police prefecture. They also presume to make "several observations" concerning their findings, including speculations concerning the
number of protesters killed, a figure which, they argue, was "very much smaller

than the hundreds of victims claimed here and there." Obviously, I am the target of this affirmation. At the Papon trial in Bordeaux, I testified that "during the period of time in question there was a minimum of two hundred killed and probably as many as three hundred."

In a democracy, it is not the role of high functionaries acting in their official capacities to write history. Let the scholars work freely in the archives, with the necessary critical spirit, cross-checking their finds with other sources. It would be totally unacceptable to use the Mandelkern report to lend credence to a new official truth concerning these events without allowing scholars to first consult all available sources.

The archives consulted in making this report are incomplete and the report is lacking in impartiality. Incomplete, as the authors themselves acknowledge, because the only archives consulted were those of the police prefecture and the department of the Seine. The fact is, however, that the events in question also took place in the former department of the Seine-et-Oise. Bodies were also found far from Paris, notably bodies carried downstream by the Seine. Incomplete as well because, as the report itself indicates, some archives have disappeared. Those of the River Authority (Brigade fluviale) have been destroyed in recent years, and it was this authority that fished out numerous bodies that were found at the time. The archives of the Service for Coordinating Algerian Affairs have also disappeared. This service "took the point" in the struggle against the FLN. Perhaps Roger Chaix, in charge of this service at the time and someone who has remained very close to Maurice Papon, has some idea as to what happened to these archives.

The list is not finished: the archives of the Center for Identification and Verification at Vincennes have disappeared as well. Just the same, one would wish to know the names of the 1,710 Algerians arrested on 17 October and who, according to the police prefecture, were still detained at Vincennes as of 6 November. One would want to know these names because, on the same 6 November, three deputies who visited the center counted only fifteen hundred detainees. So where were the two hundred missing Algerians?

It is also impossible to characterize these findings as impartial since they are the version of the facts provided by functionaries serving a hierarchy accused of involvement in the repression. It would be a serious misjudgment to believe therefore that the report contains the truth. It is indispensable that these archives be compared to others, and checked against other sources. Moreover, at certain junctures, the Mandelkern report accepts uncritically the police version of events, especially when it is a question of explaining the tragic "clashes" between the police and the demonstrators. These police accounts are false accounts, which the report echoes nonetheless. There were no "clashes" on the night of 17 October, only violent assaults by the police against peaceful demonstrators in which the police indulged in attacks based solely on the physical appearance of the victim.

The Mandelkern report discusses, among other episodes, the events that took place on the boulevards Poissonière and Bonne-Nouvelle. According to numerous testimonies, including that of the distinguished journalist Jacques Dérogy, police forces opened fire on the demonstrators on all the large boulevards. They then charged the demonstrators, coldly, without encountering any resistance. Numerous corpses of protesters lay on the ground in pools of blood, but there is no mention of these bodies in the official tally of seven killed given in the Mandelkern report. There is one exception: one finds in the report the name of Guy Chevalier, the only Frenchman to have been killed, whose death is finally acknowledged as having been caused by "numerous blows to the head from a nightstick, received during a police charge." One reads in the report as well that "gunfire was exchanged" (on the Neuilly Bridge and in the Saint-Michel–Saint-Germain area). In this instance the report reiterates false information originally generated to justify the use of arms by the police. The only gunshot victims were Algerians.

Another example of the excessive confidence the Mandelkern report places in the official version of events concerns the death of Amar Mallek, "mortally wounded by the gunfire of two policemen on 20 October at the Pierre-de-Coubertin Stadium." Maurice Papon himself explained this death as having resulted from Mallek's effort to flee and a single policeman's having gunned him down in conditions that conformed to official rules and procedures.

As it happens, the body of Amar Mallek was examined by doctors who were not attached to the police prefecture (to the best of my knowledge, this is the only instance where independent doctors examined the victims). The doctors in question concluded that Mallek died as a result of extraordinarily violent blows, and not as a consequence of gunshots.

In drawing its conclusions as to the number of people killed, the report relies in the main on the register of the Institut médico-légal (a register that I was not allowed to examine), but speculates that "perhaps some bodies were not transported to the institute at the time of the demonstrations of October and, as a result, were not counted in the official tally." However, having developed this very reasonable hypothesis, the report then dismisses its own insight in affirming that "this hypothesis is difficult to take into account." Why? We are not told. And there certainly were bodies that were *not* transported to the institute. I will mention as examples the Algerian victims held in the Sports Palace and placed under the surveillance of the Mobile Guards. What happened to these people? What service made them disappear? These questions still remain to be answered.

In the Mandelkern report one doesn't find a single trace of certain events — for example, what happened in the courtyard of the police prefecture on the night of 17 October? According to a number of police sources at the time, as many as fifty Algerians were killed there. It would of course have been surprising to find evidence of these victims in the police archives of Maurice Papon. So how can the report pretend to draw conclusions from *these* archives while calling into question the reliability of other research?

Constantin Melnik, who in 1961 was in charge of police affairs and information in the cabinet of the prime minister, Michel Debré, has testified on several occasions since 1991 that on the basis of information gathered at the time, he concluded that the death toll was between one hundred and fifty and three hundred killed. It is important to note that these figures coincide with those of Melnik's former enemies, the French Federation of the FLN, whose own sources suggest that the number killed was between two and three hundred.

If the findings of independent researchers working freely in the archives and having access to all sources suggest that I have been mistaken, and that the death toll of the repression of 17 October 1961 is, as Dieudonné Mandelkern suggests, much lower than I have written and stated on numerous occasions, then I will voluntarily recognize my error. But until that time, I will continue to affirm: in October 1961 a massacre took place in Paris that was perpetrated by police forces acting under the orders of Maurice Papon.

MONSIEUR PAPON

WILL NOT SHUT ME UP

Le Monde, 2 February 1998

Jean-Luc Einaudi

In its 20 May 1998 edition, *Le Monde* published an opinion piece I wrote entitled "For the Truth, at Last." At the conclusion of that piece I wrote, "But until that time, I will continue to affirm: in October 1961 a massacre took place in Paris that was perpetrated by police forces acting under the orders of Maurice Papon." For my having made this statement, Papon wants to have me declared "guilty of complicity in defaming a public functionary in the person of Maurice Papon, prefect of police in 1961" and wishes me to be sentenced to pay him one million francs. Accordingly, I will appear the fourth, fifth, eleventh, and twelfth of February of this year before the Seventeenth Correctional Chamber of the Paris High Tribunal.

As soon as I was aware of Papon's legal proceedings against me, my lawyer, Pierre Mairat, and I did everything possible to ensure that my trial will serve as the occasion to get at the truth of a crime that, for most of the last thirty-eight years, Maurice Papon has been trying to conceal. In order to accomplish this aim, I have called on numerous witnesses who, either through testimony in court or through written accounts, will say what they lived through, saw, or learned at the time of the events in question. Among them are a number of Algerians living in Algeria who were victims in 1961 of this savage repression and who, I hope, will receive visas from French authorities in order to come and testify in a

French court. In spite of the restraints imposed on my research as a result of being denied access to the archives of the prefect of police and the Paris prosecutor—access accorded to an historian hostile to me—I plan to establish that my writings since 1991, when I published *The Battle of Paris*, are solidly grounded in historical fact.

Just the same, why does Maurice Papon, who has refrained from undertaking legal proceedings against me in the past, do so now? The reason is that recently he has been convicted by the Bordeaux Assizes Court to ten years in prison for complicity in crimes against humanity, a sentence that he is currently appealing. It should be remembered that in October 1997, at the request of civil litigants, I testified in the context of the examination of Papon's curriculum vitae concerning what I knew of his actions as prefect of police. In seeking my condemnation in the Seventeenth Correctional Chamber of the Paris High Tribunal, Papon and his lawyer are attempting to develop an argument favorable to having the Bordeaux verdict overturned. Moreover, in cloaking himself in his role as prefect of police under General de Gaulle, Papon is attempting to protect himself beneath de Gaulle's shadow and to provoke reactions in the world of politics that will prove favorable to him. Finally, Papon is hoping to benefit from the Mandelkern report on the police archives submitted in January 1998 to Minister of the Interior Jean-Pierre Chevènement and which I have criticized as being both incomplete and lacking in impartiality.

As for myself, for years I have had no other motivation than to help shed light on the events of October 1961. My efforts coincide with those of others who, since that moment, have wanted to expose the truth, a truth that Papon has continually sought to squelch. Among others, I am thinking of Paulette Péju, whose book *Beatings in Paris* (*Ratonnades à Paris*) was confiscated; of the Maurice Audin Committee, whose newspaper, *Vérité-Liberté*, was confiscated; of Jacques Panijel, whose film *October in Paris* was seized; of François Maspero, whose review *Partisans* was confiscated.

Throughout the trial the luminous memory of my friend Claude Bourdet, who died on 20 March 1996, will be with me. Because of his commitment, he was, in my eyes, and as I told him one day, the anti-Papon. A member of the National Council of the Resistance, he remained faithful to the values of this "uncertain adventure," as he referred to the Resistance. The words that he addressed to Maurice Papon on 27 October 1961 during an extraordinary session of the Municipal Council of Paris have not ceased to reverberate. Calling for the creation of a commission to investigate the circumstances surrounding the terrible events that had just taken place, Bourdet stated: "These events deserve a serious, detailed, and impartial investigation whose integrity will guarantee that there will be no doubts as to the veracity of the findings either in France or abroad. In a matter of weeks, months, or even years, the truth will be known." Maurice Papon responded: "The police did what it had to do." There was no investigation.

Today, as one of his lawyers declared, Maurice Papon wants to shut me up. In the name of the memory of his Algerian victims, I will not be quiet, no matter what happens.

"ONE OF THE FEW TIMES SINCE THE

NINETEENTH CENTURY THAT POLICE

HAVE FIRED ON WORKERS IN PARIS"

An Interview with Benjamin Stora

Le Monde, 14–15 February 1999

Philippe Bernard

P. B.: What was occurring in the Algerian war when French Algerians decided to demonstrate in Paris on the night of 17 October 1961?

B. S.: The end of the conflict was near, because negotiations between General de Gaulle and the FLN were under way, and these negotiations would result five months later in the Évian accords. De Gaulle had made the choice of self-determination for Algeria two years before, but he wanted to deal in the negotiations from a position of power. Fundamental issues, including the fate of the Sahara and the status of the *pieds noirs*, remained to be resolved. The FLN was also motivated by the desire to deal from a position of strength. The French Federation of the FLN, which called for the demonstration, was worried about being forgotten and also wanted to make its presence felt in the negotiations. At the same time, this was a moment when a Franco-French civil war was developing. De Gaulle had just escaped an assassination attempt by the OAS and had to deal with the nervousness of his military and police forces.

This was the climate on 5 October, when the prefect of Paris police, Maurice Papon, decided to impose a curfew on Algerians, forbidding them to to go out in the evening in the ghettos in the suburbs where they resided.

To demonstrate their rejection of this decision, the French Federation of the FLN ordered the Algerians to demonstrate against the curfew on 17 October, to march on the *Grands boulevards*, the Champs-Élysées, and the Latin Quarter—in other words, the central space of the colonial metropole [*sic*]. The fear inspired by news of this order explains the extreme ferocity of the repression as well as the attitude of part of the press, which stigmatized what it described as the "North African invasion" occurring in the heart of Paris.

P. B.: Was the demonstration a surprise to the police?

B. S.: Not really, because they had been warned by their informers and the *harkis* [pro-French Algerians] who were on patrol in the Algerian communities. Hence the preparations made by the police to prevent the entry of the Algerians into the capital. Police cordons were established at the Neuilly and Bezons Bridges, which were principal points of access into the city and were among the locations where the tragedy occurred.

P. B.: How do you account for the unleashing of police violence?

B. S.: The rank and file were very nervous because police stations had been subjected to murderous machine gun attacks by Algerians. It must also be pointed out that Parisian police are known for their violence against Algerian immigrants. On 14 July 1953 the police fired on Algerians who were demonstrating with the Confédération nationale du travail to celebrate the French Revolution at the Place de la Nation. Six people were killed and fifty were wounded. Police bullets brought about more deaths on 9 March 1956, when Algerian nationalists protested against the special powers [a legislative decision requiring all young French conscripts to go fight in Algeria.]

These dramas have been erased from memory because the left was in power at the time, but they certainly forecast the paroxysm of 17 October 1961. By this time Algerians in France were perceived as a "fifth column." This reputation was reinforced by their ambiguous status. They were not considered to be completely French, even though they were nationals, nor were they considered Algerian, because their country was not recognized. They were called "Muslims" or "North Africans," and this juridical foreignness exacerbated the logic of suspicion that characterized police attitudes toward them. Finally, the Algerian war was always considered to be an operation for the maintenance of internal order, a police operation. The police thus felt themselves to be entrusted with a special mission.

P. B.: From the FLN's perspective, what was the strategic value of the demonstration?

B. S.: It was a question for the FLN of making a show of force in the heart of Paris at a moment when General de Gaulle still had thoughts of a "third way" between the FLN and French Algeria. To this must be added the desire of the French Federation of the FLN to be at the heart of Algerian nationalism. The choice had been made coercively for the Algerian émigrés in France to engage in political confrontation independent of the French left, although the French left ended up being in favor of Algerian independence. One might well wonder about the wisdom of this choice: it is possible that de Gaulle's determination to impose his will on the negotiations was underestimated, as was his will to maintain order.

P. B.: Maurice Papon blames the deaths of protesters on the night of 17 October on the settling of scores among rival Algerian factions. What do you think of this claim?

B. S.: The claim doesn't hold up for one second. In 1961 the MNA, the rival of the FLN, was beaten politically and physically. It had disappeared in the Paris region by 1959. At the time about which we are speaking, the FLN had consolidated its political power over the Algerians living in the metropole.

P. B.: But were there not Algerians who refused to follow the orders of the FLN?

B. S.: Of course, there had always been. But to imagine that the FLN would take advantage of a demonstration in the heart of Paris in order to kill people who refused to join up, that's absurd. The only possible settling of scores in Paris in 1961 were between the Algerian nationalists and the Parisian *harkis*, brigades of "blue caps" that Maurice Papon had seen at work when he was prefect of police in the Constantine region of Algeria in 1958, and whom he had had transferred to Paris. But if the *harkis* went into action on the night of 17 October 1961, it was on the side of the French police, surely not on the side of the demonstrators.

P. B.: Didn't the FLN's choice of confrontation on 17 October presuppose risks for the demonstrators?

B.S.: Frankly, no. This decision had more to do with an ignorance of the ways of French society than it did with the desire to send people to get their heads busted open. The French Federation of the FLN sincerely believed that a peaceful demonstration with women and children in the heart of Paris would show the world the desire of the Algerian people for independence. The naïveté as well as the underestimation of the consequences of this choice were total on the part of a directorate living not in France but in Germany. Under any circumstances, it was never the directorate's aim to open a second, violent front in France. The emigrant workers in the metropole were the primary financial resource of the Algerian maquis, and there was certainly no desire to destabilize the pipeline. That is why the claim that police violence was necessitated by a state of war existing in France simply doesn't hold up. The war was in Algeria, not France. Seventeen October 1961 was simply one of the rare moments in France since the nineteenth century when police fired on workers in Paris.

P.B.: Did the personality of Maurice Papon play a specific part in in these events?

B.S.: Papon is a high functionary whose hand doesn't tremble. In Bordeaux under Vichy or in the Constantine, he acted as a man of order and of authority and continued to do so in 1961. On 17 October, I believe he was obeying an order to reestablish order and at all costs to prevent Paris from becoming an echo chamber of Algerian nationalism.

P.B.: What has become of the memory of 17 October 1961 in France and in Algeria?

B.S.: For a long time the day has been commemorated in Algeria as the "Day of Immigration." Algeria is a country that legitimizes itself by claiming for itself a superheroic history and counting up its martyrs. The people are presented as the only heroes, while individuals like Mohamed Boudiaf, who led the struggle, are papered over because they are no longer politically in favor. On the French side, the date has been carefully obfuscated. The memory came to the surface again in 1991 when the children of the émigrés organized a commemorative demonstration. The *Beurs* seek the history of their parents as well as their own genealogy in French society. They wish at the same time to be French and respect the memory of their fathers, and they therefore want to inscribe 17 October in the history of France.

MAURICE PAPON DECLARES THE BLOODY

CRACKDOWN OF 17 OCTOBER 1961

AN "UNFORTUNATE EVENING"

Le Monde, 7–8 February 1999

Acacio Pereira

"Hold Paris," de Gaulle Was Alleged to Have Told the Former Paris Police Chief

V isibly well recovered from an "acute influenza" that had kept him from attending the first day of the hearing at the Seventeenth Correctional Chamber of the Paris High Tribunal, Maurice Papon, on Friday, 5 February, gave his own version of the events of 17 October 1961. On that day, a demonstration organized by the Algerian FLN to protest against the curfew imposed on Muslims was brutally put down.

Before the court, the individual who was chief of police in the capital at that time attacked Jean-Luc Einaudi for "complicity in libel" for his article published in *Le Monde* in which Einaudi claimed: "In Paris there was a massacre perpetrated by police forces acting on the orders of Maurice Papon."

Sporting a tiny white mustache, dressed in a charcoal gray suit, and wearing a black tie, Maurice Papon had prepared his speech as a professor would prepare a course. Organized in three parts, it related the "FLN offenses," the "retaliation of the French government and its police force," and "the 17 October demonstration that had the virtue of putting an end to FLN terrorism."

If we are to believe Maurice Papon, it was at this time that the FLN tried to "create urban warfare in Paris as taught by famous revolutionaries such as Mao Tse-tung, in order to create panic among the population," but also to eliminate its principal competitor, the Algerian National Movement (MNA). The chief of police had received strict orders from General de Gaulle, president of the Republic, to "hold Paris." "We were to protect the population, including Algerians exposed to the plundering and demands of the FLN," explained Maurice Papon. "We also had a duty to restore confidence in the police ranks, which were experiencing a deep unrest, in order to avoid impulsive reactions."

He pronounced the demonstration "superficially peaceful." "All the Algerians from Paris and the suburbs had been mobilized with orders to attend the gatherings unarmed," he admitted. "But [the organizers] were not content to 'invite' but pressured the workers by threatening them with punishment, and units of the FLN were present and armed." According to the former police chief, authorities constantly feared that the demonstration would become violent. "What could have happened if they were overwhelmed and swamped? It almost happened," he declared in citing "incidents" that occurred at the Neuilly Bridge and which were alleged to have brought officers and demonstrators face to face. "If the mob had not been stopped there, the columns would have gone on to invade the Champs-Elysées, becoming more and more fanatical as they went."

Maurice Papon then sprang to his feet to refute the idea of a "massacre" advanced by Jean-Luc Einaudi: "What I emphatically deny is that these events were the result of police anger. Have you seen them strangling or emasculating anyone? Look at what's happening today in Algeria. In France, we cannot do that, it's inconceivable!"

"The Mandelkern report, however, speaks of a 'violent repression,'" the chief justice of the court, Jean-Yves Monfort, reminded him. "For my part, I would remove the superlative," responded the former police chief.

In concluding, Maurice Papon gave a rather positive assessment of what he qualified as an "unfortunate evening." "The demonstration included around twenty thousand people and eleven thousand were directed to buses that would take them to a number of shelter centers," he insisted. "These individuals were examined separately, which allowed us to discover 2,454 FLN members who were repatriated."

"How can so many interrogations be explained with the limited number of police?" asked the judge. "Thanks to the willingness of those who were apprehended who were not rebellious and were very happy to be rid of this chore imposed on them by the FLN," retorted Maurice Papon.

The day before, Jean-Luc Einaudi had given a more dramatic version of these "massive roundups" during which, according to him, more than two hundred people were allegedly killed. But Maurice Papon was not about to deny his own testimony. He refuted the witnesses who stated that around fifty had died in the Court of Honor at police headquarters. "That is unreasonable and unprovable," said Papon disdainfully. "There were some scuffles and I personally went down to calm the situation." Although he later accepted the number of "around thirty dead," as reported during the court session, he denied that bodies had been thrown in the Seine by the police. "They proceeded with the identifications and had uncovered members of the MNA or Muslims who had worked with the police and been liquidated by the FLN."

Maurice Papon totally rejected all the accusations. And what of the three policemen who denounced the "massacre" carried out in the police courtyard? "A small group of left-wing activists." And the photographs by Elie Kagan taken during the demonstration? "I don't doubt at all that they were doctored." The testimony of those who were present at the extortions? "They are suspect. Why didn't they speak up at the time? They should have denounced these crimes." And the critical statements of Gérard Monate, at that time the associate secretary-general of the principal union of police? "He was known as a schemer . . ."

Concerning his final responsibility in the police crackdown on the demonstration, the former police chief limited himself to a simple explanation: "The measures taken were decided in a high place. The police chief is under the directives of the minister of the interior, indeed, of the prime minister and the head of state."

The arguments will continue on Thursday, 11 February, with the additional witnesses for the defense.

THE MAGISTRATES' COURT OF PARIS

ACKNOWLEDGES THE "EXTREME

VIOLENCE" OF THE POLICE CRACKDOWN

OF 17 OCTOBER 1961

Le Monde, 28–29 March 1998

Philippe Bernard

Maurice Papon, chief of the Paris police at the time of the demonstration on 17 October 1961 of the National Liberation Front (FLN), cannot legally claim damages from Jean-Luc Einaudi, author of a book on the subject, for having written in *Le Monde* that the bloody police crackdown on the demonstration constituted "a massacre" carried out by "the forces of order acting under orders from Maurice Papon," (*Le Monde*, 20 May 1998), even if this assertion proved to be defamatory. This was the decision of the Seventeenth Correctional Chamber of the Paris High Tribunal, presided over by Jean-Yves Monfort, in a detailed decision handed down Friday, 26 March.

The reading by the judge of the thirty-one pages of the decision, the first on this historically important subject, had the audience holding their breath for nearly an hour. In the opinion of the court those Algerian deaths on 17 October 1961 are not a historian's whim but a tragic reality worthy of a discussion about those responsible. "From the moment we admit that the official version of events of 1961 seems to have been largely inspired by reasons of state— possibly admissible because of the situation at the time—and that the extreme brutality of the crackdown at that time should today call for a different analysis that does not exclude the use of the word 'massacre,' it would be impossible to condemn an historian, whose overall research is unquestionably valid, for having lacked 'caution' when he described the facts harshly in his concluding words . . . and curtly pointed out the individual responsible."

Thus, in a paradoxical fashion, the courts, acting on a complaint of libel from Maurice Papon, were brought around to admitting for the first time the brutality of the police for whom Papon was responsible in 1961. In fact, this decision is the first legal intervention on the subject of these events that were almost completely covered up for thirty years.

The decision, which was solidly supported, qualified the incriminated phrase as "obviously " defamatory, as had the substitute, Vincent Lesclous, to the court. But the judges did not agree with the representative from the public ministry who had requested a sentence of principle. The court discharged Jean-Luc Einaudi in according him "the benefit of good faith," thanks to the "serious, timely and complete" character of his lengthy and thorough investigation, which constitutes both a homage to this guardian of memory and an indirect analysis of the 17 October events.

Pointing out that "the group of witnesses" quoted by Jean-Luc Einaudi "have not been refuted," the court finds that "the evidence presented would lead us to believe that certain members of the police force, relatively numerous, acted with extreme violence in a desire for deliberate revenge and in a climate of anger that was the result of many assaults on police officers at an earlier date," and that "this violence was not justified by the behavior of the militants on that evening." Moreover, "violence was used not only 'in anger' during the demonstrations themselves, but also 'in cold blood' in the internment centers hastily set up to house those arrested," and that "the number of victims was noteworthy, in any case larger than that of the official total."

Returning to the accusation by Jean-Luc Einaudi of the responsibility of Maurice Papon, the verdict quotes both the vengeful words of the police chief—"For each blow received, we will give ten"—and the written comments in 1963 claiming a "direct and personal responsibility" for the maintenance-of-order directives.

In all, "taking into account the information at the disposal of the hierarchy of the seriousness of the behavior described by witnesses and of its tragic consequences, of the public controversy that began the day following the events, an historian would have been forced to ask questions about the personal responsibility of the police chief."

Basing his argument on the indirect character of this accusation against the former police chief, Papon's lawyer, Maître Jean-Marc Varaut, concluded that the court "had not established either [the existence of] the massacre or the responsibility of Maurice Papon." "Disappointed," he will wait until 31 March to announce whether or not he will appeal. As for Maître Pierre Mairat, defense attorney for Jean-Luc Einaudi, "the truth is now on the march and nothing further can stop it." His client hopes that, in the wake of the decision, the prime minister also will break his silence on the events of October 1961. He hopes for this "for the sake of Franco-Algerian relations" as well as "for the descendants of the victims, who make up the youth who have come from immigration."

BIBLIOGRAPHY

Baruch, Marc-Olivier. "Procès Papon: Impressions d'audience." *Le Débat* 102 (November–December 1998), pp. 11–16.

———. *Servir l'État français: L'Administration en France de 1940 à 1944.* (Paris: Fayard, 1997).

Bédarida, François. *Touvier, le dossier de l'accusation.* (Paris: Seuil, 1996).

Best, Geoffrey. *War and Law since 1945.* (Oxford: Oxford University Press, 1995).

Billig, Joseph. *Le Commissariat général aux Questions juives (1941–1944).* 3 vols. (Paris: Éditions du Centre, 1955).

Boulanger, Gérard. *Maurice Papon: Un Technocrate français dans la collaboration.* (Paris: Seuil, 1994).

———. *Papon, un intrus dans la République.* (Paris: Seuil, 1997).

Bracher, Nathan. "Memory Null and Void? The Broken Record of Vichy Polemics in the Papon Case." *Contemporary French Civilization* 23:1 (winter–spring 1999), pp. 65–80.

Bredin, Jean Denis. "Le Droit, le juge et l'historien." *Le Débat* 32 (November 1984), p. 93.

———. "History and Justice Abused." *Memory, the Holocaust and French Justice: The Bousquet and Touvier Affairs.* (Hanover, N.H.: University Press of New England, 1996), pp. 109–13.

Bruno, Jean, and Frédéric de Monicault. *L'Affaire Papon: Bordeaux: 1942–1944.* (Paris: Tallandier, 1997).

Burrin, Philippe. *La France à l'heure allemande.* (Paris: Seuil, 1995).

———. "La France et le fascisme." *Le Débat* 32 (November 1984), pp. 52–72.

Carpi, Daniel. *Between Mussolini and Hitler: The Jews and the Italian Authorities in France and Tunisia.* (Hanover, N.H.: University Press of New England, 1995).

Cohen-Grillet, Philippe. *Maurice Papon: De la collaboration aux assises.* (Bordeaux: Le Bord De L'eau, 1997).

Colin, Marcel, ed. *Le Crime contre l'humanité.* (Ramonville Saint-Agne: Érès, 1996).

Conan, Éric. "À lire en marge du procès." *L'Express,* 2 October 1997), p. 56.

————. "Le Casse-Tête juridique." *L'Express*, 2 October 1997), pp. 54–56.

————. "Papon, les Français et Vichy." *L'Express*, 2 October 1997), pp. 28–31.

————. *Le Procès Papon: Un Journal d'audience*. (Paris: Gallimard, 1998).

————. "Un Vichysto-Résistant parmi d'autres." *L'Express*, 2 October 1997), pp. 48–50.

————. "La Vraie Vie de René Bousquet." *L'Express*, 5 October 1990), p. 32.

Conan, Éric, and Henry Rousso. *Vichy: An Ever-Present Past*. Trans. by Nathan Bracher. (Hanover, N.H.: University Press of New England, 1998). Trans. of *Vichy, un passé qui ne passe pas*. (Paris: Fayard, 1994).

Le crime contre l'humanité: Mesure de la responsabilité? Actes du cycle des conférences Droit, Liberté et Foi, Juin 1997. École Cathédrale, Institute de Formation Continue du Barreau de Paris. (Paris: CERP, 1998).

Daeninckx, Didier. *Muertres pour mémoire*. (Paris: Gallimard, 1984).

Delperrié de Bayac, Jacques. *Histoire de la milice, 1918–1945*. (Paris: Fayard, 1969).

Dossier Bousquet. *Libération*. Supplement. 13 July 1993.

Dumay, Jean-Michel. *Le procès de Maurice Papon: La Chronique de Jean-Michel Dumay*. (Paris: Fayard, 1998).

Einaudi, Jean-Luc. *La Bataille de Paris. 17 octobre 1961*. Paris: Seuil, 1991.

————. "Le Papon des ratonnades." *L'Express*, 2 October 1997, pp. 53–54.

Finkielkraut, Alain. *Comment peut-on ête Croate?* (Paris: Gallimard, 1992).

————. *The Future of a Negation: Reflections on the Question of Genocide*. Trans. Mary Byrd Kelly. (Lincoln: University of Nebraska Press, 1998).

————. *L'Ingratitude: Conversation sur notre temps*. (Paris: Gallimard, 1999).

————. *Remembering in Vain: The Klaus Barbie Trial and Crimes against Humanity*. (New York: Columbia University Press, 1992).

Finkielstein, Claire. "Changing Notions of State Agency in International Law: The Case of Paul Touvier." *Texas International Law Journal* 30:2 (1995), pp. 261–84 .

Froment, Pascale. *René Bousquet*. (Paris: Stock, 1994).

Frossard, André. *Le Crime contre l'humanité*. (Paris: Laffont, 1987).

Garaudy, Roger. *Le Procès du sionisme israélien*. (Paris: Vent du Large, 1998).

Golsan, Richard J., ed. *Memory, the Holocaust, and French Justice: The Bousquet and Touvier Affairs*. (Hanover, N.H.: Dartmouth Books: University Press of New England, 1996).

————. "Memory's *bombes à retardement*: Maurice Papon, Crimes against Humanity, and 17 October 1961." *Journal of European Studies* 28 (1998), pp. 153–172.

————. "Memory and Justice Abused: The 1949 Trial of René Bousquet." *Studies in Twentieth Century Literature* 23:1 (1999), pp. 93–110.

————. "Que reste-t-il de l'affaire Touvier? Mémoire, histoire et justice." *French Review* 72.1 (October 1998), pp. 102–12.

Gravier, Bruno, and Jean-Marc Elchardus, eds. *Le Crime contre l'humanité*. (Paris: Erès, 1996).

Greilsamer, Laurent. "Un 'collaborateur précieux.'" *Le Monde*, 9 June 1993.

Greilsammer, Laurent, and Daniel Schneidermann. *Un Certain Monsieur Paul: L'Affaire Touvier*. Rev. ed. (Paris: Fayard, 1992).

Gros, Dominique. "Un Droit monstrueux?" *Le Droit antisémite de Vichy*. *Le Genre humain* 30–31. Ed. Maurice Olender. (Paris: Seuil, 1996).

Guéry, Christian. "Une Interrogation après le procès Touvier: Le Crime contre l'humanité existe-t-il?" *Juger sous Vichy*. *Le Genre humain* 28. Ed. Maurice Olender. (Paris: Seuil, 1994), pp. 119–38).

Guicheteau, Gérard. *Papon Maurice ou la continuité de l'État*. (Paris: Mille et Une Nuits, 1998).

Haget, Henri. "Paroles de victimes." *L'Express*, 2 October 1997, pp. 38–44.

Hartog, François. "L'Historien et la conjoncture historique." *Le Débat* 102 (November–December 1998), pp. 4–10.

Hellman, John. *The Knight-Monks of Vichy France: Uriage 1940–1945*. (Montreal: McGill-Queen's University Press, 1993).

Hoffmann, Stanley. "Cinquante ans apres." *Esprit* 181 (May 1992), pp. 38–42.

———. "A Symposium on Mitterrand's Past." *French Politics and Society* 13.1 (winter 1995), p. 7.

Husson, Jean-Pierre. "L'Itinéraire d'un haut fonctionnaire: René Bousquet." *Vichy et les Francais*. Ed. Jean-Pierre Azéma and François Bédarida. (Paris: Fayard, 1992), pp. 292–93.

Jankélévitch, Vladimir. *L'Imprescriptible: Pardonner? Dans l'honneur et la dignité*. (Paris: Seuil, 1986).

Jeanneney, Jean-Noël. *Le Passé dans le prétoire: L'Historien, le juge et le journaliste*. (Paris: Seuil, 1998).

Judt, Tony. "Truth or Consequences." *New York Review of Books*, 3 November 1994, pp. 11–12.

Julliard, Jacques. *L'année des fantômes: Journal 1997*. (Paris: Bernard Grasset, 1998).

Keijman, Georges. "L'Histoire devant ses juges." *Le Débat* 32 (November 1984), pp. 112–13.

Klarsfeld, Arno. *La Cour, les nains et le bouffon*. (Paris: Robert Laffont, 1998).

———. *Papon: Un Verdict français*. (Paris: Ramsay, 1998).

———. *Touvier, un crime français*. (Paris: Fayard, 1994).

Klarsfeld, Serge. Interview with Marie-Amélie Lombard. *Le Figaro*, 9 June 1993.

———. *Vichy-Auschwitz: Le Role de Vichy dans la solution finale de la questions juive en France*. 2 vols. (Paris: Fayard, 1985).

Klarsfeld, Serge, and Henry Russo. "Histoire et justice: Débat entre Serge Klarsfeld et Henry Rousso." *Esprit* 181 (May 1992), pp. 16–37.

Kupferman, Fred. *Le Procès de Vichy: Pucheu, Pétain, Laval.* (Brussels: Complexe, 1980).

Lacouture, Jean. *Mitterand, une histoire de Français. Tome 2: Les Vertiges du sommet.* (Paris: Seuil, 1998).

Laughland, John. *The Death of Politics: France under Mitterrand.* (London: Michael Joseph, 1994).

Lambert, Bernard. *Dossier d'accusation: Bousquet, Papon, Touvier.* (Paris: FNDIRP, n.d.).

Maier, Charles. *The Unmasterable Past: History, the Holocaust, and German National Identity.* (Cambridge: Harvard University Press, 1988).

Maillard, Jean de. "À quoi sert le procès Papon" *Le Débat* 101 (September–October 1998).

Marrus, Michael, and Robert Paxton. *Vichy France and the Jews.* (New York: Schocken, 1983), pp. 250–52.

Matisson, Maurice-David, and Jean-Paul Abribat. *Psychanalyse de la collaboration: Le syndrome de Bordeaux: 1940–1945.* (Paris: Hommes et Perspectives, 1991).

Mayer, Arno J. *Why Did the Heavens Not Darken? The "Final Solution" in History.* (New York: Pantheon, 1990).

Mitterrand, François, and Elie Wiesel. *Mémoire à deux vois.* (Paris: Odile Jacob, 1995).

Mongin, Olivier. "La France de Mitterrand ou le royaume de l'anachronisme." *Esprit* (November 1994).

Morgan, Ted. *An Uncertain Hour: The French, the Germans, the Jews, the Barbie Trial, and the City of Lyon, 1940–1945.* (New York: William Morrow, 1990).

Noiriel, Gérard. *Sur la "crise" de l'histoire.* (Paris: Belin, 1996).

Novick, Peter. *The Resistance versus Vichy: The Purge of Collaborators in Liberated France.* (New York: Columbia University Press, 1968).

Papon, Maurice. *Les Chevaux du pouvoir.* (Paris: Plon, 1988).

Paris, Erna. *Unhealed Wounds: France and the Klaus Barbie Affair.* (New York: Grove Press, 1985).

Paxton, Robert O. "A Symposium on Mitterrand's Past." *French Politics and Society* 13.1 (winter 1995), pp. 19–21.

———. *Vichy France: Old Guard and New Order, 1940–1944.* (New York: Columbia University Press, 1982).

Poirot-Delpech, Bertrand. *Papon: Un Crime de bureau.* (Paris: Stock, 1998).

Le Procès de Maurice Papon. Compte Rendu Sténographique. 2 vols. Les Grands Procès Contemporains. (Paris: Albin Michel, 1998).

Rajsfus, Maurice. *La Police de Vichy: Les Forces de l'ordre au service de la Gestapo.* (Paris: Cherche Midi, 1995).

Rassat, Michèle-Laure. *La justice en France.* (Paris: Presses Universitaires de France, 1985).

Reisman, W. Michael, and Chris T. Antoniou, eds. *The Laws of War: A Collection of Primary Documents of International Laws Governing Armed Conflict.* (New York: Vintage, 1994), p. 319.

Rémond, René, et al. *Paul Touvier et l'Église: Rapport de la Commission historique instituée par le cardinal Decourtray.* (Paris: Fayard, 1992).

Rémy, Dominique, ed. *Les Lois de Vichy: Actes dits "lois" de l'autorité de fait se prétendant "gouvernement de L'Etat français."* (Paris: Romillat, 1992).

Rousso, Henry. *La hantise du passé: Entretien avec Philippe Petit.* (Paris: Textuel, 1998).

————. "Une Justice impossible: L'Épuration de la politique antijuive de Vichy." *Annales* 48:3 (May–June 1992), pp. 745–70.

————. "Pour les jeunes, un passé très présent." *L'Express,* 2 October 1997, pp. 32–34.

————. *Le Syndrome de Vichy: De 1944 à nos jours.* (Paris: Seuil 1987). Trans. *The Vichy Syndrome: History and Memory in France since 1944.* Cambridge, Mass.: Harvard University Press, 1991.

Ryan, Donna F. *The Holocaust and the Jews of Marseille.* (Urbana: University of Illinois Press, 1996).

Schneidermann, Daniel. *L'Étrange procès.* (Paris: Fayard, 1998).

Slitinsky, Michel. *L'Affaire Papon.* (Paris: Alain Moreau, 1983).

————. *Procès Papon: Le Devoir de justice.* (Paris: Éditions de l'Aube, 1997).

Sweets, John. *Choices in Vichy France: The French under Nazi Occupation.* (New York: Oxford University Press, 1986).

————. *The Politics of Resistance in France, 1940–1944: A History of the Mouvements Unis de la Résistance.* De Kalb: Northern Illinois University Press, 1976.

Taguieff, Pierre-André. "L'Abbé Pierre et Roger Garaudy. Négationnisme, antijudaïsm, antisionisme." *Esprit* 8–9 (1996), pp. 205–16.

Taylor, Telford. *The Anatomy of the Nuremberg Trials: A Personal Memoir.* (Boston: Little, Brown, 1992).

Thenault, Sylvie. "Le 17 octobre 1961 en question." *Jean Jaurès Cahiers Trimestriels* 148 (July–September 1998), pp. 89–104.

Thibaud, Paul. "l'Homme au-dessus des lois." *Le Débat* (Septembre–November 1994), p. 116.

————. "Un temps de mémoire?" *Le Débat* 96 (September–October 1997), pp. 166–83.

Thomas, Yann. "La véité, le temps, le juge et l'historien," *Le Débat* 102 (November–December 1998), pp. 17–36.

Tigar, Michael, et al. "Paul Touvier and the Crime against Humanity." *Texas International Law Journal* 30:2 (1995), pp. 286–310.

Todorov, Tzvetan. *Les Abus de la mémoire.* (Paris: Arléa, 1995).

————. "Letter from Paris: Racism." *Salmagundi* 88–89 (fall 1990–winter 1991), p. 3.

Trémolet de Villers, Jacques. *Paul Touvier est innocent.* (Paris: Dominique Martin Morin, 1990).

Varaut, Jean-Marc. *Plaidoirie de Jean–Marc Varaut, devant la cour d'assises de la Gironde au procès de Maurice Papon, fonctionnaire sous l'occupation.* Paris: Plon, 1998.

Vergès, Jacques, and Étienne Bloch. *La Face cachée du procès Barbie.* (Paris: Samuel Tastet, 1983).

Vidal-Naquet, Pierre. *Assassins of Memory: Essays on the Denial of the Holocaust.* Trans. Jeffrey Mehlman. (New York: Columbia University Press, 1992).

———. "Ce qui accable Papon." *Le Nouvel Observateur,* 23–29 October 1997, pp. 56–57.

———. *Mémoires 2, le trouble et la lumiére 1955–1998.* (Paris: Seuil/la Découverte, 1998).

———. *Réflexions sur le génocide: Le Juifs, la mémoire, et le présent. Tome III.* (Paris: Seuil, 1995).

Voléry, Anne. "La Bataille sans nom." *Carnet d'échanges* 1 (May 1999), pp. 7–15.

Weill, Nicolas. "Penser le procès Papon." *Le Débat* 103 (January–February 1999), pp. 100–10.

Weisberg, Richard H. *Vichy Law and the Holocaust in France.* (New York: New York University Press, 1996).

Wexler, Leila Sadat. "The Interpretation of the Nuremberg Principles by the French Court of Cassation: From Touvier to Barbie and Back Again." *Columbia Journal of Transnational Law* 32.2 (1994), pp. 349, 288–380.

Wood, Nancy. "Memory on Trial in Contemporary France: The Case of Maurice Papon." *History and Memory* 11:1 (spring–summer 1999), pp. 41–76.

Zuccotti, Susan. *The Holocaust, the French, and the Jews.* (New York: Basic, 1993).

APPENDIX:

CHRONOLOGY

3 September 1910 Maurice Papon, the youngest of three children of Arthur and Marie Papon, is born in Gretz-Armainvilliers in the Seine-et-Marne department. A good student, Papon studies letters at twelve as a resident at the Lycée Montaigne in Paris. He will later attend the Lycée Louis-le-Grand

1929 Papon passes the baccalauréat exam, and begins university studies in literature and law.

February 1931 Papon is a militant participant in the Radical-Socialist youth movement in Paris. The Radical-Socialist Party is center-left in its politics. Papon also begins government service, working in the cabinet of Jacques-Louis Daumesnil, named minister of air in the cabinet of Pierre Laval. Daumesnil is a friend of Papon's father.

1932 Papon marries Paulette Asso, with whom he will have three children, born between 1934 and 1948.

June 1936 Papon works in the cabinet of the undersecretary of state, François de Tessan (also a friend of Arthur Papon), in Léon Blum's Popular Front government. His responsibilities include Moroccan and Tunisian affairs.

3 September 1939 France, along with Great Britain, Australia, and New Zealand, declares war on Germany.

10 May 1940 Germany launches its western offensive.

14 June 1940 Paris falls to the Germans.

16 June 1940   Premier Paul Reynaud resigns. Marshal Philippe Pétain, who will head the Vichy regime, requests an armistice from the Germans. On 22 June the French government signs the armistice with Nazi Germany at Rethondes.

10 July 1940   The French parliament votes full governing powers to Philippe Pétain and his *État français* (French State). In so doing, the Third Republic votes itself out of existence.

22 July 1940   The Vichy government creates a commission to review the naturalizations of immigrants and of foreign Jews in particular, since 1927. According to Serge Klarsfeld, this is the first cornerstone of "Vichy's anti-Jewish edifice."[1] Subsequent measures dated 16 August and 10 September restrict the medical and legal practices to children born of French fathers. Although not explicitly anti-Semitic, the measures further marginalize Jewish immigrants and others fleeing from Nazi Germany and Eastern Europe.

27 August 1940   Vichy repeals the "Marchandeau Law," which outlawed any press attack on "a group of persons who belong by origin to a particular race or religion when [that attack] is intended to arouse hatred among citizens or residents." Henceforth anti-Semitic propaganda becomes a staple of many collaborationist newspapers and magazines.

October 1940   Called for military service in August 1939 at the outset of the "Phony War" and serving as a lieutenant in the French army in Tripoli, Papon is demobilized after returning to Clermont-Ferrand for medical reasons. He debates joining with de Gaulle and the Free French but eventually opts to serve Vichy, going to the new French capital in November. He goes to work in Vichy's Ministry of the Interior, where he works for Maurice Sabatier, under whom he will later serve in Bordeaux.

4 October 1940   The first of Vichy's anti-Jewish Statutes is promulgated. It calls for the arbitrary arrest and detainment in French concentration comps of foreign Jews and severely restricts the civil rights of French Jews. Jews are henceforth excluded "from top positions in the public service, from the officer corps and from the ranks of noncommissioned officers, and from professions that influence public opinion: teaching, the press, radio, film, and the theater."[2]

February 1941   Papon is promoted and given the title of subprefect

29 March 1941   Without seeking prior approval from the German military authorities, the Vichy government creates the Commissariat-General of Jewish Affairs under the direction of Xavier Vallat, a well-known anti-Semite and a fierce nationalist who believes Jews cannot be assimilated culturally. The idea of a central office for dealing with Jewish affairs and the "Jewish question" initially came from the Germans, who had their own list of potential commissioners in mind. Among them were Louis Darquier de Pellepoix, who would later head the agency, and the notoriously anti-Semitic writer and pamphleteer Louis-Ferdinand Céline.[3]

14 May 1941   The first of Vichy's roundups of foreign Jews is carried out by French police. More than 3,700 Jews are arrested and their civil status reviewed. Most are subsequently interned in French concentration camps at Pithiviers and Beaune-la-Rolande and later deported to Auschwitz.

2 June 1941   The Second Jewish Statute is promulgated. It has been carefully prepared for several months in cabinet meetings at Vichy. According to historians Michael Marrus and Robert Paxton, it is "a properly French initiative without direct German intervention." The Second Jewish Statute and subsequent ancillary measures limit Jews to comprising 2 percent of the liberal professions and 3 percent of students enrolled in institutions of higher education. They also call for a detailed census of all Jews in the Unoccupied Zone, "a grave step which was to have fatal consequences later when Jews were being rounded up and deported." On 22 July an "aryanization" law empowers the state "to place all Jewish property in the hands of a non-Jewish trustee who had the authority to liquidate it if it was deemed unnecessary to the French economy, or to sell it to a non-Jewish producer."[4]

20 August 1941   A second roundup, occurring over several days, is carried out by the French police. The roundup is undertaken at he behest of the Nazis and in reprisal for Communist agitation following the German invasion of the Soviet Union.

12 December 1941   A third roundup of Jews is carried out by the French and German police. This time, numerous Jews are executed in Paris and elsewhere in an effort to discourage the increasing number of anti-German attacks carried out by the Resistance.

20 January 1942   The Wannsee Conference decides on the "Final Solution." Reinhard Heydrich, head of the Reich Central Security Office (RSHA) announces to the assembled participants the targeted figures for deportations of Jews from each European country. For France, the proposed figure is 865,000 individuals, "broken down into 165,000 for the occupied zone and 700,000 for the unoccupied zone."[5] The responsibility for organizing the Final Solution in France falls to SS captain Theodor Dannecker, chief of the Gestapo's Jewish Office in Paris. The age limits on those to be deported are set at between sixteen and forty, because it is the Germans' intention to disguise the deportations as labor convoys.

18 April 1942 Two days after his return to power at Vichy (16 April) Pierre Laval names René Bousquet secretary-general for police in the Ministry of the Interior. Bousquet, in turn, designates Jean Leguay as his representative in the Occupied Zone.

6 May 1942 Louis Darquier de Pellepoix is named commissioner-general of Jewish affairs. Darquier replaces Xavier Vallat, whom the Germans consider too soft, to carry out the "massive internment and deportation of families, and not just men" that will soon be taking place.[6] During a meeting in Paris with Reinhard Heydrich in early May, René Bousquet learns of the pending deportations of Jews from the Occupied Zone and inquires whether it would be possible to include Jews interned in camps in the Unoccupied Zone in the deportations.

26 May 1942 Papon is named secretary-general of the Gironde prefecture (Bordeaux) under the prefect Maurice Sabatier. Among other assignments, Papon is placed in charge of Jewish affairs.

1 June 1942 Jews from the age of six on are required to wear the yellow star in the Occupied Zone.

3 July 1942 At a meeting of the cabinet in Vichy, Laval, Pétain, and the cabinet approve Bousquet's agreements with the Germans the previous day.

4 July 1942 In a meeting with Dannecker, Pierre Laval confirms official French acceptance of the 2 July agreements. Laval also asks that children under the age of sixteen be allowed to accompany their parents during the deportation of foreign Jews from the Unoccupied Zone. Later, on 10 July, Laval presents this as a humanitarian act to the Vichy Council of Ministers, with Pétain himself present.

15 July 1942 Bousquet issues orders to the prefect of the Paris police concerning the roundup to begin the next day.

16–17 July 1942 The so-called Vel d'hiv roundup of foreign Jews by French police takes place in Paris. Beginning at 4 A.M. on Thursday, 16 July, French policemen carrying carefully prepared index cards with the names and addresses of those to be arrested begin their sweeps; 12,884 men, women, and children are arrested and herded into an indoor bicycle racing stadium known as the Vélodrome d'hiver, kept in abominable conditions for several days, and then deported. The code name for the roundup is "Spring Wind." Bousquet specifically orders that all children over the age of ten are to be rounded up with their parents and not to be "left with neighbors." All those rounded up are foreign Jews, mostly refugees from Eastern Europe, except those children born in France and naturalized as French citizens as a result of their births being declared to the appropriate French authorities.

18 July 1942   The first convoy of Jews, numbering 161 persons in all, leaves Bordeaux. Between this date and May 1944, ten convoys carrying some 1,500 men, women, and children will leave Bordeaux to go to Drancy in Paris. From there, they are sent to the East to their deaths. Papon's role in organizing and expediting these convoys serves as the primary basis for the accusation of complicity in crimes against humanity.

29 July 1942   First accord between Bousquet and Karl Oberg, head of the SS in France. This accord, which concludes with a letter from Oberg dated 29 July, gives greater autonomy to the French police in allowing them to establish reserve units in the Occupied Zone and in guaranteeing that henceforth any orders from the Germans will only be issued through official channels. The French are also exempted from carrying out the unpleasant talk of designating hostages, and all persons handed over to the occupier by French authorities will not be executed as hostages. The Germans also agree to share information in cases that concern the French. Marrus and Paxton note that in exchange, the French police agree "to act vigorously against 'communists, terrorists, and saboteurs' and to assure 'the repression of all the enemies of the Reich, carrying on this struggle itself, on its own responsibility.'"[7]

18 August 1942   René Bousquet gives instructions to regional prefects concerning the roundup of foreign Jews in the Unoccupied Zone. Dates for the roundups are set, and exemptions for children between the ages of two and sixteen are suspended. Bousquet reminds the prefects of the "absolute necessity of taking the most severe measures to ensure the efficacy of the operation."

26–31 August 1942   Roundups of foreign Jews in the Unoccupied Zone. On orders from Bousquet's office, children between the ages of two and sixteen are deported along with their parents.

19 September 1942   Bousquet issues instructions allowing French Jews to be deported from the Occupied Zone.

11 November 1942   Following the Allied landings in North Africa, the Germans invade the Unoccupied Zone.

31 December 1942   By this date, 41,951 Jews have been deported from France to Auschwitz.

30 January 1943   Creation of the Milice, or Militia, paramilitary units created by Vichy to fight the Resistance, under the leadership of Joseph Darnand, a decorated veteran of World War I.

May 1943   Papon orders Gaullist graffiti erased from the bathroom walls in the Bordeaux prefecture and the perpetrator arrested. This episode, cited in the press at the time of Papon's trial for crimes against humanity as evidence that Papon was anti-Gaullist and did not serve the interests of the Resistance, is shown during the trial neither to prove nor disprove this claim.

July 1943   Alois Brunner, appointed to oversee the Final Solution in France, sets about seizing control of the deportations from the Vichy authorities. With the aid of Parisian collaborators, he launches a violent press campaign against Laval and Bousquet, labeling them protectors of the Jews. On 2 July he seizes control of the Drancy deportation center from French authorities. According to Marrus and Paxton, "Vichy thereby lost control of the key point in the administrative network of the deportation. Thereafter, the French police and bureaucracy were excluded from any influence on the composition of convoys to the east."[8] Arrests of French and foreign Jews are henceforth carried out by German squads and members of the various French Fascist movements, including members of the Parti populaire français and the Francistes.

November 1943   Papon agrees to shelter a Jewish member of the Resistance, Roger Bloch.

December 1943   A German internal memorandum specifies that Papon should now be considered pro-American. Earlier, the Germans considered Papon a solid ally.

1 January 1944   Joseph Darnand succeeds Bousquet and assumes the new title of "Secretary-General for the Maintenance of Order."

6 January 1944   Philippe Henriot is named state secretary for information and propaganda at Vichy.

10 January 1944   Murder of Victor Basch, former head of the Human Rights League, and his wife by the Milice. As head of the Milice's S-2 unit (intelligence and operations) for the Rhône and Savoy regions, Paul Touvier is known to have been involved in the crime, although lack of evidence led to its being dropped from the charges against him at his 1994 trial for crimes against humanity.

May 1944   First contacts between Papon and the Gaullist leader Gaston Cusin. Papon offers Cusin and the Gaullists his services.

6 June 1944   Allied landings in Normandy begin. Shortly thereafter, German authorities arrest René Bousquet and send him to Germany by private car. He is lodged in a villa, where his wife and son are allowed to join him.

28 June 1944   In the morning, three members of the Resistance, disguised as miliciens, gun down Vichy's propaganda minister, Philippe Henriot, at his residence in Paris. The news is announced over Vichy's radio at 12:40 P.M. by Pierre Laval himself. Enraged miliciens in Mâcon murder seven citizens in their homes in reprisal. Other reprisals are carried out by the Milice in Toulouse, Clermont-Ferrand, Grenoble, and Voiron. In Lyon, Paul Touvier orders the roundup of seven hostages, and tells his men to arrest Jews. Before dawn on the morning of 29 June seven hostages are taken by the Milice under the orders of Touvier to the cemetery of Rillieux-la-Pape, stood against a wall, and executed at about 5 A.M. It is for these murders, and these murders alone, that Touvier will finally stand trial for crimes against humanity in March and April 1994.

August 1944   Liberation of Bordeaux. Papon is named Cusin's cabinet director in the new Liberation government.

25 August 1944   Paris is liberated.

September 1944 Representing Cusin at a public rally, Papon reminds the crowd of the tragic fate of the deportees.

2 September 1944   Liberation of Lyon. Paul Touvier avoids arrest by hiding out in the home of the Abbé Vautherin. Touvier begins a long period in hiding, punctuated by robberies, arrests, and escapes. From the beginning, he is frequently sheltered and protected by members of the Catholic clergy.

6 October 1944   Papon is presented in the local newspaper as a Resistance member from the beginning of the Occupation.

18 May 1945 After returning voluntarily from exile, René Bousquet is incarcerated at Fresnes prison.

10 September 1946 Touvier is convicted of treason in absentia by the court of justice in Lyon. He is sentenced to death and *dégradation nationale* (loss of civil rights). His possessions are subject to confiscation. During this period Touvier is on the run with several members of his family, hiding out primarily in Montpellier in the southwest and then in Paris. On 29 June he is wounded during a holdup attempt.

January 1947 Papon is named prefect of Corsica. During his trial he will claim that while in Corsica he helped the Israelis secure arms.

4 March 1947 The court of justice at Chambéry (Touvier's hometown) sentences Touvier to death and *dégradation nationale* in absentia. He is convicted this time for "intelligence with the enemy."

20 June 1949 A court in Lyon sentences Touvier, who fails to appear, to five years in prison and ten years of *interdiction de séjour* (Touvier will not be permitted to live in the area for ten years) after he is convicted of armed robbery.

23 June 1949 After three and a half years in prison (at the beginning of his prison term, Bousquet prepares the notes for his former boss Laval's defense) and a brief period of release under surveillance, René Bousquet stands trial before the High Court of Justice. He is given a symbolic sentence of five years' loss of civil rights, which is immediately commuted for "acts of resistance." Following his release, Bousquet begins a successful career as a businessman, most notably at the Bank of Indochina, where he will become a director for international affairs in 1952 and associate director-general in 1960.

October 1949 Papon is named prefect of the Constantine region in Algeria.

5 January 1951 A general amnesty law is passed for those sentenced to *dégradation nationale* and prison terms of less than fifteen years.

24 July 1953 A second amnesty law is passed that affects all but the perpetrators of the most serious crimes committed during the Occupation. According to Henry Rousso, the second amnesty law marks the official end of the postwar Purge. Henceforth, sentences meted out to former collaborators returning from exile are extremely mild compared to those handed down in the immediate postwar period.

14 April 1954   A law is passed designating the last Sunday in April as "A National Day of Remembrance for the Victims and Heroes of the Deportation."

June 1954   Papon is named secretary-general of the Protectorate of Morocco.

March 1956   Back in Paris, Papon is named councilor in the Ministry of the Interior.

May 1956   Papon is named inspector-general of administration in the eastern region of Algeria.

March 1958   Papon is named prefect of Paris police by the Socialist Félix Gaillard. Considered to be a "man of the Socialist Party," Papon is nevertheless maintained in place when Charles de Gaulle returns to power in June 1958.

17 October 1961   A massive demonstration of Algerians called by the FLN to protest a curfew imposed on Algerian immigrants by Papon in his capacity as prefect of police is brutally suppressed by the Paris police. Between fifty and three hundred Algerians are killed. Some are shot, others are beaten to death, and some of the bodies are thrown into the Seine. They are fished out of the water over the next several days. Thousands of Algerians are rounded up and taken to detention centers where they are held indefinitely, often in appalling conditions. Many are deported to Algeria. Papon, in concert with other government officials, acts to hush up these events. In October 1997, during his trial for crimes against humanity for his actions during the Occupation, Papon says only thirteen or fourteen Algerians were killed, and not by the police.

8 February 1962   Following a number of spectacular terrorist acts committed in Paris by the OAS (Organisation armée secrète, the terrorist group supporting French Algeria), a number of unions linked to the CGT (Confédération générale du travail) decide to organize a huge rally at the Bastille to protest the government's "complicity" in these acts, evident in the relative impunity with which the terrorists are allowed to function. It is the decision of the Ministry of the Interior and Prefect of Police Papon to suppress the rally. The protesters are therefore greeted by heavily armed police, and violent confrontations ensue. A large group of protesters, attempting to escape a police charge, descend the stairs at the Charonne metro stop, hoping to board a train. The gates at the entrance are closed, however, and as more panicked protesters descend the stairs, many are trampled and unable to breathe. Meanwhile, the police attack and beat those still trying to escape. All told, eight people are killed and sixty more wounded. The Ministry of the Interior blames the protesters, claiming the Communists especially organized charges against the "forces of order" and wounded many. These claims are challenged in the press and elsewhere. Many years later, the prime minister at the time, Michel Debré, will praise Papon for his role in the affair, saying, "his devotion to the state deserves great praise in my opinion."

26 December 1964   Crimes against humanity, as defined in the *United Nations Resolution of 13 February 1946*, are declared imprescriptible in French law.

1965   According to numerous sources, Bousquet, an acquaintance of François Mitterrand through mutual friends, supports the latter's unsuccessful bid for the presidency. Bousquet's contributions include securing the support of the Toulouse newspaper the *Dépêche du Midi*, as well as financial contributions for Mitterrand's campaign.

1967   The statute of limitations goes into effect on the 1946 and 1947 convictions of Paul Touvier, who has avoided punishment by remaining in hiding. A National Identity Card under the name "Paul Touvier *alias* Berthet" is delivered to him on 7 December at the address of the archdiocese of Lyon. Although the death penalty has lapsed, Touvier is still not allowed to reside in the twelve departments of southern France and cannot lay claim to family property owned there or appear publicly in his hometown of Chambéry.

January 1967   Papon becomes an executive for the Sud-Avion airline company.

June 1968   Papon becomes Gaullist deputy from the Cher region.

28 January 1970   The prosecutor of the State Security Court asks Jacques Delarue, an historian and specialist on the Occupation, to conduct an investigation into Touvier's past and to assess the fairness of Touvier's earlier convictions. On 10 June Delarue submits his findings, concluding that Touvier's actions were "nefarious, unscrupulous, and inexcusable" and that his past convictions were fully justified.

April–July 1970   In their continuing efforts to have Touvier pardoned, members of the Catholic clergy, Monsignors Duquaire and Gouet, accompanied by Touvier himself, pay visits to officials of the Pompidou government. Those involved in the discussions include Edouard Balladur, prime minister in 1994 at the time of Touvier's trial.

6 August 1970   After conducting an investigation into the circumstances of Touvier's convictions in 1946 and 1947 the minister of the interior recommends against a pardon for Touvier.

1971   Papon is treasurer for the Gaullist UDR party.

3 September 1971   Paul Touvier's friend and supporter Monsignor Duquaire is received by Anne-Marie Dupuy, the principal private secretary of President Georges Pompidou. "Reticent" in her reaction to Duquaire's affirmations of Touvier's innocence and his statements concerning the "injustice" of the Delarue report, Dupuy is moved by the fate of Touvier's family. She would later affirm: "Monsignor Duquaire touched the mother in me. His comments on [Touvier's] children moved me."

23 November 1971   Despite the recommendations against the pardon by Delarue and others, Georges Pompidou grants a pardon to Touvier, influenced in part by sympathy for his family encouraged by Anne-Marie Dupuy. Instructions are that the pardon is to be handled as discreetly as possible.

1972   Public outcry over the Touvier pardon begins, following the publication on 5 June of an article in *L'Express* by Jacques Dérogy exposing the pardon, entitled "Exclusive: *L'Express* has found the Torturer of Lyon."

21 September 1972   At a press conference Pompidou explains his reason for pardoning Touvier, stating, "Hasn't a moment come to draw a veil over the past, to forget a time when Frenchmen didn't like one another?" Few are convinced, and former members of Resistance groups prepare to press charges against Touvier for crimes against humanity.

9 November 1973   Two accusations of crimes against humanity are brought against Touvier before the examining magistrate of Lyon. The accusations are brought by Joë Nordmann and Ugo Iannucci on behalf of Georges Glaeser, the son of one of the victims of Rillieux-la-Pape, and Rosa Vogel, daughter of a deported guardian of the grand synagogue of Lyon, respectively. Over the course of the next several years, the issue will provoke a lengthy legal battle.

April 1978   Nearing the end of his political career, Papon is named minister of budget under Valéry Giscard d'Estaing.

28 October 1978   *L'Express* publishes an interview with Louis Darquier de Pellepoix, the former minister of Jewish questions under Vichy, now living in exile, who claims René Bousquet was responsible for the deportation of Jews and especially the Vel d'hiv roundups. Bousquet's role in the Final Solution had been revealed earlier by Joseph Billig in his 1955 book *Commissariat général aux Questions juives*, but the information was not widely disseminated until the Darquier interview.

15 November 1978   Serge Klarsfeld files a complaint alleging crimes against humanity against Jean Leguay, René Bousquet's representative in the Occupied Zone from May 1942 to the end of 1943, who, as Bousquet's representative, was responsible for the deportation of large numbers of Jews.

12 March 1979   Jean Leguay is indicted by investigating magistrate Martine Anzani for crimes against humanity. This indictment marks the first time that the suspension of the statute of limitations for crimes against humanity is applied to a French citizen.

May 1981   The satirical political newspaper *Canard enchaîné* publishes an article, "Papon, aide de camps," on Papon's role in the deportations of Jews from the Bordeaux region during the Occupation. The article appears between the first and second rounds of the presidential elections, and apparently helps François Mitterrand to victory by tilting the Jewish vote in his favor. Mitterrand is consulted before the publication of the article and, according to reliable accounts, approves its publication. Ironically, Mitterrand's own Vichy past will become the subject of intense controversy in the nineties.

June 1981   The RPR (Rassemblement pour la République) Party refuses to sponsor Papon's candidacy in legislative elections in the Cher region.

8 December 1981   The first accusations of crimes against humanity are brought against Papon by relatives of the victims of the deportations. Several days later, an honor jury of former Resistance members, convened at Papon's request, confirms Papon's participation in the Resistance, but also asserts that he should have abandoned his post in Bordeaux by July 1942. Papon's having remained in his post beyond this point resulted in his having to carry out policies which, for the jury, violated "[our] conception of honor." But the jury concludes that to legally pursue Bordeaux officials for following orders from May 1942 to the Liberation would be "perfectly unjustified." Maurice Sabatier, Papon's former boss in Bordeaux, claims all responsibility for the anti-Jewish actions of the Gironde prefecture during the period in question.

July 1982   A first judicial investigation into Papon's role in the deportations opens and is handed over to the investigating magistrate Minvielle.

December 1982   A second investigating magistrate, Jean-Claude Nicod, is named to the case.

January 1983   Papon is charged with crimes against humanity for the first time.

April 1983   Papon sues the families of the victims for calumny. He also tries to have *L 'Affaire Papon*, a book written by Michel Slitinsky, the son of one of the victims of the deportations from Bordeaux, seized by government authorities. He is unsuccessful. (However, a preface written for Slitinsky's book by Gilles Perrault, which describes Papon as "a true bastard," "the symbol of a certain rottenness," and possessed of a "triumphant ignominy," is suppressed from all further editions by order of the court.)

January 1985   A report requested of three "experts" finds Papon to be innocent of all personal responsibility in the deportations from Bordeaux and affirms that Papon deserves recognition for saving a number of individuals from being deported. The credibility of two of the three experts is challenged by the families of the victims, who claim that the respective pasts of these experts during the Occupation are themselves not above criticism.

5 October 1985   The magistrate's initial investigation for the trial of Klaus Barbie is completed.

20 December 1985   The Court of Appeals modifies the definition of crimes against humanity, which henceforth can include crimes committed against members of the Resistance.

9 July 1986   A second investigation of Barbie's file is concluded.

11 February 1987   The judicial investigation of Papon's past is ordered dropped by the Court of Appeals, due to an error made by the examining magistrate. The decision raises eyebrows in several quarters, because the error by the examining magistrate (questioning Papon's superior in Bordeaux, Maurice Sabatier, without indicting him) appears to be insufficient reason to drop the case.

11 May–4 July 1987   The trial of Klaus Barbie takes place before the Assizes Court in Lyon.

8 July 1988   New charges of crimes against humanity are brought against Papon by another examining magistrate, François Braud, who later abandons the dossier when promoted at the end of 1989.

20 October 1988   Papon's superior in Bordeaux, Maurice Sabatier, is indicted. Sabatier dies six months later.

24 May 1989   Paul "Lacroix" (Touvier) is arrested by the French police at the priory of Saint-François in Nice.

2 July 1989   Jean Leguay dies of natural causes. After ten years, the protracted investigation of his case is complete and is about to be handed over to a Paris court. Breaking with custom, the statement declaring the case closed due to Leguay's death also confirms his guilt on charges of crimes against humanity.

13 September 1989   Represented by Serge Klarsfeld, the Association of the Sons and Daughters of Deported Jews lodges a complaint against René Bousquet, charging him with crimes against humanity. The case is handed over to the Indictments Division of the Court of Appeals in Paris.

February 1990   A new magistrate, Anne Léotin, is named to the Papon case.

16 May 1990   The Indictments Division delivers the materials of the Bousquet case to the prosecutor-general, Pierre Truche, who had recently prosecuted the case against Klaus Barbie.

June 1990   Papon sues the magazine the *Nouvel Observateur*, describing himself as a new "Captain Dreyfus." He wins the suit, but decides to drop the case when the magazine appeals. Papon fears a reversal of the decision.

25 September 1990   The prosecutor-general Pierre Truche orders the Indictments Division to begin its investigation of the charges against Bousquet.

10 September 1990   Doing a complete about-face, Pierre Truche asks the Indictments Division to declare itself incompetent to handle the Bousquet case and proposes that the case be handled instead by the High Court of Justice of the Liberation, the Purge court that originally judged Bouquet in 1949 and no longer exists. Truche is apparently acting on the orders of the newly appointed special delegate to the Ministry of Justice, Georges Kiejman, who is himself acting at the behest of the president of the republic, François Mitterrand. The action is clearly a delaying tactic to avoid bringing Bousquet to trial. When asked to justify his action following public outcry, Kiejman claims in a statement made in *Libération* on 22 October to be acting in the name of "civil peace."

19 November 1990   Despite Truche's request, the Indictments Division declares itself competent to proceed with the Bousquet case. Bousquet appeals the decision three days later.

31 January 1991   The Criminal Chamber of the High Court of Appeals rejects Bousquet's appeal. The last obstacle to the indictment of Bousquet for crimes against humanity is removed.

3 April 1991   The court's decision to indict Bousquet is made public.

July–August 1991   The neofascist magazine *Le Choc du mois* publishes a dossier entitled *Mitterrand et la cagoule,* underscoring the president's prewar right-wing activism and his service to Vichy.

8 July 1991   A new penal code is passed that includes a new definition of crimes against humanity, convictions for which are subject to life imprisonment.

11 July 1991   Paul Touvier is ordered released from prison by the Indictments Division of the Court of Appeals in Paris on the grounds that his continued detention "is no longer necessary to the discovery of the truth." The decision causes public consternation and outrage: given Touvier's record, some speculate that the former *milicien* will once again go into hiding. The prosecutor-general in Paris announces his intention to appeal the decision.

23 October 1991   Maurice Papon holds a press conference in which he announces that he has written a letter to the president of the republic demanding to be judged or acquitted of the charges against him, eight years having passed since judicial procedures involving charges of crimes against humanity were instituted against him.

6 January 1992   A distinguished panel of historians headed by René Rémond delivers its report on Paul Touvier's links to the Catholic church and its hierarchy to Monsignor Decourtray, the archbishop of Lyon, who had requested the report after Touvier's arrest in June 1989. Although the report does not fault the church as a whole, it sharply criticizes the activities of many church authorities who helped

Touvier evade justice. The report is published in book form as *Paul Touvier et l'Église* by Fayard in March 1992.[9]

13 April 1992   The Court of Appeals in Paris acquits Paul Touvier of charges of crimes against humanity, arguing that the charges do not apply to a servant of Vichy, which was not, according to the judges, a regime that practiced "ideological hegemony." According to the December 1985 definition of crimes against humanity as defined in French law, only actions performed on behalf of such a regime are to be considered crimes against humanity. The public outcry is immediate and intense and is fueled by the fact that the three judges who handed down the decision are known for their right-wing sympathies.

6 July 1992   The press reveals new indictments against Maurice Papon and René Bousquet, announced on 19 and 22 June, during the course of the investigation of charges against Papon by the courts in Bordeaux. According to Éric Conan and Henry Rousso, these indictments are "the indirect consequence of the outrage provoked even among the magistrates, by the acquittal of Touvier." [10]

16 July 1992   The fiftieth anniversary of the Vel d'hiv roundup is commemorated at the site of the former velodrome. François Mitterrand, who attends the ceremony, is heckled by some members of the crowd (two days earlier, Mitterrand had denied that the French Republic was in any way responsible for the crimes of Vichy).

27 November 1992   The Criminal Chamber of the High Court of Appeals partially overturns the April acquittal of Touvier. The charge retained against Touvier concerns his order to execute seven Jews at the cemetery at Rillieux-la-Pape in June 1944.

3 February 1993   A national day commemorating "racist and anti-Semitic persecutions committed under the authority of the French State (1940–1944) is decreed. The commemoration will occur annually on 16 July, if that date is a Sunday, and if not, the first Sunday following that date."

8 June 1993   Christian Didier, a deranged and unsuccessful writer who had tried to kill Klaus Barbie in 1987, enters René Bousquet's Paris apartment and guns him down. He then flees to a hotel in Lilas near Paris, where he calls a press conference and states, "I had the impression I was crushing a snake."

17 March 1994   The trial of Paul Touvier for crimes against humanity begins in Versailles under tight security. As an added precaution, the synagogue in Versailles is placed under police protection.

20 April 1994   Touvier is convicted of crimes against humanity and sentenced to life in prison. He appeals the verdict immediately. Following the conviction of Touvier, numerous demands are made to put Maurice Papon on trial.

18 May 1994   A plaque commemorating the murder of the seven Jewish hostages at the cemetery of Rillieux-la-Pape is destroyed by persons unknown.

24 May 1994   The Indictments Division of the Court of Appeals of Versailles refuses a request made on 11 May to free Paul Touvier.

14 June 1994   The Correctional Tribunal of Bordeaux agrees to delay the trial of Papon until a ruling is made on Papon's complaint against Gérard Boulanger, author of *Maurice Papon: Un Technocrate français dans la collaboration* and the lawyer for several of the civil litigants in Papon's case. Boulanger is accused of "public defamation of a government functionary."

12 September 1994   As a result of the scandal provoked by the publication of Pierre Péan's *Une Jeunesse française: François Mitterand, 1934–1947*, the president of the Republic appears on French national television to explain his role at Vichy and his postwar friendship with René Bousquet.[11]

December 1995   After several more charges are filed, the prosecutor in Bordeaux decides to try Papon in front of the Assizes Court.

28 January 1997   Papon's last appeal for a dismissal of charges is rejected.

8 October 1997   The trial of Maurice Papon for crimes against humanity opens in Bordeaux.

2 April 1998   Maurice Papon is found guilty of complicity in the "illegal arrest" of thirty-seven people and of the "arbitrary detention" of fifty-seven more in the context of the deportation of Jews by train convoys leaving Bordeaux in July 1942, August 1942, October 1942, and January 1944. He is also found guilty of the arbitrary detention of one Léon Librach. Papon is acquitted on charges of complicity to murder those deported to the East. In other words, Papon is found innocent of having knowledge at the time of the aim and purpose of the Final Solution. Papon is sentenced to ten years in prison, which he appeals immediately.

May 1998   Following an investigation undertaken in October 1997 at the behest of the minister of the interior, Jean-Pierre Chevènement, State Councilor Dieudonné

Mandelkern issues a report claiming that some thirty-two protesters were killed on the night of 17 October 1961. In its article on the Mandelkern report (included in this volume) *Le Monde* argues that the most important information contained in it concerns the incompleteness of the archives relating to the events themselves. For example, no copies of Prefect of Police Maurice Papon's report can be found either at the Paris prefecture of police or at national police headquarters. Similarly, the archives of the River Authority (*Brigade fluviale*), which would have contained figures concerning the number of bodies fished out of the Seine, had been destroyed years before. Not surprisingly, the report is widely criticized by experts for its lack of thoroughness and its speculative nature. (See the essay by Jean-Luc Einaudi in this volume.)

February 1999   The "Other Papon Trial," as the magazine *L'Express* labels it, gets under way in Paris. This time, Papon is the accuser and the historian Jean-Luc Einaudi the defendant. At issue is a statement made in *Le Monde* by Einaudi asserting that the Paris police had massacred Algerian protesters in October 1961 "under the orders of Maurice Papon." Papon sues Einaudi for "defamation of a government functionary."

In late March the president of the Seventeenth Correctional Chamber of the Paris High Tribunal, Jean-Yves Monfort, delivers his verdict finding in favor of the accused. While Monfort acknowledges that the passage in question "is not lacking in ambiguity," he concludes that it must be considered in the broader context of Einaudi's research, which is considered to be both rigorous and carried out "in good faith." Einaudi announces that the judgment is "a victory for the victims of October 1961."

21 October 1999   Papon's appeal is rejected by the Court of Appeals. An international warrant for Papon's arrest is issued, the convicted man having fled to Switzerland before his appeal is heard. Within days, he is arrested by Swiss police in Gstaad, Switzerland, and turned over to French police. He begins his prison sentence at the Fresnes prison in Paris

NOTES

1. Serge Klarsfeld, *Vichy-Auschwitz: Le Role de Vichy dans la solution finale en France.* 1942 (Paris: Fayard, 1983), p. 13.

2. Michael Marrus and Robert Paxton, *Vichy France and the Jews* (New York: Schocken, 1983), p. 3.

3. Ibid., pp. 81–84.

4. Ibid., pp. 98, 100, 101.

5. Susan Zuccotti, *The Holocaust, the French, and the Jews* (New York: Basic, 1993), pp. 95–96.

6. Serge Klarsfeld, *Vichy-Auschwitz 1942*, p. 50.

7. Marrus and Paxton, *Vichy France and the Jews*, p. 244.

8. Ibid., p. 330.

9. René Rémond et al., *Paul Touvier et l'Église: Rapport de la Commission historique instituée par le Cardinal Decourtray* (Paris: Fayard, 1992).

10. Éric Conan and Henri Rousso, *Vichy, un passé qui ne passe pas* (Paris: Fayard, 1994), p. 295.

11. Pierre Péan, *Une Jeunesse française: François Mitterrand 1934–1947* (Paris: Fayard, 1994).

CONTRIBUTORS

Philippe Bernard is a journalist for *Le Monde*.

Nathan Bracher is Associate Professor of French in the Department of Modern and Classical Languages at Texas A&M University.

Philippe Burrin is Professor of International History at the Graduate Institute of International Studies in Geneva, Switzerland. He is best known in the United States as the author of *France Under the Germans: Collaboration and Compromise* (New Press, 1997).

Michel Dubec is a legal psychologist who works in the French courts.

Jean-Luc Einaudi is an historian and journalist and leading authority on the Algerian experience in France.

Alain Finkielkraut, one of France's foremost intellectual figures, has had several of his works translated into English, including *Dispatches from the Balkan War and Other Writings* (Nebraska, 1999), *The Future of a Negation* (Nebraska, 1998), *The Imaginary Jew* (Nebraska, 1997) and *The Defeat of the Mind* (Columbia University Press, 1996).

Christopher Flood is Director of European Studies at the University of Surrey, United Kingdom.

Richard J. Golsan is Professor of French in the Department of Modern and Classical Languages at Texas A & M University and is author most recently author of *Vichy's Afterlife*, forthcoming from Nebraska. He has edited several collections, including *Fascism's Return: Scandal, Revision, and Ideology Since 1980* (Nebraska,

1998) and *Memory, the Holocaust, and French Justice: The Bousquet and Touvier Affairs* (UPNE, 1996).

Eberhard Jäckel is Professor of Contemporary History and director of the Historical Institute of the University of Stuggart. His works that have been translated into English include *Hitler's Worldview* (Harvard University Press, 1981) and *Hitler in History* (UPNE, 1989).

Vann Kelly is Associate Professor in the Department of French and Italian at the University of Kansas.

Annette Lévy-Willard is a political writer and editor at the newspaper *Libération* in Paris.

François Maspero is a novelist and essayist.

Pierre Nora is editorial director of the publishing house, Éditions Gallimard, editor of the journal *Le Débat*, and director of studies at Ecole Hautes Etudes Bibliothèque Sciences Sociales Humaines.

Robert O. Paxton is Mellon Professor Emeritus of the Social Sciences at Columbia University. He is author of *Vichy France* (Columbia University Press, 1982) and *French Peasant Fascism* (Oxford University Press, 1997). He testified as an expert witness in both of Maurice Papon's trials.

Acacio Pereira is a reporter for the newspaper *Le Monde*.

Henry Rousso is Director at CNRS for the Institute of Modern History, Paris. His work that has been translated into English includes *The Vichy Syndrome* (UPNE, 1991) and *Vichy: An Ever-Present Past* (UPNE, 1998), which he co-authored with Eric Conan.

Leila Nadya Sadat is Professor of Law at the Washington University School of Law in St. Louis.

Benjamin Stora is Professor of History at l'Institut d'Histoire du Temps Présent in Paris and a leading historian of the French-Algerian War.

Zeev Sternhell is Leon Blum Professor of Political Science at the Hebrew University in Jerusalem. His works translated into English include *The Founding Myths of Israel: Nationalism, Socialism, and the Making of the Jewish State* (Princeton, 1998) and *The Birth of Fascist Ideology* (Princeton, 1994).

Tzvetan Todorov, one of France's leading intellectuals, is best known in the United States for his books *Facing the Extreme: Moral Life in the Concentration Camps* (Metropolitan/Henry Holt, 1997) and *The Conquest of America: The Question of the Other* (Harper, 1992).

Jean-Marc Varaut is the lawyer who served as the main defense counsel for Maurice Papon at the Bordeaux trial and is an authority on the Nuremburg Trials.

Nancy Wood is Senior Lecturer in Media and European Studies history at the University of Sussex, United Kingdom. She is author of *Vectors of Memory*, which is forthcoming from Berg Publishers.

Michel Zaoui is the lawyer who represented the civil parties during the initial trial of Maurice Papon.

ACKNOWLEDGMENTS

Philippe Bernard, "The Magistrates' Court of Paris Acknowledges the 'Extreme Violence' of the Police Crackdown of 17 October 1961," trans. Lucy Golsan, copyright © Routledge, 1999. Originally published in *Le Monde* in 1997 as "Le Tribunal correctionnel de Paris reconnaît 'massacre' du 17 octobre 1961." Used with permission.

———— "One of the Few Times since the Nineteenth Century That Police Have Fired on Workers in Paris: An Interview with Benjamin Stora," trans. Richard Golsan, copyright © Routledge, 1999. Originally published in *Le Monde* in 1999 as "L'Une des rares fois . . . (entretien avec Benjamin Stora)." Used with permission.

———— "According to the Mandelkern Report Thirty-Two Were Killed during the Night of 17 October 1961," trans. Lucy Golsan, copyright © Routledge, 1999. Originally published in Le Monde in 1998 as "Selon le rapport Mandelkern, trente-deux personnes ont été tuées dans la nuit du 17 au octobre 1961." Used with permission.

Lucas Delattre, "Nazism, Vichy, and the Papon Trial Seen by a German Historian: An Interview with Eberhard Jäckel," trans. Richard Golsan, copyright © Routledge, 1999. Originally published in *Le Monde* in 1997 as "Le Nazisme, Vichy et la procès Papon vus par un historien allemand (entretien avec Eberhard Jackel)." Used with permission.

Michel Dubec, "Maurice Papon and Criminal Pathology," trans. Lucy Golsan, copyright © Routledge, 1999. Originally published in *Le Monde* in 1997 as "Maurice Papon et la pathologie criminelle." Used with permission.

Jean-Luc Einaudi, "Monsieur Papon Will Not Shut Me Up," trans. Richard Golsan, copyright © Routledge, 1999. Originally published in *Le Monde* in 1999 as "M. Papon ne me fera pas taire." Used with permission.

———— "October 1961: For the Truth, at Last," trans. Richard Golsan, copyright © Routledge, 1999. Originally published in *Le Monde* in 1998 as "Octobre 1961: Pour la vérité enfin." Used with permission.

Alain Finkielkraut, "Papon: Too Late," trans. Lucy Golsan, copyright © Routledge, 1999. Originally published in 1996 in *Le Monde* as "Papon, trop tard." Used with permission.

Laurent Greilsamer and Nicolas Weill, "Maurice Papon Was Tried Long Ago in History's Court: An Interview with Henry Rousso," trans. Lucy Golsan, copyright © Routledge, 1999. Originally published in *Le Monde* in 1998 as "Le Tribunal de l'histoire a jugé Vichy depuis longtemps (entretien avec Henry Rousso)." Used with permission.

Thomas Firenczi, "The Papon Investigation Brings to Light the True Role of France in Nazi Europe: An Interview with Philippe Burin," trans. Lucy Golsan, copyright © Routledge, 1999. Originally published in *Le Monde* in 1996 as "L'Affaire Papon met en évidence le spécificité de la France dans l'Europe nazie (entretien avec Philippe Burin)." Used with permission.

Annette Lévy-Willard and Béatrice Vallaeys, "Those Who Organized the Trains Knew There Would Be Deaths: An Interview with Robert O. Paxton," trans. Lucy Golsan, copyright © Routledge, 1999. Originally published in *Libération* in 1997 as "Ceux qui organisaient les trains savaient qu'il y aurait des morts." Used with permission of Annette Lévy-Willard and *Libération*.

François Maspero, "Are We All Guilty?" trans. Lucy Golsan, copyright © Routledge, 1999. Originally published in *Le Monde* in 1997 as "Tous coupables?" Used with permission.

Robert O. Paxton, "Vichy on Trial," copyright © 1997 by the New York Times Co. Reprinted by permission.

Acacio Pereira, "Maurice Papon Declares the Bloody Crackdown of 17 October 1961 'An Unfortunate Evening,'" trans. Lucy Golsan, copyright © Routledge, 1999. Originally published in *Le Monde* in 1999 as "Maurice Papon qualifie de 'malheureuse soirée.'...." Used with permission.

Henry Rousso, "Letter to the President of the Bordeaux Assizes Court," trans. Richard Golsan, copyright © Routledge, 1999. Used with permission of the author.

Zeev Sternhell, "Maurice Papon Was Not Alone," trans. Lucy Golsan, copyright © Routledge, 1999. Originally published in *Le Monde* in 1997 as "Papon n'était pas seul." Used with permission.

Tzvetan Todorov, "Letter from Paris: The Papon Trial," trans. John Anzalone, from *Salmagundi*, No. 121–122 (winter/spring 1999), pp. 3–9. Used with permission of the author and *Salmagundi*.

Nicolas Weill and Robert Solé, "Today, Everything Converges on the Haunting Memory of Vichy: An Interview with Pierre Nora," trans. Lucy Golsan, copyright © Routledge, 1999. Originally published in *Le Monde* in 1997 as "Tout concourt aujourd'hui au souvenir obsédant de Vichy (entretien avec Pierre Nora)." Used with permission.

Michel Zaoui and Jean-Marc Varaut, "The Papon Trial, Three Months Later," trans. Lucy Golsan, copyright © Routledge, 1999. Originally published in *Le Monde* in 1998 as "Procès Papon, trois mois après." Used with permission.

INDEX